When should I travel to get the best airfare?
Where do I go for answers to my travel questions?
What's the best and easiest way to plan and book my trip?

frommers.travelocity.com

Frommer's, the travel guide leader, has teamed up with **Travelocity.com**, the leader in online travel, to bring you an in-depth, easy-to-use resource designed to help you plan and book your trip online.

At **frommers.travelocity.com**, you'll find free online updates about your destination from the experts at Frommer's plus the outstanding travel planning and purchasing features of Travelocity.com. Travelocity.com provides reservations capabilities for 95 percent of all airline seats sold, more than 47,000 hotels, and over 50 car rental companies. In addition, Travelocity.com offers more than 2,000 exciting vacation and cruise packages. Travelocity.com puts you in complete control of your travel planning with these and other great features:

Expert travel guidance from Frommer's—over 150 writers reporting from around the world!

Best Fare Finder—an interactive calendar tells you when to travel to get the best airfare

Fare Watcher—we'll track airfare changes to your favorite destinations

Dream Maps—a mapping feature that suggests travel opportunities based on your budget

Shop Safe Guarantee—24 hours a day/7 days a week live customer service, and more!

Whether traveling on a tight budget, looking for a quick weekend getaway, or planning the trip of a lifetime, Frommer's guides and Travelocity.com will make your travel dreams a reality. You've bought the book, now book the trip!

Travelocity.com
A Sabre Company

other titles in the

irreverent guide

series

Frommer's

irreverent guide to Amsterdam

4th Edition

By
David Downie

HUNGRY MINDS, INC.

a disclaimer

Please note that prices fluctuate in the course of time, and travel information changes under the impact of the many factors that influence the travel industry. We therefore suggest that you write or call ahead for confirmation when making your travel plans. Every effort has been made to ensure the accuracy of information throughout this book and the contents of this publication are believed correct at the time of printing. Nevertheless, the publishers cannot accept responsibility for errors or omissions or for changes in details given in this guide or for the consequences of any reliance on the information provided by the same. Assessments of attractions and so forth are based upon the author's own experience and therefore, descriptions given in this guide necessarily contain an element of subjective opinion, which may not reflect the publisher's opinion or dictate a reader's own experience on another occasion. Readers are invited to write to the publisher with ideas, comments, and suggestions for future editions.

Your safety is important to us, however, so we encourage you to stay alert and be aware of your surroundings. Keep a close eye on cameras, purses, and wallets, all favorite targets of thieves and pickpockets.

Published by HUNGRY MINDS, INC.

909 Third Avenue
New York, NY 10022

ISBN 0-7645-6568-0
ISSN 1085-4703

Interior design contributed to by Tsang Seymour Design Studio

special sales

For general information on Hungry Minds' products and services please contact our Customer Care Department within the U.S. at 800-762-2974, outside the U.S. at 317-572-3993 or fax 317-572-4002.

For sales inquiries and reseller information, including discounts, premium, and bulk quantity sales, and foreign-language translations, please contact our Customer Care Department at 800-434-3422 or fax 317-572-4002.

Manufactured in the United States of America

what's so irreverent?

It's up to you.

You can buy a traditional guidebook with its fluff, its promotional hype, its let's-find-something-nice-to-say-about-everything point of view. Or you can buy an Irreverent guide.

What the Irreverents give you is the lowdown, the inside story. They have nothing to sell but the truth, which includes a balance of good and bad. They praise, they trash, they weigh, and leave the final decisions up to you. No tourist board, no chamber of commerce will ever recommend them.

Our writers are insiders, who feel passionate about the cities they live in, and have strong opinions they want to share with you. They take a special pleasure leading you where other guides fear to tread.

How irreverent are they? One of our authors insisted on writing under a pseudonym. "I couldn't show my face in town again if I used my own name," she told me. "My friends would never speak to me." Such is the price of honesty. She, like you, should know she'll always have a friend at Frommer's.

Warm regards,

Michael Spring

Michael Spring
Publisher

contents

introduction

Self-censorship, PC conformism, and neo-conservatism may be the watchwords in much of Europe these days, but not in Amsterdam. More than ever, that old Amsterdam saying, "Our hearts are on our tongues," reaffirms Amsterdammers' claim to extreme forthrightness. Throughout this revised, fourth edition I follow the heart-on-tongue principle, adding cheek whenever possible.

Wonderful, wild, too-good-to-be-true Amsterdam, and its sometimes self-consciously cool, cultivated denizens, lend themselves to tongue-in-cheek treatment. Few Europeans are so ready to make fun of themselves, their history, language, and customs as the inhabitants of this small, flat, watery capital of a small, flat, watery country. So much for the stereotype of the dour Dutch: Amsterdammers are disarmingly friendly, fun—and irreverent.

In fact, the Dutch as such do not exist; the Netherlands is a collection of provinces with distinct personalities. Amsterdammers are as different from their countrymen as a Scotsman is from a Londoner, or a Milanese from a Sicilian. The governmental capital, The Hague, is stiff and conservative; war-damaged Rotterdam is industrial and hard-edged; Amsterdam, the symbolic capital, where Dutch figurehead monarchs from the House of Orange have been crowned since 1813, is casual and liberal, with an anything-goes spirit. Stunningly well-preserved,

Amsterdam revolves around tourism, conventions, and high tech, with Schiphol Airport the city's second-largest employer. The biggest employer is the seemingly recession-proof government, whose tolerant quality-of-life policies help make this city so livable and so loved, even by visitors who detest big government.

Like Florence, A'dam is a city of art. Truth be told, only half a dozen of its 42 dynamic and ever-expanding museums are world-class: the Rijksmuseum, Vincent van Gogh Museum, Stedelijk Museum, Rembrandt House Museum, Historical Museum, and Maritime Museum—still an impressive roster for a cosmopolis of just 730,000 souls, a city so compact you can stroll across it in a couple of hours. Within the Centrum alone—the center-city bounded by the 19th-century Singelgracht canal—there are nearly 6,800 centuries-old canal houses squeezed into a semicircle the size of a small American town. Their bricks stand balanced on wooden pilings driven through the mud into more-or-less solid ground.

Though most locals are proud of their showcase city, which has modernized while maintaining its monuments, they manage to poke fun at its founding. There is no illustrious Roman pedigree ("Here a wretched race is found," noted Pliny the Elder, "inhabiting either the more elevated spots or artificial mounds" where no Romans in their right minds would set foot); there's not even a lost Viking to pep up the history books. The whole thing started, it seems, when some fishermen and their dogs drifted down the Amstel River some time in the early 1200s. They slogged up a muddy bank and had a stiff drink, thus laying the foundations of a tavern around which the entire metropolis would grow.

And grow it did: Bright, beaverlike fishermen dammed the river at—you guessed it—Dam Square, thereby reclaiming huge quantities of mud, and devised a clever, inspired name for the settlement: Amstellodam (or Amstelledamme), which means—you guessed it again—Dam on the Amstel River. By 1275, Count Floris V of Holland, whoever he was, had granted this previously unknown fishing village special trading privileges. An official charter was drawn up in 1300.

Things really got going in Amstellodam when the founding fathers and their dog were joined by a few founding mothers bearing *genever* (gin) and salted herrings. The humble herring was responsible for the city's early prosperity: Local fishermen knew how to catch, preserve, and market it better than anyone else in Europe. Tobacco arrived a few centuries later, and soon the institution of the tobacco-stained, fly-blown Bruine Kroeg—better known as the brown cafe—was born. Brown cafes worth their stains haven't been washed or painted since—thus their name—and are marvelous time tunnels to the Golden Age of Rembrandt's Amsterdam—via hippiedom, circa 1968, though the hippie scene is now as dead and buried as Count Floris V.

The talents and resources of the early immigrants fueled everything from diamond polishing (still an important industry) to shipbuilding and international trade. The 1602 creation of the East India Company by natives and immigrants ushered in the so-called Golden Age of the 17th century, when Amsterdam briefly reigned as Europe's most populous and powerful city. As the company's headquarters, Amsterdam in effect ruled a vast commercial empire, with satellites in South Africa, Indonesia, Sri Lanka, Goa, and China. As the company grew embarrassingly rich, so too did Amsterdam. Today, the East India Company is reviled by young Amsterdammers guilty about their checkered colonial past, but like it or not, the corporation helped make Amsterdam the handsome, prosperous cosmopolitan capital it is today. It also helped create the city's signature red-light district (the "RLD"): Practical-minded city governors saw the RLD as the best means to prevent sailors from raping the wives and daughters of locals (and it helped that it also generated considerable income, as it still does today).

During its heyday in the 17th century, the city burst through its medieval corset of walls and spilled outward in concentric semicircles; the Grachtengordel—literally, the "girdle of canals"—was built to handle this midriff bulge. First came the grandest canal of all, the Herengracht, whose Golden Bend (between Leidsestraat and Vijzelstraat) sprouted scores of mansions. The slightly less grand Keizersgracht followed, then the notably less grand Prinsengracht. The word "Grachtengordel" came to signify both the canals (a noun) and the fat-cat society living there (an adjective); it still does. Along these picturesque arteries thousands of opulent palaces, churches, and public buildings sprang up. Miraculously, most are still there, and some members of the same merchant-prince dynasties—notably the Six family—still live in them.

At the same time, beyond the Grachtengordel to the northwest, the helter-skelter Jordaan neighborhood grew, its name a corruption of the French *jardin* (garden), left behind by Napoléon Bonaparte when his invading army annexed the Netherlands from 1795 to 1813. The French forced the Amsterdammers to name and number the canals and streets, thus

making obsolete the city's endearing gablestones, which identi-
fied each home's owners with a picture-book bas-relief depiction
of the family trade. Poetically, the Jordaan's urban garden bears
the names of flowers: Rozengracht, Egelantiersgracht, Bloemstraat, and so on. Unless you're an architecture buff, the rest of the
city is beautiful but unremarkable—counterclockwise, the Old
West, Old South, New South, and East quarters, all added in the
19th and early 20th centuries.

Amsterdam may look like a museum, but it lives in the
present like no other European city. The economy has been
booming since the mid-1990s and looks set to weather the
post–September 11th period with aplomb. A whole new section of the city on the IJ River waterfront west of Centraal Station has been built since 1999 and occupies two large artificial
islands: Java and Borneo. There's also a new cruise ship port
facility to handle the increasing number of seagoing visitors.
Furthermore, A'dam deserves its reputation as both the sex,
drugs, and rock 'n' roll capital of the Continent, as well as
Europe's gay capital, thanks again to the centuries-old tradition of tolerance and a natural bent for commerce. You can
smoke small quantities of hash and marijuana, or nibble magic
mushrooms, in some 250 "smoking coffee shops"; prostitution
is legal so long as services are performed in registered whorehouses (prostitutes are covered by social security and now have
their own labor union); homosexuality has been legal for
almost 200 years. The number of cafes—many exquisitely
cozy, others wild and woolly—boggles the mind. Experimental music, dance, and theater flourish. Streets are animated
and amazingly safe day and night, because people live, work,
and play all over town instead of scurrying to the suburbs when
darkness falls. The presence of two large universities explains
only in part the number of young people living here. In fact,
A'dam is a talent magnet, drawing ambitious artists and businesspeople from all over Europe. Environmental consciousness is high, too (particularly if the problem is not in
Amsterdam's backyard). It's no coincidence that Greenpeace
International—a fine-tuned Dutch business with a multi-
million-dollar budget—is based here.

The ironic old Dutch saying, "Everything is possible, but
you're not supposed to enjoy it," seems hopelessly dated today.
Modern Amsterdammers seem untouched by Calvinism. The
cliché about a Calvinistic obsession with cleanliness is patently
false, too: The city's two liveliest squares, Leidseplein and
Rembrandtplein, often are merry pig sties. And don't be sur-

prised if the tabletop at your favorite cafe or restaurant is sticky with spilled beer.

Sound like paradise? Well, sort of. On the other hand, the weather is abysmal—consistently rainy and often cold—and prices continue to climb, despite a strong dollar. Environmental consciousness? Yes, car traffic is limited; the air (outside) is clean. But many of the estimated 5,000 houseboats in town flush raw sewage directly into the chocolate-brown canals. Locals smoke like chimneys; most cafes, restaurants, and clubs are blue with pollution, and nonsmoking sections are still not respected. Because it is legal here, prostitution is refreshingly unhypocritical as it eliminates pimps and keeps prostitutes off the streets. But the architecturally stunning red-light district is squalor itself. Toleration of soft drug use may sound enlightened; unfortunately, many smoking coffee shops and magic mushroom shops are dives controlled by organized crime.

The local strain of tolerance does not mean loving acceptance, either. While most Amsterdammers are cosmopolitan and curious, plenty are bigots. Citizens of ex-colonial origin—Indonesians, Surinamese, black Africans—sometimes say the Singelgracht is really a moat designed to keep them out. Central Amsterdam may be beautiful, clean, and safe, but suburbs like Bijlmermeer—80-percent immigrant—are seedy and dangerous. The opposite of white flight has occurred: Old-money families and new-money yuppies have stayed in the high-rent, fortresslike old city, while immigrants and the poor are exiled to outlying neighborhoods or suburbs, with soulless modern architecture and housing projects that incubate crime.

But let's be fair. Amsterdam remains one of the most alluring and prosperous cities on earth. One breed of visitor can stay in a chain hotel, take canal-boat cruises, tiptoe through tulip fields, buy clogs, and never see a prostitute, nightclub, or smoking coffee shop. A different sort can wear spiky leather to S&M workshops, cruise live-sex shows, and stay stoned day and night in dens of depraved carnality. You can also opt for a world-class hotel, dine in epicurean restaurants, take in concerts at the Concertgebouw or Bimhuis jazz club, shop for peerless antiques, and spend glorious days with the Dutch Masters in the Rijksmuseum.

Amsterdam today remains unquestionably the Continent's most compact, sophisticated cosmopolis. The European Union and single currency (the euro) have finally become a reality, and, as predicted, the Dutch are proving themselves to be the standard-bearers: multilingual, multicultural, rich, and disarmingly tolerant. Irreverence fits them to a tee. Enjoy!

Central Amsterdam Neighborhoods

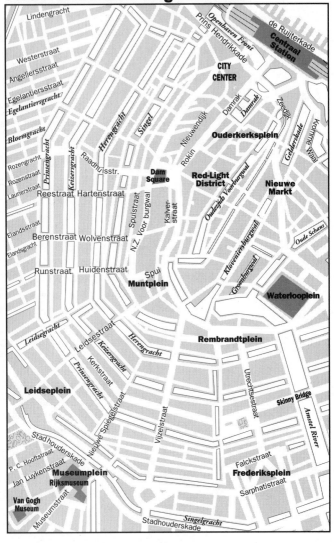

you probably didn't know

How to tolerate the Dutch sense of tolerance...
The Dutch in general, and Amsterdammers in particular, are very tolerant people. And they're the first to let you know that. Their extreme tolerance can sometimes be hard to take. The only thing Amsterdammers won't tolerate is intolerance, so rule number one is: Never criticize tolerance. The locals put up with prostitution; sex between (consenting) children ages 12 to 16; soft drugs and the attendant sleaze; millions of tourists; astronomical taxes; overcrowding (the city has one of the highest population densities in the world); huge numbers of immigrants and refugees; heavy smoking everywhere; frightful drivers; spoiled children; and dog dirt. On the international scene, they must put up with big, boorish neighbors like France and Germany, who are always telling them what to do when it comes to drugs, prostitution, immigration, and cooking. Among other things, this means that you, too, as a visitor, are fully expected to put up—graciously— with the aforementioned. This applies particularly when in restaurants, clubs, and cafes where the combined cigarette, cigar, dope, and pipe smoke is as thick as Dutch pea soup (see When smoke gets in your eyes, below).

How to swallow a fish like the locals... Some nations love shrimp heads, others tree grubs, others still raw oysters that slither down your throat. The Dutch have a peculiar predilection for herring, raw or pickled, which they gobble in a variety of ways. Go to the zoo to see how the seals do it, or observe the Dutch at one of the countless sidewalk fish stands in practically every city, town, and village in the Netherlands. Outside Amsterdam, herring is held by the tail and swallowed whole (gutted and cleaned already, of course). Little ado is made about bones and fins. Amsterdammers instead chop their herring into three or four pieces and eat them off a napkin or small plate. They can always spot out-of-towners by the way they eat fish.

How to avoid having your digital camera stomped... The red-light district is in one of the oldest parts of town, roughly from Warmoesstraat east to Nieuwemarkt Square, and from the Zeedijk (a street) south to Dam Straat (which, within the red-light district, changes its name to Oude Doelenstraat, and changes again to Oude Hoogstraat). It's architecturally appealing, historically significant, and seedy as hell. Regulating prostitution is a good idea for many reasons, including lower health risks, but concentrating it in one area has its downside. Contrary to what you'd expect, the district is pretty much safe by night when tittering tourists pour in for some sordid entertainment, but it can get dicey in the early morning when the Venus business is slow and the shops haven't opened yet. Druggies and pickpockets lurk in the district's narrow alleys and prey on jet-lagged tourists out for a 7am stroll. Stow away your camera at any time of day or night, and for Godsakes, don't take snapshots of the ladies in the picture windows. They don't want their photos taken because, as locals point out, "their daddies don't know" how they earn a living. If you are spotted taking snapshots you're liable to have your fancy digital unit stomped, along with parts of your anatomy. Business-minded readers will want to know that these painted ladies rent their windows for 8-hour shifts (typically they pay about 75 euros), during which time they take in 200 to 400 euros. Services begin with the poetically named "s--k and f--k" (condom required), for 25 to 40 euros, and proceed from there to your wildest desires. The prostitutes' union is called The Red Thread.

The once-infamous Zeedijk, which curves along the eastern edge of the district, is less dicey than it was even a few years ago. But it still attracts drug dealers and addicts, purse-snatchers, and other charming fauna. In general, use common sense: Don't stagger around the district when you're high; keep close track of your wallet or purse; don't flash your cash; and avoid the local dope peddlers, who sell low-quality wares and sometimes operate in cahoots with muggers. (Smoking coffee shops, described below, are much safer bets if you just want to enjoy some hash or marijuana.) Remember that Amsterdammers call the bridge that crosses Oudezijds Achterburgwal canal at Oude Hoogstraat the "Pillenbrug" (Pill Bridge) because so many druggies still hang out there, despite police efforts to move them on. The cat-and-mouse game continues into the new millennium.

How to define the indefinable gezellig... The Dutch make a cult of *gezellig*. *Gezellig*-ness (or *gezelligheid*) is the opposite of the other Dutch cult, that of efficiently run businesses and anything-goes commerce. The word is unpronounceable, and there's no English equivalent—cozy, homey, friendly, snuggly, cute, and swell all come close but don't quite get it. If you take something *gezellig* and stuff it into *gezellig* surroundings, *gezellig* becomes both form and function, medium and message. A well-worn brown cafe, a local restaurant, a living room with fireplace and friendly hound, even a good people-person, or a wonderful experience can be *gezellig*. Got that?

How to enjoy your hash and grass without being arrested... Tolerance may be a byword in Amsterdam, but so is ambiguity. For example, it's currently illegal to possess, use, or sell drugs, hard or soft. But if you have 5 grams of hash (or marijuana) or less, and a "small amount" of magic mushrooms, strictly for personal use, and you are 18 or older, you probably won't be hassled. Probably. However, you aren't allowed to buy or sell the stuff or smoke it outside so-called smoking coffee shops (which may stock no more than 500 grams). If the police want to, they can confiscate anything you have and fine you, but they seem to do this only when dope users behave obnoxiously. The authorities crack down indeed on hard-drug dealers and anyone causing a public nuisance. Currently there are some 250 smoking coffee shops in town (see Nightlife), down from 450 in 1995, which must follow certain "guidelines"—i.e., no hard drugs, no public nuisances, no sales to minors, and no transactions involving more than 5 grams. If a place breaks these rules, it will be shut down immediately, and its license to operate as a coffee shop revoked forever (nearly 200 licenses have been pulled in the last 5 years). Magic mushrooms and so-called "smart drugs," the trend since the late '90s, are natural or synthetic hallucinogenics sold in specialized shops with names like "Conscious Dreams"; as long as users do not make trouble for others they are ignored by the authorities. You can find out everything you ever wanted to know about dope and evolving legal issues at the **Hash and Marijuana Museum** (see Diversions for details). To speak to an official about drug use (and abuse), call **City Hall** at 020/552–9111; the operator will direct you to the info office; you can also call the Dutch Ministry of Justice (070/370-7911, www.minjust.nl/). Beware: A lot of Amsterdammers are fed up with pot smokers and the scruffy image they've given the city. Smoking weed in non-smoking establishments—many now display a "No Drugs" sign, in English—will make you most unpopular; you'll probably be asked to leave.

What the Jamaican flag really stands for... For one thing, the term "coffee shop" is never used nowadays by a normal cafe. You quickly learn to recognize the smoking variety. Sometimes it's the smell. Sometimes it's the name (Homegrown Fantasy, Smokey, Mellow Yellow, Grasshopper, etc.). Or the clientele—bleary-eyed, touristy, and/or trendy. Sometimes it's the use of palm trees or fronds (marijuana leaves cannot be shown) or the Jamaican flag on the shop front. Most often it's the decor—modern, slick, the opposite of *gezellig* brown cafes—and the music—grunge, funk, whatever is currently in fashion—played very loud. Bear in mind when you light up that organized crime has bought into most smoking coffee shops—an estimated 90 percent of them—which are ideal for money laundering.

When smoke gets in your eyes... Tobacco and dope pollution pose a serious challenge in all public places—hotel rooms, restaurants, cafes, lobbies, shops, businesses, and even (though it's illegal) public transportation. It's tough to avoid cig addicts and airborne Dutch pea soup. Many big hotels now have nonsmoking rooms (or entire floors); at others, call ahead and request management to air the room and bring in clean blankets. Fast food, vegetarian, and luxury and/or hotel restaurants often have nonsmoking sections (though they're not always respected). The only way to survive at cafes is to sit outside (often not an option, given the weather). Cafe de Jaren, one of the few spots with a nonsmoking room, got rid of it in 1999 because managers were unable to keep smokers at bay. See the Accommodations and Dining chapters for (short) lists of establishments with (theoretical) nonsmoking areas.

How to ride—and not lose—a Dutch bike... There are about 500,000 bicycles in this city of three-quarters of a million. You can rent one cheaply—about 2.50 to 3.50 euros per day—and you'll usually be asked to leave an ID card or passport as collateral. But bouncing over the cobbles on a rigid Dutch bike, some with back-pedal brakes, in the rain, is no picnic. To begin with, car, bike, and tram traffic is chaotic. Pavements are often slippery, uneven, and furrowed with tram tracks that seem expressly designed to trap tires. Cross them at an angle if you value your life (trams don't like to stop for clumsy bikers). Bikes do not have the right of way in Amsterdam. Never ride two abreast or without reflectors both fore and aft, or you'll risk getting a ticket (though the police have better things to do than bother bikers). Keep a plastic bag handy to cover your seat when you park your bike: It rains a lot in these parts.

Pickpockets

Violent crime is rare, but pickpocketing continues to be big business in Amsterdam, with thousands of cases reported annually. The police declare the last three months of each year as open season on foreign pickpockets, implementing special sting operations all over town that routinely net hundreds of professionals, all of them foreigners: South Americans, Africans, and East Europeans. The police warn known local pickpockets to stay home during such raids. Why? To break several international crime rings operating in Amsterdam and other European cities. (Local criminals are only too happy to oblige.) The prime locations for pickpocketing are Dam Square, Damrak, Centraal Station, and the red-light district. The technique: The pickpocket slips his hand into your back pocket and pushes you violently forward behind the shoulders. Your wallet is swiped as you fall. Sometimes the culprits work in teams: One distracts you as the other removes your valuables. The police often set up information booths in Dam Square to inform visitors of risks. Take note.

AMSTERDAM | YOU PROBABLY DIDN'T KNOW

Bike thieves are legion—witness the cheap deals at flea markets and on the so-called "Fietsenbrug" or "Bridge of Stolen Bikes" (its real name is the Sleutelbrug, next to A'dam University on the edge of the red-light district). You can pick up a stolen two-wheeler for as little as 10 euros. Locals readily admit that "after you've had your bike stolen five times, you too become a bike thief." They always use two locks, usually lug their bikes indoors, and offer up prayers to ward off their fellow thieves. Some hang their bikes off upper-story balconies, anti-black-bear style. Avoid chaining your bike to a tree —you might harm the tree, and the Dutch, like most right-thinking folk, prefer not to harm trees. If you rent from one of the dozens of bike-hire agencies in town, ask about their theft policy. All of them supply at least one lock; most supply two. Generally, if the bike is stolen it's your responsibility, and it'll cost you 100 to 200 euros. Only a few agencies offer theft insurance. Most hotels do not have a guarded bike-parking area.

On the other hand, there are plenty of bike lanes (marked with an obvious symbol or the word *Fietspad*), and cycling is a wonderful way to see the city—just ask Queen Beatrix, an avid cyclist. Though she lives near The Hague, she sometimes pedals through Amsterdam. You can spot her by her beautiful, classic Dutch bike and discreet police escort (a posse of about 20, also on bikes).

How to whiz around town... Forget the Amsterdam Metro—it serves suburbs you'll never see (unless you're heading to the ballpark, i.e, the Ajax soccer stadium). Most visitors don't realize, however, that trams (street-cars) provide a fun, fast, and cheap way to rollercoaster around town, which makes them very popular with locals. The Circle Tram (number 20) circles central A'dam, stopping at major sights and some big hotels. Those in the know buy either a *strippenkaart* (punch-as-you-go "strip tickets," which contain varying numbers of horizontal divisions, called strips, that are time-stamped when used), or a day, week, or month pass, all valid for any city transportation. They're sold at the GVB transit authority office in front of the main train station, at tobacco shops, post offices, VVV tourist info offices, and some train station ticket windows. The per-unit cost declines the more units you buy, so work out how many days you'll be in town and the distances (zones) you think you'll want to cover. Tickets are also sold onboard the trams, but cost slightly more per strip. There are 11 zones in greater Amsterdam; knowing exactly how many strips to punch is an art not easily mastered. A typical central-city ride is one zone, for which you punch two strips; two zones require three strips, and so forth (always one strip more than the total number of zones). Once stamped, the ticket is valid for one hour on trams, buses, and Metro/light rail lines. If you have any doubts about the number of strips needed for your trip—even locals some-times do—ask the driver or conductor to stamp your ticket for you and to tell you when you've reached your desired stop. Keep in mind that there are two types of trams in town: On those with conductors (lines 4, 6, 7, 10, and 13), drivers can't sell or stamp tickets, and they're likely to bark at you if you ask them to. A small sticker at the front of the tram will tell you to board at the rear if a conductor is pre-sent. If in doubt, get on the back and work your way up to the front to buy your ticket. But the best way to know where to jump on is simply to watch where the locals are lining up. To alight, remember to press the "deur open" button, then step on the bottom tread to keep the doors from slam-ming shut on you.

How to avoid being eaten alive by mosquitoes in summer... Canals hold water. Mosquitoes breed in water. Amsterdam has a lot of canals. Therefore Amster-dam has a lot of... mosquito nets. In fact, mosquitoes can make a summer visit miserable. How to beat the bugs? Stay in a hotel with screens (ask before reserving), bring a net with you to drape around your bed, or buy one at specialty shops like **Klamboe Unlimited** or **Marañon** (see Shopping). The size of a large poncho or a rolled-up double sheet, mosquito nets are easy to travel with.

How to ice-skate like the locals... As Breughel might say if he were alive today, if you skate on thin ice, you can expect to sink through into dirty, cold canal water. You'll know when the time is right to strap on your gear and venture onto the icy waterways: When the locals migrate from easy pond (or rink) skating in parks (the Vondelpark and Oosterpark) and squares (the Leidse-plein becomes a rink), and begin zipping up and down the solid sections of the canals. They stay away from the edges and the areas around bridges, and so should you. If you're a serious skater, you're best off bringing your blades from home, since most Amsterdammers own their own and skates are difficult to rent (see Getting Outside).

How to order and drink Dutch genever (gin)...

Genever—Dutch gin—is a potentially lethal concoction made from molasses and juniper berries. This is the national spirit, in the widest sense of the term, and comes in three basic varieties: *jong* (young), *oud* (old), and *zeer oud* (senile). Sometimes it has delightful flavorings—*bitterje* (with angostura bitters), *citroenjenever* (lemony), or *bessenjenever* (sweetened with blackcurrant syrup). Belly up to the bar of a brown cafe or *Proeflokaal* tap house (see Dining and Cafes for details), lean over your brimming, tulip-shaped glass, and slurp. When the glass is properly overflowing, it's called a *kamelenrun* (the one that broke the camel's back), or an *over het IJ-kijkertje* (view over the River IJ). The hip, if generic, way to ask for one is a *borrel* (a shot). There's a whole vocabulary to accompany *genever* (also spelled with a "j"): *recht op en neer* ("straight up"), *pikketanussie* (something akin to "cheers"), and half a dozen other unpronounceable (and probably obscene) terms. Many locals knock back their booze with a beer chaser, called a *kopshoot*, literally "a blow to the head." Fitting.

How to navigate the gay capital of Europe...

Admittedly, "Gay Amsterdam" doesn't ring quite as poetically as "Gai Paris," but this is where the action is. Homosexuality has been legal since 1811, and the age of consent (since 1971) is a low 16. In 1987 the city erected the world's first memorial to gays and lesbians persecuted by the Nazis, the so-called Homomonument, three rose-colored granite triangles spilling across the small square behind Westerkerk and into the waters of the Keizersgracht canal. It has since become a rallying point for the gay community. Scores of clubs, bars, restaurants, and hotels all over town cater to every imaginable taste and tendency (though most are oriented toward gay men). Gays are thoroughly integrated into business, journalism, politics, and the arts; nonetheless, four largely gay districts exist. **Reguliersdwarsstraat**, between Rembrandtplein and Koningsplein, and **Amstel,** on the south riverbank between Vijzelstraat and the Blauwbrug, attract a young, hip crowd. **Warmoesstraat**, which traverses the red-light district on its western edge, draws more of a leather, S&M, and cling-wrap-jeans bunch. **Kerkstraat**, between Leidsegracht and Vijzelstraat, is tame, and appeals to quieter, older gays. A lot of gay venues welcome straights, and some are among the city's liveliest. Local lesbians have a limited club scene; mostly, they hang out in cafes and at ad hoc all-night parties listed in local magazines (*Day by Day* and *Gay & Night Magazine* are published in English). Lesbian (and gay/lesbian) bars, cafes, and discos like **Saarein II** (tel 020/623–4901; Elandsstraat 119), **You 2** (tel 020/421–0900; Amstel 178), and **GETTO** (tel 020/421–5151; Warmoesstraat 51), or book shops like **Xantippe** (tel 020/623–5854, xantippe@xs4all.nl; Prinsengracht 290) and **Vrolijk** (tel 020/623–5142, www.vrolijk.nl; Paleisstraat 135) also provide fliers advertising these parties. All the latest gay info is available at www.gayamsterdam.com or www.switchboard.nl. (See Accommodations, Nightlife, and Hotlines for more on gay Amsterdam.)

What passes for an age of consent... Tolerance and ambiguity blend in the question of the age of consent for both heterosexual and homosexual intercourse. Legally, it is 16. However, a difficult-to-interpret law, passed in December 1991, makes nonviolent sexual acts among persons aged 12 to 16 an affair to be dealt with by parents. If complaints are made by either the children or parents, the case can be referred to the Council of Youth Protection or to the police. Such complaints can be filed for up to 12 years after the alleged act. The law was intended to allow cases of sex among teenagers of about the same age to be resolved outside the legal system and was in no way intended to encourage sex between adults and children. Nonetheless, the result has been that child prostitutes and "rent-a-boy" agencies continue to do business.

How to greet (or take leave of) an Amsterdammer... When you meet locals for the first time and are introduced, you shake hands. Thereafter no more handshaking is expected until you meet up again after a considerable period of separation. With their constant clasps and kisses, the French and (especially) Italians seem to embarrass the Dutch. Ditto Americans with their countless hearty handshakes. In Amsterdam, once you've made friends, you exchange three pecks (really just a smacking of the lips) on the cheeks. The proper order is left-right-left. Three times. Never two or four. Men do this with women; women with men; women with women; but not men with men, unless they are gay (or Italian).

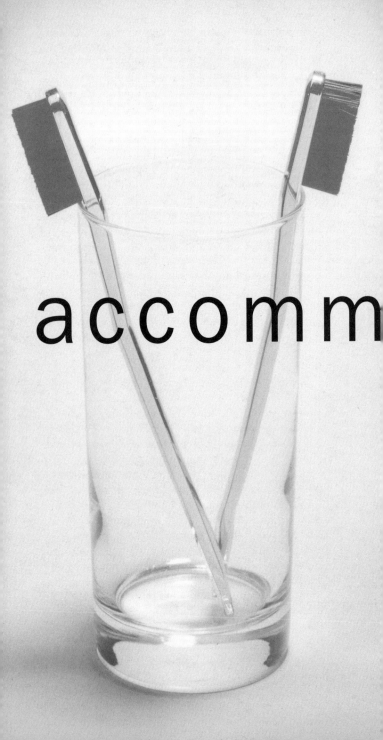

accomm

1

odations

The Internet and
21st century have
taken Amsterdam
by storm, but
many of its hotels
still belong to
earlier epochs.

Don't mind the labyrinthine corridors and the lace-draped window that looks onto a wall. Call it *gezellig,* i.e., cozy. The Dutch obsession with coziness applies doubly to hotels in Amsterdam. Ask Amsterdammers what counts in a hotel and you're likely to hear them say "atmosphere" or "character," rather than "luxury," "comfort," or "convenience." What locals might consider a great room can be cramped, cluttered, nearly inaccessible, and impregnated with the smell of stale tobacco. Happily, the Dutch are also a nation of neatniks, and, like the Swiss, worship efficiency. So, many A'dam hotels are homey, squeaky-clean, and professionally run.

If Dutch "charm" doesn't come high on your list, most international chain hotels are here, as well as the home-grown AMS and Golden Tulip groups. Since the late 1990s, Amsterdam has two super-luxury hotels—the **Amstel Inter-Continental** and **The Grand Amsterdam**—that rank among Europe's best, plus a constellation of bona fide charmers like the **Ambassade, 717,** and **Blakes**. The city has a startling capacity to accommodate all tastes; you'll be delighted to discover hotels sleazy and sublime, catering to backpackers, gays, philosophers, musicians, S&M aficionados, dope smokers, and cyclists.

Amsterdam's so-called canal-house hotels—centuries-old, converted private homes facing the capital's 100-plus waterways—are the most sought-after properties. Most are small, *gezellig,* family-run gems. Only a few, such as **Ambassade** and **Estheréa,** have elevators, and the staircases in many are like ladders, leading to rooms where average Americans bump their heads and sleep with their feet hanging off the beds. Don't forget that there are dozens of leafy gardens and courtyards in town; often a room overlooking one of these, on the back side of a canal house or other hotel, is preferable to a potentially noisy canal-side room with a view.

Almost all one-, two-, and three-star hotels include in the room price a copious Dutch buffet breakfast (ham, cheeses, rolls, butter, jam, croissants, fruit juices). Some four-star and almost all five-star hotels charge extra—up to 30 euros—for continental breakfast, and considerably more for a Dutch or American breakfast. Bed-and-breakfasts are not common. Nonsmoking rooms are few and far between, found primarily in luxury and business establishments; even these sometimes smell of smoke, since the Dutch simply ignore smoking prohibitions. Be aware that in some Dutch hotels, especially family-run operations, double rooms could have twin beds pushed together. Calvin would approve.

Winning the Reservations Game

Most of the hotels listed here have been inspected and rated by the Benelux Hotel Classification system, which assigns them stars—not according to quality, but simply according to the number of rooms and the facilities provided (such as elevator, garage, and special services). You're likely to land in one of the reported 29,500 Benelux beds in some 300 A'dam hotels.

But Amsterdam is an expensive city, and many of those beds are pricey (around 40 percent are in four- or five-stars). This overabundance at the high-end continues to ramp up competition, bringing prices down for travelers who know to ask for a favorable room rate. No one pays "rack rates" (standard list prices) anymore for upper-end rooms. Because of the continuing price war, you can often get a five-star room for the list price of a four-star room, or a four-star room for the price of a three-star. Tourist-class and budget hotels are harder to crack, especially those in canal houses, which are very popular.

The best approach is to call, fax, or e-mail several hotels, ask what their standard rates are, then ask for the corporate rate, the weekend rate, the special discount rate, the winter (and bad-weather) rate (which ought to be available nine months of the year), the advance-booking rate, and any other rate you can think of. There's always a better rate available (except during the Christmas and New Year's holidays and the last week of April, when the queen's birthday celebrations occur). The Dutch are a nation of traders and are used to dickering. Book as far ahead as possible: The prospect of your custom will soften up even the toughest managers, and you'll also be able to request the kind of room you prefer. The longer your proposed stay, the more leverage you have. Visitors sometimes negotiate a room rate based on a lengthy stay—of a week or more—then switch gears and convince the hotel to apply that rate to their actual (shorter) stay. Dutch hoteliers whine and complain about such underhanded methods, but use them themselves when traveling.

Reserving through a travel agent in the United States will probably get you a good rate, too, since many hotels belong to international reservations systems (Accor, Bilderberg, Carlton, CIGA, Concorde, Golden Tulip International BV, Hilton, Holiday Inn, Mercure, Swissotel, Utell International, and so forth). The various branches of the **Amsterdam Tourist**

Office (called the VVV—pronounced fay, fay, fay) will book rooms for you at the last minute, but you must go in person to one of their offices and pay a fee of about 3 euros per person (later deducted from your hotel bill). The main VVV offices are inside Centraal Station and opposite it at Stationsplein 10 (tel 0900–400–4040; 55 euro cents per minute; www.amsterdamtourist.nl, reservations@amsterdamtourist.nl, or www.visitamsterdam.com and www.holland.com). Branch offices are at Leidseplein 1 (corner of Leidsestraat), Stadionplein, and the main arrivals hall at Schiphol Airport (marked "Holland Tourist Information"). A further possibility for same-day reservations is the **Holland Tourist Information Office** located at Damrak 35, in central Amsterdam, or Hotel Bookings, a private web site: www.bookings.nl. (See Hotlines for these offices' opening hours.)

Is There a Right Address?

It depends entirely upon what you're looking for. Of the dozen or so distinct neighborhoods within the A10 beltway, which separates Amsterdam from the suburbs, none is bad or dangerous.

The city's core, inside the Singelgracht canal, is, unsurprisingly, called the Centrum. Fanning out from it in a wide semicircle are, counterclockwise, the Oud West (Old West), Oud Zuid (Old South), De Pijp, and Oost (East); beyond the Old South is the Nieuw Zuid (New South). Distances are short: A fast walker can cross from Centraal Station to the New South in an hour and a quarter; a tram or taxi takes 15 to 20 minutes.

The Centrum, the biggest and most interesting district, is really a mosaic of neighborhoods. If you don't mind noisy sex-tourism crowds (both gay and straight), winking red neon lights, and hash or grass smoke wafting from the dozens of smoking coffee shops, check out the several top hotels on the edge of the **red-light district**, a few hundred yards from the train station, abutting Dam Square and the main shopping streets Rokin, Damrak, and Kalverstraat. Despite its reputation for prostitution, drug dealing, and petty crime, this area is perfectly safe if you know how to navigate it (see You Probably Didn't Know), and in any case, all the upscale hotels here are beyond the carefully contained sleaze zone. From them you can walk in minutes to anywhere in the center of town.

Just west of the red-light district, and still in the heart of the Centrum, is a boomerang-shaped neighborhood sometimes referred to as the **Dam** or **Spui.** Stretching from Centraal Station to the flower market at Munt Plein, it offers a maze of tiny alleys and several appealing squares, and a handful of the city's best restaurants, spread along Spuistraat. However, the neighborhood's main arteries—Damrak, Rokin, and Nieuwezijds Voorburgwal—are noisy, with heavy tram traffic and crowds of pedestrians. Most of the canals here have been covered over; the exception is the Singel, originally the medieval city's moat, along which you'll see several fine hotels.

Beyond the Singel is the celebrated **Grachtengordel** neighborhood, clustering around three semicircular canals—Herengracht, Keizersgracht, and Prinsengracht—built in Amsterdam's 17th-century Golden Age. "Grachtengordel" in Dutch has also come to mean "chic," "plugged-in," "monied," etcetera, and here you'll find tony restaurants and cafes, boutiques for the megabucks crowd, and the antique dealers' quarter on Nieuwe Spiegelstraat (see Shopping). The location is great for exploring the adjacent Jordaan neighborhood and also puts you within striking distance of museums and the city's two liveliest squares, Rembrandtplein and Leidseplein. You may have to book far in advance to get into Grachtengordel hotels, but it's worth it.

Still within the Centrum, on the district's eastern edge, is the **Jordaan**, a wonderful part of town with narrow streets and narrower buildings, quiet, shady canals, and scads of one-of-a-kind boutiques, cafes, and neighborhood restaurants. Unfortunately, there are only a few hotels here, and they're strictly downscale properties.

The prosperous **Old South** neighborhood, beyond the Singelgracht, is looking better all the time, especially if you want quiet nights. The "big three" museums—the Rijksmuseum, Van Gogh Museum, and Stedelijk Museum of Modern Art—are here, as well as the handsome Vondelpark, a great place to bike, jog, roller-blade, or picnic. There are quiet streets and turn-of-the-century architecture, plus great shopping, but it's just far enough out that it becomes hard to wander the central city neighborhoods' marvelous streets at night—one of the great joys of staying in Amsterdam. The same (and more so) applies to the **New South**, an even more prosperous and farther-flung neighborhood dotted with interesting Amsterdam School architecture. The Hilton is here, as well as a few four-star places strung along Apollolaan. If you stay in the New South you'll have to rely on taxis and trams to get around.

But if easy access to the airport and countryside are your priorities, then go for it.

The Lowdown

In search of canal-house coziness... Just because a building overlooks a canal doesn't mean it's a canal house, or there would be hundreds in Amsterdam. True canal-house hotels occupy old private residences—usually from the 17th or 18th century—*and* have canal-side rooms with views. A few bare-bones canal houses have steep stairs, no elevators, and no facilities to speak of. Still, these are only-in-Amsterdam hotels, which is why visitors put up with their inconvenience. Don't be put off by appearances at cheap and cheery **De Admiraal**, a beer-can's throw from Rembrandtplein—some rooms have showers or baths down the hall, but all include color TVs and are comfortably furnished, with polished plank floors. The pleasant breakfast room is filled with green plants and lit by a dreamy Persian lamp. Close by, popular **Seven Bridges** is an intimate perch overlooking one of Amsterdam's most picturesque waterways—but be prepared for slightly inflated prices. It's so small, affable owners Gunter Glaner and Pierre Keulers serve you breakfast in your room. Not a bad thing, given the comfy old furnishings, the houseplants, and views (ask for a canal-side room on an upper floor—not in the attic or the basement). The flower market, a few blocks away, seems to have opened an annex in the lobby of **Agora**, an upscale two-star in a 1735 house decorated with Persian throw rugs, feathery armchairs, and scattered antiques. A pocket-sized back garden adds to the charm. Next door at **The Waterfront,** new owner Willem Van der Ham has totally remodeled and upgraded this once-notorious spot with maghogany furniture, bay windows, thick carpets, and drapes—but it's still two stars and affordable. At **Amsterdam Wiechmann** visitors choose between *gezellig*, antique-filled canal-side doubles or less expensive and more anonymous modern rooms. This narrow canal house has a memorable lobby, with delftware hanging on the walls and the kind of Oriental carpets you see draped over tables in many of Amsterdam's old-fashioned brown cafes. The breakfast room looks like a greenhouse, and there's a suitably snug bar and lounge. The modest

Hegra's most distinctive feature may well be its step-gable facade; it sure isn't the dull, though tidy, decor or stern staff. The low price and handy central location, however, may make you very forgiving. Pricier but spanking new and full of Calvinistic Minimalist charm is **'t Hotel,** a three-star overlooking lovely Leliegracht.

Higher-end canal houses mix charm with practical touches like elevators, bars, and restaurants, though you still shouldn't expect perks like swimming pools, fully equipped health centers, or convention facilities. Near Westerkerk, **Toren**, upgraded in 1999 from two to four stars, has a 17th-century marble entrance hall and a lovely breakfast room with a painted, molded ceiling. Canal-side rooms have nice views, but consider instead a room looking onto the attractive garden. There are antiques, fireplaces, and cozy public areas. **717**, a canal "guest house" with five-star prices and persnickety managers, exudes luxe, calm, and voluptuousness amid antiques, contemporary art, and designer textiles. **Estheréa**, a comfy four-star, is increasingly cozy since many rooms have been redone in 2000–2001 with pastel colors and quirky light fixtures. **Ambassade** has museum-quality antiques, a new library of books by author-guests, and a heady location on the famous Golden Bend—locals call it the "Mini Amstel" (see "The grande dames" below) because it offers luxury *and* character: marble bathrooms, prints and oils by minor Dutch masters, crystal chandeliers, and antique armchairs. The Sheraton-owned **Hotel Pulitzer**, sprawling along Prinsengracht and dotted with hidden gardens and courtyards, is downright opulent, in a predictably plush corporate style that's totally un-*gezellig*.

For tourists who want clogs, windmills, and tulips... If gawking at Amsterdam from a tour bus suits you, book rooms at the **Grand Hotel Golden Tulip Krasnapolsky**. Commonly known as the "Kras'" (can a nickname tell all?), this Victorian grande dame saw its heyday about 100 years ago; the Polish tailor-turned-hotelier who founded it started out in 1866 with the Wintertuin (Winter Garden) restaurant and went on to build a grand hotel around it. The Krasnapolsky now fills several city blocks, drawing package sightseers and conventioneers to its cavernous interior, which has been remodeled countless times. Another give-away name is **Golden Tulip Barbizon Palace**. Visitors on whirlwind tours of windmills and tulip fields will like the comfortable rooms and facilities here—the rooms are basically decorated in cookie-cutter traditional, though some have exposed oak rafters. The over-the-top faux marble colonnade in the lobby looks like it was lifted from a Cinecittà sandals-and-toga movie set (*Hercules Against Rome*, perhaps). Across the center of town, at the immense **Amsterdam Renaissance Hotel** (a Marriott property as of 1999), there's plenty of space to stow souvenirs in the forgettable rooms and to break in your clogs at the Boston Club Disco, a local hotspot.

For enemies of clogs, windmills, and tulips... There's not even room to park tour buses in front of the **Ambassade,** a canal-house hotel that occupies 12 17th-century properties on the handsome Herengracht. The discreet, anonymous owner collects antiques, and it shows in the total lack of kitsch. Each room is different, and that appeals to the literary crowd usually found here (many Dutch publishers and agents book rooms for their star writers—there's now a charming author-guest library on the ground floor). Crystal chandeliers and enormous rooms make you feel like a pearl in an oyster; a few even have canopy beds. **717,** a super-luxury "guest house," has eight suites only, authentic Dutch Masters and antiques, and owners who would probably faint if you even *mentioned* clogs or tulips. Savvy business travelers and other well-heeled guests stay at the **Estheréa,** an upscale canal-house hotel with a great location overlooking the Singel. Between gazing from your window at surrounding mansions and chatting up your hosts, a friendly family of experienced Dutch hoteliers, you'll feel more like an Amsterdam resident here than a tourist. The lobby of **'t Hotel,** a new canal-house hotel, doubles as an antiques shop. **Toren,** a small, luxurious four-star, has antiques, a garden, and an exclusive atmosphere. Lovers of spare luxury—and chic black decor and dress—will want to check out **Blakes,** with its garden court and top-rated restaurant.

The grande dames... Back in 1866, when the **Grand Hotel Golden Tulip Krasnapolsky** opened for business, things like heated winter terraces, modern plumbing, central heating, and electric lights were unknown. The Kras' was the first in Amsterdam in all these departments. Time hasn't stood still: Much of the charming decor of old is gone, there is no more "grand" even in the name, and the location on rather tacky Dam Square isn't what it used to be. The Victorian gentry who frequented the Kras' would probably go elsewhere today, yet there's a bit of the grande dame left, especially off season, when the Winter Garden is a joy and there are no tulips in bloom to attract the bus crowds. In an earlier incarnation, the **Amstel Inter-Continental** (sans "Inter-Continental") was the Krasnapolsky's direct rival, opening a year later in 1867. After a $50-million renovation that took years, the Amstel reopened in the mid-1990s and is now in a class all its own, with sky-high prices to match. Liveried doormen flank the marble grand hall, and if you're on a shopping spree, diamonds are available at the boutique. Dutch royals have staged family celebrations in the opulent Spiegelzaal (the Mirror Room) and the list of celeb guests is long. The **Hotel de L'Europe**, built in 1896, was the top hotel in town for most of the 20th century. Haughtily perched over the river and Munt Plein, it looks much as it probably did the day it opened. Despite a late-1990s renovation and all the usual trappings of luxury—the faux Empire furniture, thick carpets, molded plaster decorations, and doorman with epaulets and striped trousers—it remains behind the Amstel and **The Grand Amsterdam**. Though the Grand Amsterdam hotel itself is new, it boasts a historic site—it started out as the 15th-century convent of St. Cecilia and served as city hall until 1992. (Queen Beatrix and Prince Claus were married upstairs in 1966.) Planted on two beautiful courtyards just south of the red-light district, this newest of the grand hotels goes in for muted colors and understated luxury.

In search of the indefinable *gezelligheid*... In a city where coziness means floral arrangements, knickknacks, antique furniture, grandfather clocks, and pianos (baby grands are best), a young Irish couple has taken over but preserved cozy **Canal House**, occupying five old houses on (and behind) one of the city's prettiest canals. It still wins hands-down in most *gezelligheid* categories. Quiet, quaint, and cute are the operative words. Most clients are American or British; many swoon over the memorable breakfast room with its parquet floors, molded plaster ceilings, and baby grand piano. Luckily, back rooms are just as snug, and even quieter. **Hotel Washing-**

ton's armchairs, polished parquet floors, red runners, and carved banister exude Edwardian comfort. It's the kind of seriously quiet place where you nod and whisper to your fellow guests, gay and straight, as classical music plays softly in the background: the Concertgebouw Auditorium is nearby and most guests are musicians or music-lovers. The book-lined salon and vaguely colonial terrace of **De Filosoof**—a one-of-a-kind hotel with philosophy as a theme—are quintessentially cozy, though some of the rooms are anything but (the Heidegger Room is thoroughly black). The Aristotle Room has a classical pediment; the Plato Room is black and white, with trompe-l'oeil decorations; and so forth. One of the co-owners, Ida Jongsma, is a former high school philosophy teacher. When **Toren** jumped from two stars to four (in 1999), out came the red bedspreads and heavy fabrics, the roaring fireplaces, and the twinkling chandeliers: cozy-luxe *gezellig,* with class.

Taking care of business... If you're looking for a big, American-style hotel, with big, no-nonsense rooms and all the business facilities you'll need, try the **Amsterdam Renaissance Hotel** (formerly a Ramada, now a Marriott hotel). The **Hilton Amsterdam** is still a favorite business hotel, thanks to its safe, rather boring notions of executive luxury. Where its younger business-hotel competitors offer clients personal computers and fax machines, the Hilton still staunchly lists typewriters among equipment available. In addition to its seven-story atrium lobby and tidy theme-decor rooms (Scandinavian, Oriental, Old Dutch, art deco), the **Radisson-SAS Hotel Amsterdam** has a business and conference center in its south building. You may not even have to leave your comfortable room at the **Golden Tulip Barbizon Palace**, right across from Centraal Station: Telephones come with computer interfaces, and more technology is available at the front desk. Then, when working hours are over, you can amble downstairs to the Henry Hudson Club lounge—though a bit starchy, it's not bad at all if you fancy relaxing with a book by a crackling fire in winter.

If you don't need the apparatus of a big hotel, look into the practical, family-run **Estheréa**, which draws a mix of discreet businesspeople and well-heeled families. The hotel overlooks the Singel, between Dam Square and the floating flower market, and offers nice canal views; free Internet access. Venture off the buttoned-down track and stay at **Bilderberg Hotel Jan Luyken**, a quietly confident four-star in a Dutch art-nouveau building near Museumplein. It was remodeled top to bottom in 2001 with a corporate "boutique-design" theme and attracts a VC/VP clientele.

For travelers with old money... The owner of the extraordinary three-star **Ambassade** knows that old-money travelers hate to spend more than they have to. For the price of a closet at the five-star competition, you can get a suite with a sitting room and two bedrooms here. Half the museums in town would love to get hold of the china and grandfather clocks in the hotel's common areas. If money's no object, then by all means settle into **The Grand Amsterdam**. Keen to have an instant pedigree, this recently founded hotel quietly and rather disingenuously touts the building's 600-year history (in fact, much of the complex dates to the early 1900s). The desk staff dress and behave like good Dutch ladies and gentlemen, whispering what others shout. Black-and-gray marble floors grace the vaulted lobby, and the rooms feature a subdued palette of salmon, teal, and saffron. Guests take tea (or more interesting drinks) in a leafy inner courtyard and meals at Café Roux (see Dining), brainchild of restaurateur Albert Roux of London's famous Le Gavroche. The **Amstel Inter-Continental,** with its 1867 birthdate and megabuck rebirth ($50 million) in the mid-'90s, modestly calls itself "a favorite with cosmopolitan society—from royalty and the aristocracy to luminaries in the arts and international affairs." Indeed—as long as they have fat wallets. If you're worried about denting the old trust fund, instead check out the **Hotel de L'Europe**, little changed since its 1896 birth. Less sumptuous than either the Amstel or The Grand, this remodeled oldster is on the rebound. Don't worry, it's sufficiently coddling. The lobby's centerpiece is still a Sun King–style clock, but the highly polished floor now reflects molded plaster decorations lightened of dust.

For travelers with new money... The **Amstel Inter-Continental** has just enough old-school cachet to attract both Golden Age spenders and the aggressively nouveau. Rock stars and groupies with euros to burn monopolize the palatial health club and pool. Water taxis drop shiploads of crocodile bags on the private dock, and deeply tanned torsos

ACCOMMODATIONS | THE LOWDOWN

ACCOMMODATIONS | THE LOWDOWN

draped in gold chains and diamonds are spotted in mid-winter in the magnificent arcaded lobby. Some guests probably wish the pianist in the swank La Rive restaurant would stop with the classical stuff already and play "New York, New York" or "Volare." The endless roster of glitzy visitors is the talk of the town (Red Hot Chili Peppers, Janet Jackson, Madonna, Jagger, Spielberg…). Naturally, a chauffeured Rolls Royce and historic saloon boat are at your disposal. The immense **Grand Hotel Golden Tulip Krasnapolsky** is especially popular if you want to show the locals that you own (or have rented) a large luxury car and are going to drive through Amsterdam despite traffic restrictions, right into the garage at the Kras', at the center of the universe on Dam Square. The landmark Dutch art-nouveau **American Hotel** on lively Leidseplein likes to call itself "the entertainment hotel," because minor rock stars and groupies who can't quite manage the Amstel book into its spacious rooms (redone in mock art deco, many have views over Leidseplein or the Singelgracht canal). Guests abuse the 24-hour room service and pose in the famous Nightwatch Bar, feeling wonderful when the bartender remembers their names and favorite drinks. (He remembers everyone's name and favorite drink.) The hip new-rich are fighting over the 20-odd rooms of super-luxe **Blakes,** in a 17th-century former theater/almshouse/lawyers' office converted into a showcase for British designer Anouska Hempel's megabuck Asian-Spartan-look rooms (mostly black). Call it Rigor Mortis?

Dowdy but lovable… Even the name sounds nice and sweet: **Acacia**. It's the kind of place where first-time travelers meet gentle, middle-aged folks wearing sandals and white socks. Owners Hans and Marlene van Vliet are young, have kids, and like people, and their tiny, triangle-shaped Jordaan hotel is simple and clean. The staircase is as steep as they come (naturally there's no elevator) and there are no TVs in the rooms, but then you'll be too busy reading up on Amsterdam to worry about Dutch TV. The **Amsterdam Wiechmann Hotel**, a narrow canal-house hotel, has too much character to be prim, but the lady at the desk will protect you from undesired elements: "No one not registered is allowed in the rooms," she booms. **The Bridge Hotel** has a grand lobby but plain-Jane rooms and a mousy-friendly staff. **Owl** is the kind of place where you might run into birdish maiden aunts who've brought their nieces up from the provinces: It's a pleasant, family-run three-star hotel with two-star prices, just one block from the Vondel-park on a quiet residential street. With a pastel color scheme, the no-nonsense, summery style matches the garden setting. Tidy **Van Onna** is a cheap one-star on peaceful Bloemgracht canal in Jordaan. All rooms are furnished with modern, metal-frame chairs, tables, and beds; the bathrooms are squeaky-clean but eccentric: The shower heads stick out over the toilets and drain in the middle of the floor. At the **Van Ostade Bicycle Hotel**, a little hotel wedged into a narrow, early-1900s building in the blue-collar De Pijp neighbor-hood, guests are encouraged to pedal their days away sight-seeing. A bike hangs from the facade of the hotel, and its owners, Jos and Clemens, are keen cyclists and will rent you two-wheelers for about 3 to 4 euros a day (fractionally cheaper than commercial rates). Renovated in 1995, the place is clean both literally and figuratively: A "No Drugs" sign adorns the front door.

For those who hate surprises... If you're used to the plush, overstuffed, thick-carpeted brand of luxury found at the Sheraton hotels worldwide, you'll be delighted by the **Hotel Pulitzer**. Occupying 24 old canal houses in the shadow of Westerkerk, this ex-CIGA luxury hotel has a warren of inner gardens and courtyards, some with a pri-vate entrance on one of the canals. The **Radisson-SAS Royal Hotel**, in Old Amsterdam south of the red-light district, offers typical SAS theme rooms—choose between faux Scandinavian, old Dutch, Oriental, or art deco. There's a pleasant enough restaurant (the De Palm-boom Brasserie), a brown cafe (the Pastorie Bar, set in a transplanted 18th-century landmark vicarage), and a glassed-in atrium lobby with a fountain. The 11-story, boomerang-shaped **Hilton Amsterdam** in the far-flung New South could be a Hilton anywhere, and that's prob-ably its strongest point (it's got big rooms and reliable ser-vice). God only knows why, but John Lennon and Yoko Ono enacted their celebrated "Bed-In" here in 1969, and the hotel has been successfully marketing their suite ever since. The **Golden Tulip Schiller Hotel**, a seven-story turn-of-the-century property overlooking Rembrandt-plein, remains a monument to its original owner, Fritz Schiller, a slightly mad amateur painter whose kitschy land-scapes adorn the lobby, cafe, and rooms to this day. Remod-eled top to bottom in 1997, Mr. Schiller's marvel now belongs to the ever-expanding Golden Tulip chain; wisely,

ACCOMMODATIONS | THE LOWDOWN

they kept the art. A certain amount of character remains
in the comfy leather armchairs and sofas in the vaulted
lobby and in the wood-panelled, crepuscular Schiller Cafe,
once a literary hangout but now a comfortingly rear-guard
hideout for friendly middle-aged locals.

Luscious love nests... The hushed, antiques-filled
salons, library, and canal-view rooms of the **Ambassade**,
on the Herengracht's Golden Bend, are ideal for soulful
yearnings. Middle-aged and older romantics who don't
make noise when making love will find a cozy, antique-
feathered nest at **Canal House**, overlooking Keizersgracht, almost next door to Westerkerk. If you always
wanted to float that romantic proposal but didn't know
how, you can rent a cute little houseboat covered with
flowers from the **Acacia**, in the supremely romantic Jordaan, and make love on the leafy Lijnbaansgracht. Gays
who prefer a mixed clientele, lots of green plants, and
comfy old furniture favor **Seven Bridges** or **De Admiraal**,
two tiny canal-house hotels near Rembrandtplein. **Toren**,
a plush four-star with red bedspreads, antiques, fireplaces,
and crystal chandeliers, also has a pocket-sized garden for
sniffing roses and tiptoeing through tulips. Westerkerk is
nearby, in case you want to tie the knot before (or after)
parting the thick curtains. The marble entrance hall is
nearly 400 years old, and if the breakfast room with the
molded, painted ceiling ain't romantic, nothing is ("Hey,
aren't those cupids flying around up there?").

Rooms with a view... There are no skyscrapers or tall
buildings in central Amsterdam, and the only high-rise
hotels are so far out that the scenery isn't worth seeing.
This is a flat city of intimate, keyhole views—a tree-
lined bend in a canal, a stretch of wide river—rather
than Empire State Building–style oohs and ahs. The
Amstel Inter-Continental luxuriates on the east bank
of the Amstel River, just south of the old locks that reg-
ulate the flow of water through the city's canals, and
from the rooms' French windows, guests have a panorama
of river traffic, city lights, and drawbridges. The **Hotel
de L'Europe** also overlooks the Amstel River and some
rooms have loveseat-sized riverside balconies—make
sure you get one so you can watch the trams slink by and
the private boats pull up to the hotel's dock. **Seven
Bridges**, a small canal-house hotel, gets a special mention

because it overlooks Reguliersgracht, one of the city's prettiest waterways; you actually get 15 bridges at a glimpse, but who's counting? Another upscale canal house, **Estheréa**, has several beautifully redecorated rooms with large windows three-abreast looking out at gorgeous Singel houses and mansions, while **Ambassade** does much the same over the Herengracht or Singel.

Homes away from home... You can count the actual B&Bs in town on the fingers of one hand, though simple Dutch hotels practically count as B&Bs, because bread rolls, ham, and cheese are generally included in the price of the room. Two small guesthouse-residences do, however, fit the bill. The simply-named but sumptuous **Nr 40** doesn't call itself a B&B but functions like one. Owner Tony van der Veen converted the 1893 Herenhuis mansion, one block from the northern edge of the Vondelpark's panhandle, into four full-service studio apartments, rentable by the day, week, or longer. Each room has a minibar, fax-answering machine, and stereo. Chic designer furniture mixes with antiques. In 1998, the affable Van der Veen expanded into the next-door house, adding two large, split-level one-bedroom apartments with a shared garden. **717**, a "guest house," with eight suites, exudes luxury and the kind of homey starchiness that millionaire silver-spooner neatniks will love—a place for every antique, and every antique in its place. Indeed!

Convention hotels with flair... The **Golden Tulip Barbizon Palace** is a city within a city, including a conference center in the startlingly handsome, 15th-century St. Olof's chapel across the street, reached via a tunnel. Unconventional conventioneers will be delighted to know that the red-light district and S&M/gay Warmoesstraat are a block away, and though it's sanitized, the hotel's Bar Bizonder is an improvement on the kind of coffee shop found in most convention hotels. The **Amsterdam Renaissance Hotel** also has a former church now used as a convention center (is business a religion around here, or what?): the circular, 17th-century Koepel church, the only wholly round building in town. Formerly the Ramada Renaissance, now a Marriott hotel, this thoroughly American-style complex is shoehorned into a series of converted warehouses and other buildings just off the Singel, near Centraal Station. Saying that it has charm would be stretching it—this is a business hotel, after all, but Marriott has redecorated with coziness (and red) as a theme, and quirky architecture adds interest.

To relive the Golden Age... If you want to know what the canal house of a wealthy Netherlands family probably looked like circa the late 1700s, book a room at **Ambassade**, on Herengracht's snooty Golden Bend. Antiques dealers' hands tremble when they spot the 1750 grandfather clock by celebrated clockmaker Jan Theo van Kempen in the salon (little ships dance on the waves as the seconds tick by). A china cabinet displays delftware and other valuable pieces that would make handsome souvenirs, if only you could convince the hotel's owner, a collector, to part with them. At **717**, a boutique "guesthouse," you'll feel like a pearl in a 17th-century Dutch still life, nested among antiques in a period townhouse, with neo-Calvinist staff to match.

In search of the perfect pool... Amsterdam is not a city for hotel-bound sports fanatics. Most buildings are centuries old, and space is at a premium, so hotels simply don't have room for fitness centers and pools. One of the nicest things to happen when the **Amstel Inter-Continental** underwent its $50-million restoration was the remaking of the health club. The pool is now arguably the city's best, an admittedly smaller version of the one at Hearst Castle, but you get the idea. There's a big Jacuzzi, a sauna and Turkish bath, and a rather modest weight room. A small army of muscular masseurs, beauticians, and trainers is there to pummel and pamper you. The **Hotel de L'Europe** has fallen behind in terms of sheer luxury, but it has a pond-sized colonnaded pool with a coffered ceiling (with some nutty garden statuary scattered around). Sybarites staying at **The Grand Amsterdam** are probably more interested in trying out the Molton Brown aromatherapy bath milk in their two-tone art-deco marble bathrooms; nonetheless, hidden under the 600-year-old complex's beautiful courtyards in the heart of Old Amsterdam is the grandly named "Spa at The Grand," which offers a smallish pool not intended for swimming laps and a serviceable sauna and steam bath. It's not a bad place to sweat off the pounds you put on by eating at the Café Roux. For a totally different atmosphere, tucked away in the basement of the **Golden Tulip Barbizon Palace** is the Fitness Center and Health

Club, where you'll find dynamic businesspeople pumping iron, jogging in place, tanning, and dashing from the sauna to the Turkish bath and then into the hands of a masseur. Phew! The only thing that's missing is the pool. Stay at the **Amsterdam Renaissance Hotel** (now a Marriott property), off the Singel, near Centraal Station, and guess what you get? The Splash Fitness Club! It has the same amenities plus a hot whirlpool bath and aerobics classes, though *still* no swimming pool, despite the splashy name. The **Golden Tulip Barbizon Schiphol**, a modern business/luxury complex a few minutes from the airport, offers the same kind of fitness center as in town, but—at last!—with an honest-to-God splashing swimming pool.

The royal treatment... The owners of multigenerational, family-run **Estheréa** may be sartorial look-likes for Prince Willem Alexander and hisbride Maxima, but sisters Esther and Caroline Esselaar are a mine of info on restaurants and culture in A'dam, and brother Jan-Willem and his desk staff remember your name and room number, are authentically friendly, and never seem obsequious. Free coffee and tea are served in the lobby. At **Acacia**, Hans and Marlene van Vliet will draw you up lists of their favorite restaurants, cafes, parks, herring stands, canals, foods, books, hairdressers.... Coming from hotelier families, they seem to have hospitality in their blood. Many of their clients are repeat customers who appreciate the laid-back atmosphere of this small, extremely simple hotel with triangular rooms (it's a corner building, shaped like a wedge of cheese). You can also rent a houseboat from them. If you're really nice, they might even invite you for a ride on their motorboat. The quiet but efficient staff of **The Bridge Hotel** are the kind of folks who seem genuinely honored (and somewhat surprised) to have such nice people like you as guests. This modest property (don't be fooled by the misleadingly grand marble entrance) looks out on the locks on the Amstel River that control the flow of Amsterdam's canal water. A handful of the large, spare, casually decorated rooms and new top-floor apartment offer views of the river or Nieuwe Prinsengracht canal.

For cheap sleeps... Don't bother to take your hiking boots off before tramping up to **Acacia**: You'll need them to scale the Matterhorn of a staircase. Its superb location—in the

Jordaan, overlooking peaceful Lijnbaansgracht—offsets the spartan lodgings. **Van Onna**, on Bloemgracht, is good and cheap; though rooms are tiny, the staircases are plenty wide to allow for giant tortoise-style packs to get through. On the posh Herengracht, the one-star **Hegra** has supremely simple, plain, sturdy furniture. No elevator, again, but there is a cheapo-tolerant atmosphere. The **Van Ostade Bicycle Hotel** is the quintessential place for penurious students and sandal-shod young bikers. Rooms are spartan but neat as a pin, and there's a no-drugs policy. You can buy your daily picnic at the nearby Albert Cuypstraat street market. Cheapest of all (though you might not sleep) are the dormitory-style **The Bulldog Low Budget Hotel** and **Kabul Young Budget Hotel**. Good luck!

Lavender lodgings... Amsterdam's hotels are used to welcoming people of myriad sexual persuasions, and many small, charming hotels here are gay-owned or -managed. It's illegal for a proprietor to deny lodging due to sexual orientation; this goes both ways. A dozen or so self-styled gay hotels in town may discourage straights from staying in them (some are hardcore places for S&M aficionados, and others practice or tolerate male prostitution). Most other gay properties are simply hotels that happen to be plugged into the gay circuit, though the atmosphere is such that if you're not one of the guys or girls, you might feel uncomfortable. **De Admiraal** is considered particularly gay-friendly, though it's not a gay hotel per se, but an unpretentious canal-house hotel. Ditto the nearby **Seven Bridges,** a charmer. These small one-stars are around the corner or down the block from Rembrandtplein and within shouting distance of Reguliersdwarsstraat. Upscale **New York**, which was extensively remodeled in the late 1990s, is set in a canal house on Herengracht, a quarter mile from Centraal Station. All rooms come with refrigerator and color TV, and guests can borrow VCRs free of charge. Front rooms have views over this atmospheric corner of town, which has the sole disadvantage of being far from most gay venues. Still, the rooms are decorated with a splash of glitz, the bar stays open until 11pm, and condoms are sold at the reception desk.

Party scenes... Most Amsterdam party hotels are in the red-light district and specialize in beyond-the-pale activities. If you want to book into one, just slip on your leather and chains, pack your condoms, and fill your pockets with joints. Don't worry, you can't miss them. The rest is up to you. Or, you can nibble at the edges of exotica by staying at the **Kabul Young Budget Hotel**, stuffed into an old building on the gay stretch of Warmeosstraat in the red-light district. Rooms range from monastic singles to 16-bed dormitories equipped with lockers and not much else. **The Bulldog Low Budget Hotel**, above a smoking coffee shop, is redolent of grass and hash, lit by fluorescent strips, and offers bunk beds with a 24-hour rotation of gamey puffers. Zounds! In either of these hotels, sleep should not be a priority, and anyone squeamish about body or dope odors will want to look elsewhere. Hey, the price is right, and you asked for it.

Family values... You can wheel the rented station wagon right into the garage at the **Amsterdam Renaissance Hotel** and feel at home. After all, this is a Marriott hotel, and the kiddies will never know they've left the theme park. They'll also have a blast running through the huge lobby and tripping up all the dazed conventioneers in the round, 17th-century Koepel church congress center. The location, a few hundred yards from Centraal Station, means easy access to trams and trains and buses. For moms and pops with money to burn, the **Golden Tulip Barbizon Palace** is another sort of theme park—corporate Dutch—with 19 rebuilt old houses kids can explore. The proximity of the red-light district, a block or so away, is no problem, since Centraal Station is across the street, with trams, trains, and so forth to all the places you'll want to go, including the zoo. There's a top-flight coffee shop–style restaurant for the well-behaved, and don't overlook the souvenir shop in the lobby. No such attractions are found at the **Estheréa**; but the Esselaar family likes kids, has produced many of late, and has equipped nine beautifully redecorated rooms with spiffy Murphy beds that brats get a kick out of. The big, comfy, practical rooms are furnished with child-resistant wooden built-ins. Extra beds, and children's toys, are available. The double sinks will come in handy, no doubt, and so will the elevator (only four canal-house hotels have one). Though there's no restaurant, the desk staff can order in food for you if you're too exhausted to go out, and kids will love the croissants that are part of the Dutch breakfast (not included in the room price). Across town at the **Owl**, near Vondelpark, you'll be happy to discover a small backyard in which to turn the children loose.

This small, family-run, three-star hotel is in a converted turn-of-the-century mansion, which has been so thoroughly transformed that you might be in a pastel Miami resort hotel. Best of all, it's on a quiet residential street, safe from traffic hazards, with the park one block away (it's minutes from Museumplein, if your youngsters are so inclined).

When smokes gets in your eyes... Nonsmoking rooms are hard to find (and often smell of smoke anyway). All are in top-end luxury or business establishments. Here's the lineup: Tied for first place are **Golden Tulip Barbizon Schiphol** (at the airport), with 260 smoke-free rooms, and **Hilton Amsterdam,** with three smoke-free floors. **Radisson-SAS Hotel Amsterdam** has 106; **Amsterdam Renaissance Hotel** has 75; **Golden Tulip Barbizon Palace** comes in at 45; and **The Grand Amsterdam** offers a mere 15.

When you've got a plane to catch... Schiphol Airport is so close to town, and so well served by trains, buses, and freeways, that it's ridiculous to stay there just to shave 15 minutes off your travel time. The same goes for the huge RAI convention center, which is nearby. Sure, there's a fleet of boring airport hotels five minutes away from the departures hall, seven minutes from RAI, but you can get to either place in less than half an hour from just about any hotel in central or south Amsterdam. However, if you insist on being within earshot of whining jet engines, or are simply passing through town on the way to another destination, opt for the **Golden Tulip Barbizon Schiphol**, a vast business/luxury hotel offering the kind of extras you'll find at the Golden Tulip Barbizon Palace near Centraal Station. You get a swimming pool and fitness center, plus tennis and squash courts. A free 24-hour shuttle whisks you to the airport or, should you wish to go to town, the train station. A cheaper option is the **Ibis Amsterdam Airport**, a French-run, anonymous modern hotel housed in a tinted-glass cube. The facilities are adequate, and there's a free airport shuttle.

When everything else is filled... "Bigger is better" must have been the motto of the people who built the **Amsterdam Renaissance Hotel**, a sprawling, American-owned property filling several skillfully converted warehouses and other buildings. With 400-plus comfortable, if bland, modern rooms (totaling over 500 beds), they'll almost always be able to find space for you, no matter how many conventioneers they have under their roof. It's only a few hundred yards from Centraal Station and has a garage, which comes in handy if you're driving through town. Faded, sprawling **Grand Hotel Golden Tulip Krasnapolsky** gets first prize for total number of beds (almost 900). Little did the Polish tailor-turned-hotelier who founded this landmark property in 1866 know that his name, writ rather large, would now be spread across several city blocks, between Dam Square and the red-light district. If you're set on canal-house charm, the **Hotel Pulitzer** has the most rooms (230) and beds (338) of all the canal-house hotels—it can't hurt to check here for last-minute cancellations.

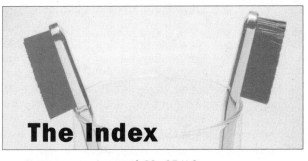

The Index

Note:	1 euro=$.88–.95 U.S.
$$$$$	over $250
$$$$	$200–$250
$$$	$125–$200
$$	$80–$125
$	under $80

Acacia. This flatiron-shaped, family-run hotel has strictly spartan rooms, but a great location in the Jordaan, overlooking leafy Lijnbaansgracht. At slightly higher rates, houseboat and studio apartment rentals are also available.... *Tel 020/622-1460, fax 020/638-0748, acacia.nl@wxs.nl or www.hotelnet.nl. Lindengracht 251, 1015 KH, tram 3, bus 18 to Nieuwe Willemsstraat. 5% surcharge for credit cards. 14 rms, 5 rms in houseboat, 2 studios. $* **(see pp. 28, 30, 33)**

Agora. A small, comfortable canal-house hotel near the Bloemenmarkt, run by Els Bruijnse and Yvo Muthert. Many rooms have been remodeled and upgraded since 2001. No restaurant; no elevator.... *Tel 020/627-2200, fax 020/627-2202, agora@worldonline.nl or home.worldon line.nl/~agora. Singel 462, 1017 AW, trams 1, 2, 5 to Koningsplein. 15 rms. $$* **(see p. 22)**

Ambassade. 12 gorgeous 17th-century canal houses on the so-called Golden Bend of Herengracht, the Algonquin of A'dam: Rushdie, Boyle, Ford, Seth, and Le Carré are among the literary lights who stay here. No restaurant; no pretentions; discreet class; CNN, library. "Float & Massage" spa next door.... *Tel 020/555-0222, fax 020/555-0277, info@ambassade-hotel.nl or www.ambassade-hotel.nl. Herengracht 341, 1016 AZ, trams 1, 2, 5 to Spui. 59 rms. $$$* **(see pp. 23, 24, 27, 30, 31, 32)**

American Hotel. A magnificent Dutch art-nouveau landmark hotel built between 1900 and 1902, overlooking Leidseplein. Unfortunately, the rooms, heavily remodeled and "improved" in the 1980s and 1990s, have lost much of their charm. Fitness center, solarium, and sauna.... *Tel 020/556-3200, 800/327-0200, fax 020/556-3222, american@interconti.com. Leidsekade 97, 1017 PN, trams 1, 2, 5 to Leidseplein. 188 rms. $$$$$* **(see p. 28)**

Amstel Inter-Continental. For many, this is the best hotel in town, with more bang for the buck than The Grand. Though located on the eastern bank of the Amstel River beyond Frederiksplein, in an unanchored and rather uninteresting area, the Amstel is perfectly *grachtengordel*: Marble grand halls, salons hung with crystal chandeliers, and vast rooms done up in silken fabrics (make sure to get one overlooking the river). The Royal Suite is $2,750 per night. High tea is an institution in the handsome upstairs salon, and La Rive restaurant gets top marks.... *Tel 020/622-6060, 800/327-0200, fax 020/622-5808, amsha_conc@interconti.com or www.interconti.com. Professor Tulpplein 1, 1018 GX, trams 6, 7, 10 to Sarphatistraat. 79 rms. $$$$$* **(see pp. 25, 27, 30, 32)**

Amsterdam Renaissance Hotel. Owned by Marriott since 1999, this is a huge, sprawling, American business hotel composed of reconverted warehouses; the round, 17th-century Koepel church (used for conventions); and a covered courtyard. The charm factor has been improved with red decor, old prints and paintings, and cozy furniture.... *Tel 020/551-2066, 800/HOTELS I, fax 020/627-5245,*

www.renaissancehotels.com. Kattengat 1, 1012 SZ, trams 1, 2, 5, 13, 17, buses 21, 170, 171, 172 to Nieuwezijds Voorburgwal and Nieuwendijk. 405 rms. $$$$$
(see pp. 24, 26, 31, 33, 35, 36)

Amsterdam Wiechmann Hotel. A narrow canal-house hotel with a charming lobby straight out of a Vermeer painting. Some *gezellig* canal-side double rooms are furnished with antiques. Breakfast room, bar, and lounge; no restaurant.... *Tel 020/626-3321, fax 020/626-8962, www.channels.nl /wiechman. Prinsengracht 328–332, 1016 HX, trams 13, 17 to Westerkerk. 36 rms. $$* **(see pp. 22, 28)**

Bilderberg Hotel Jan Luyken. This Dutch art-nouveau four-star—totally remodeled in 2001—is within striking distance of the designer boutiques on P.C. Hooftstraat. There's a pretty patio garden, a comfortable bar and lounge, but no restaurant. Spa center.... *Tel 020/573-0730, 800/223-9868, fax 020/676-3841, jan-luyken@bilderberg.nl or www.janluyken.nl. Jan Luykenstraat 58, 1071 CS, trams 2, 5 to Rijksmuseum. 63 rms. $$$$* **(see p. 27)**

Blakes. Anouska Hempel's ultra-chic, 26-room designer hotel (modeled on Blakes and The Hempel in London), where East (Asian furnishings) meets West (English silk and style) in a uniquely neo-spartan temple to trendiness. Housed in a reconverted 1637–1772 Grachtengordel property (theater, almshouse bakery, then law offices). Garden court, gorgeous public areas haunted by well-heeled, black-clad jet-setters.... *Tel 020/530-2010, fax 020/530-2030, hotel@blakes.nl or www.slh.com/blakesam. Keizersgracht 384, 1016 GB, trams 13, 14, 17, buses 21, 170, 171, 172 to Westerkerk. 26 rms. $$$$$* **(see pp. 24, 28)**

The Bridge Hotel. This small, friendly hotel overlooks the locks on the Amstel River. Rooms and the top-floor apartment are tidy but spare, with linoleum or carpeted floors, rattan chairs, and blond wood furniture. No restaurant.... *Tel 020/623-7068, fax 020/624-1565, postbus@thebridgehotel.demon.nl or www.thebridgehotel.demon.nl. Amstel 107–111, 1018 EM; tram 4 to Keizersgracht, trams 6, 7, 10 and Metro to Weesperplein. 27 rms. $$* **(see pp. 28, 33)**

The Bulldog Low Budget Hotel. Strip fluorescent lights, the smell of hash and grass wafting up from the smoking coffee

ACCOMMODATIONS | THE INDEX

shop downstairs, spartan rooms, and dormitories stuffed with bunk beds. Talk about *gezellig....* *Tel 020/620-3822, fax 020/627-1612, hotel@bulldog.nl or www.bulldog.nl. Oudezijds Voorburgwal 220, 1012 GJ, all trams and buses to Centraal Station. 95 beds. $* **(see pp. 34, 35)**

Canal House. A young Irish couple runs this hybrid Dutch/Victorian inn, on one of the city's prettiest canals, near Westerkerk. No kids under 12 or pets are allowed. One of few canal-house hotels with an elevator; there's a cozy bar but no restaurant.... *Tel 020/622-5182, fax 020/624-1317, info@canalhouse.nl or www.canalhouse.nl. Keizersgracht 148, 1015 CX, trams 13, 14, 17, buses 21, 170, 171, 172 to Westerkerk. 26 rms. $$$* **(see pp. 25, 30)**

De Admiraal. This tiny, bargain-basement one-star near Rembrandtplein may look dubious from the outside, but it's cheerful, with a few atmospheric canal-view rooms (ask for #6, with wraparound windows). Gay friendly. No restaurant; no elevator.... *Tel 020/626-2150, fax 020/623-4625. Herengracht 563, 1017 CD, trams 4, 9, 14 to Rembrandtplein. 9 rms. $* **(see pp. 22, 30, 34)**

De Filosoof. As the name implies, the theme of this unusual small hotel, a stone's throw from the Vondelpark, is philosophy. The garden, veranda, and book-lined lounge encourage mingling. Upgraded to three stars in 2000. No restaurant; elevator.... *Tel 020/683--3013, fax 020/685-3750, filosoof@xs4all.nl or www.xs4all.nl/~filosoof. Anna van den Vondelstraat 6, 1054 GZ, tram 1, 6, buses 171, 172 to Overtoom and Constantijn Huygensstraat. 25 rms. $$$* **(see p. 26)**

Estheréa. Family-owned and -run for the last 50-odd years, this canal-house hotel overlooking the Singel is a thoroughly professional property, with many tastefully redecorated rooms. Elevator but no restaurant. CNN.... *Tel 020/624-5146, 800/223-9868, fax 020/623-9001, estherea@xs4all.nl or www.estherea.nl. Singel 303–309, 1012 WJ, trams 1, 2, 5 to Paleisstraat. 70 rms. $$$$* **(see pp. 23, 24, 26, 31, 33, 35)**

Golden Tulip Barbizon Palace. There's something for everyone in this quintessentially Dutch theme-park of a business hotel. The neutrally attired rooms have thick, flowery curtains and old oak rafters. Remodeled in 1999–2000, with about 45 nonsmoking rooms.... *Tel*

020/556-4564, 800/344-1212, fax 020/624-3353, sales@gtbpalace. goldentulip.nl or www.goldentulip hotels.nl/ GTBPALACE. Prins Hendrikkade 59–72, 1012 AD, trams and buses (all lines) to Centraal Station or Prins Hendrikkade. 274 rms. $$$$ **(see pp. 23, 26, 31, 32, 35, 36)**

Golden Tulip Barbizon Schiphol. Best left to visitors in transit and conventioneers at the RAI convention center nearby. Brasserie Barbizon is for those too tired to leave the hotel; ditto The Point cocktail bar. 260 nonsmoking rooms.... *Tel 020/655-0550, 800/344-1212, fax 020/653-4999, info@gtschiphol.goldentulip.nl or www.goldentuliphotels.nl/ gtschiphol. Kruisweg 495, 2132 NA Hoofddorp, trains to Schiphol. 419 rms. $$$$* **(see pp. 33, 36)**

Golden Tulip Schiller Hotel. Gorgeous turn-of-the-century hotel overlooking Rembradtplein. Square-side rooms have best views, but can get noisy.... *Tel 020/554-0700, fax 020/624-0098, www.goldentulip.com. Rembrandtplein 26–36, 1017 CV, trams 4, 9, 14 to Rembrandtplein. 92 rms. $$$$* **(see p. 29)**

The Grand Amsterdam. Possibly Amsterdam's top super-luxury hotel. Exudes confidence, from the marble-paved, vaulted lobby to the immense, tastefully decorated rooms. Pity they've only got 15 nonsmoking rooms.... *Tel 020/555-3111, 800/SOFITEL, fax 020/555-3222, hotel@the grand.nl or www.sofitel.com. Oudezijds Voorburgwal 197, 1001 EX, trams 4, 9, 16, 24, 25 to Spui. 182 rms. $$$$$* **(see pp. 25, 27, 32, 36)**

Grand Hotel Golden Tulip Krasnapolsky. The most exclusive place in town, it's now a business, convention, and package-tourism hotel, comfortable if undistinguished. The plant-filled Winter Garden (1879) is still a joy in winter, and the Reflet Brasserie has a striking 1883 decor; otherwise the hotel's bars and restaurants are forgettable. 95 nonsmoking rooms; garage; fitness center.... *Tel 020/554-9111, fax 020/622-8607, info@krasnapolsky.nl or www.krasnapolsky.nl. Dam 9, 1012 JS, trams 4, 9, 16, 24, 25 to Dam Square. 469 rms. $$$$* **(see pp. 23, 24, 28, 37)**

Hegra. Modest is the operative word for this narrow, 17th-century canal-house hotel located on the Herengracht near Dam Square, the flower market, and Leidseplein.... *Tel*

020/623-7877, fax 020/623-8159. Herengracht 269, 1016 BJ, trams 1, 2, 5 to Paleisstraat or Spui. 11 rms. $
(see pp. 23, 34)

Hilton Amsterdam. Could be a Hilton anywhere. Even the views—over the Nooder Amstel Kanaal, a parking lot, or tree-lined boulevards—are comfortingly bland. A big draw is the nearby (1 mile away) freeway to Schiphol Airport.... *Tel 020/710-6005, 800/445-8667, fax 020/710-6080, www.hilton.com. Apollolaan 138–140, 1077 BG, trams 5, 24 to Apollolaan. 271 rms. $$$$$* **(see pp. 26, 29, 36)**

Hotel de L'Europe. This 1896 grande dame offers an excellent, though noisy, location at Munt Plein overlooking the Amstel, plus all the trappings of luxury. The lobby and many rooms have been remodeled and upgraded in the last 5 years.... *Tel 020/531-1777, 800/223-6800, fax 020/531-1778, hotel@leurope.nl or www.leurope.nl. Nieuwe Doelenstraat 2–8, 1012 CP, trams 4, 9, 16, 24, 25 to Spui. 166 rms. $$$$$* **(see pp. 25, 27, 30, 32)**

Hotel Pulitzer. The only full-blown luxury hotel in the Grachten-gordel neighborhood; the restrained decor is lovely in an opu-lent, corporate way, and though this is now a Sheraton hotel (since 1999), it's still less atmospheric than other canal-house hotels.... *Tel 020/523-5235, 800/325-3535, fax 020/627-6753, www.ittsheraton.com. Prinsengracht 315–331, 1016 GZ, trams 13, 14, 17, buses 21, 170, 171, 172 to Westerkerk. 100 rms and suites. $$$$$* **(see pp. 23, 29, 37)**

Hotel Washington. Clean and classy, the simple, tasteful rooms here overlook a verdant street or an intimate garden. No elevator; no restaurant.... *Tel 020/679-7453 and 020/679-6754, fax 020/673-4435. Frans van Mierisstraat 10, 1071 RS, trams 3, 5, 12, 16 to Concertgebouw. 17 rms. $$* **(see p. 25)**

Ibis Amsterdam Airport. Reasonably priced and near the air-port, this is a standard, modern chain hotel, with no char-acter but perfectly good facilities for travelers in transit. Free airport shuttle. Red Baron Bar (the name tells all); gift shops.... *Tel 020/502-5100, fax 020/657-0199. Schipholweg 181, 1171 PK Badhoevedorp, trains to Schiphol, then taxi or shuttle. 638 rms. $$* **(see p. 36)**

Kabul Young Budget Hotel. An Amsterdam institution. Not for light sleepers. No elevator; no restaurant.... *Tel 020/ 623-7158, fax 020/620–0869. Warmoesstraat 38–42, 1012 JE, trams and buses (all lines) to Centraal Station. 23 rms.* $ **(see pp. 34, 35)**

New York. Still the city's most upscale gay and lesbian hotel, totally remodeled in the late '90s. No elevator; no restaurant; private garage.... *Tel 020/624-3066, fax 020/620-3230. Herengracht 13, 1015 BA, buses 18, 22 to Droogbak. 15 rms.* $$ **(see p. 34)**

Nr 40. This luxury B&B offers 4 full-service studio apartments, elegant dining room wood-paneled lounge, and a small roof garden. Next door are 2 split-level, 1-bedroom garden apartments with faxes and answering machines.... *Tel 020/618-4298, fax same as tel, number40@scarlet.nl. Roemer Visscherstraat 40, 1054 EZ, trams 3, 12 to Vondelpark. 6 studio apartments.* $$$ **(see p. 31)**

Owl. A converted turn-of-the-century mansion, this family-run, 3-star hotel is tidy and pastel, and no-nonsense. No restaurant; TV lounge/bar and garden.... *Tel 020/618-9484, fax 020/618-9441, manager@owl-hotel.demon.nl. Roemer Visscherstraat 1, 1054 EV, trams 1, 2, 5 to Leidseplein. 34 rms.* $$ **(see pp. 28, 35)**

Radisson-SAS Hotel Amsterdam. Even though it's just south of the red-light district in Old Amsterdam, it looks like it could be anywhere.... *Tel 020/623-1231, 800/333-3333, fax 020/520-8200, guest.amsterdam@radissonSAS.com or www.radisson.com/amsterdam. Rusland 17, 1012 CK, trams 4, 9, 16, 24, 25 to Spui. 243 rms.* $$$$ **(see pp. 26, 29, 36)**

Seven Bridges. This *gezellig* canal-house hotel has gone upmarket, with only 8 remodeled rooms (inlaid wood, marble, and handmade furniture). No elevator; no restaurant.... *Tel 020/623-1329. Reguliersgracht 31, 1017 LK, trams 16, 24, 25 to Keizersgracht. 9 rms.* $$$ **(see pp. 22, 30, 34)**

717. 8 luxurious, vast suites in a top-end, antique-stuffed Grachtengordel "guest house." Library, private dining and conference rooms. Breakfast, tea, coffee, drinks, and wines included in price.... *Tel 020/427-0717, fax 020/423-0717,* info@717hotel.nl or www.717hotel.nl. Prinsengracht 717, 1017 JW, trams 4, 16, 24, 25 to Prinsengracht. 8 suites. $$$$$ **(see pp. 23, 24, 31, 32)**

't Hotel. Opened in late 2000, this charming 3-star overlooking a lovely Leliegracht near the Jordaan has 8 luxury rooms done in a neo-Calvinistic, Minimalist style: simple wooden furniture, cream-colored walls, burgundy carpets, and tiled baths. The lobby doubles as an antiques shop.... *Tel 020/422-2741, fax 020/626-7873, th.broekema@ hetnet.nl or www.bookings.nl/hotels/thotel. Leleigrachct 18, 1015 DE, trams 13, 14, 17 to Westerkerk. 8 rooms. $$$* **(see pp. 23, 24)**

Toren. This 2-building canal-house hotel was remodeled in 1999, jumping from 2 to 4 stars, and gaining an elevator. There's a marble entrance hall, Old Dutch decor, crystal chandeliers, fireplaces, and an attractive garden. No restaurant.... *Tel 020/622-6352, fax 020/626-9705, hotel.toren@tip.nl or www.toren.nl. Keizersgracht 164, 1015 CZ, trams 13, 17 to Westerkerk. 44 rms. $$$$* **(see pp. 23, 24, 26, 30)**

Van Onna. This unusual 1-star occupies 3 separate buildings on a lovely side canal. From front rooms you get canal views and glimpses of Westerkerk over the roofs. No elevator; no restaurant.... *Tel 020/626-5801. Bloemgracht 102/104/108, 1015 TN, trams 13, 17 to Westerkerk. No credit cards. 30 rms. $* **(see pp. 29, 34)**

Van Ostade Bicycle Hotel. Rooms in this narrow, turn-of-the-century building are tidy but spartan. No elevator (and the stairs are steep); no restaurant; parking garage.... *Tel 020/ 679-3452, fax 020/671-5213, bicyclehotel@capitolon line.nl. Van Ostadestraat 123, 1072 SV, trams 12, 25 to Ceintuurbaan. No credit cards. 16 rms. $* **(see pp. 29, 34)**

The Waterfront. Overlooking the Singel a hundred yards from the flower market, this narrow canal-house hotel has cheerful new owners who've remodeled top to bottom.... *Tel 020/421-6621, fax same as tel, hotel@waterfront. demon.nl or www.waterfront. demon.nl. Singel 458, 1017 AW, trams 1, 2, 5 to Koningsplein. 11 rms. $$* **(see p. 22)**

Accommodations in the
Museumplein Area & Amsterdam South

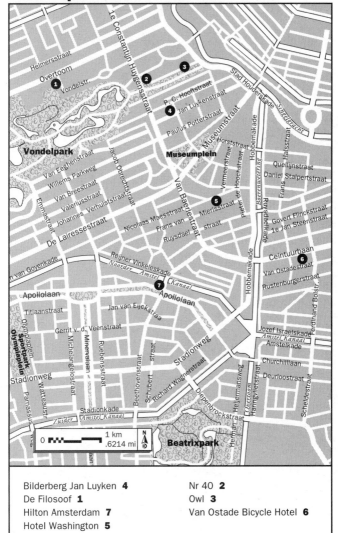

Bilderberg Jan Luyken **4**

De Filosoof **1**

Hilton Amsterdam **7**

Hotel Washington **5**

Nr 40 **2**

Owl **3**

Van Ostade Bicycle Hotel **6**

Accommodations in Central Amsterdam

46

Acacia **1**
Agora **15**
Ambassade **13**
American Hotel **17**
Amstel Inter-Continental **29**
Amsterdam Renaissance
  Hotel **4**
Amsterdam Weichmann
  Hotel **16**
Blakes **6**
The Bridge Hotel **28**
The Bulldog Low Budget
  Hotel **20**
Canal House **10**
De Admiraal **25**
Estheréa **12**
Golden Tulip
  Barbizon Palace **18**
Golden Tulip Schiller Hotel **24**
The Grand Amsterdam **21**
Grand Hotel Golden Tulip
  Krasnapolsky **5**
Hegra **11**
Hotel de L'Europe **23**
Hotel Pulitzer **9**
Kabul Young Budget Hotel **19**
New York **2**
Radisson-SAS
  Hotel Amsterdam **22**
Seven Bridges **27**
717 **26**
't Hotel **3**
Toren **7**
Van Onna **8**
The Waterfront Hotel **14**

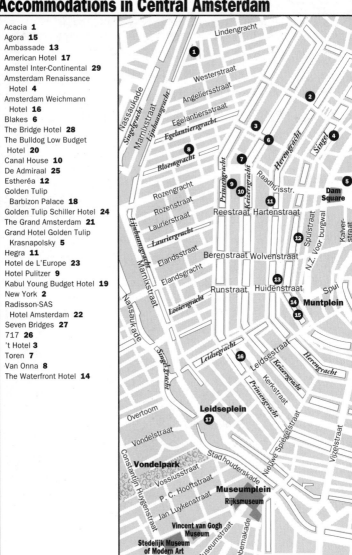

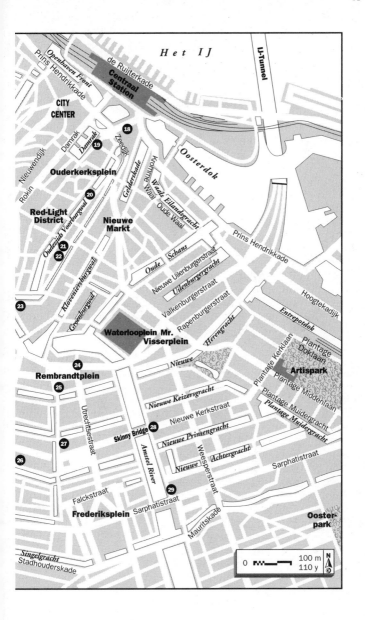

Het IJ

IJ-Tunnel

de Ruijterkade

Centraal Station

Openhaven Front

Prins Hendrikkade

CITY CENTER

Nieuwendijk

Damrak

Damrak

18

19

Zeedijk

Geldersekade

Oosterdok

Ouderkerksplein

Rokin

20

Oudezijds Voorburgwal

Red-Light District

Nieuwe Markt

Kromme Waal

Waale Eilandsgracht

Oude Waal

Oude Schans

21

Oudezijds Achterburgwal

22

Nieuwe Uilenburgerstraat

Uilenburgergracht

Prins Hendrikkade

Kloveniersburgwal

Valkenburgerstraat

23

Groenburgwal

Rapenburgerstraat

Hoogtekadijk

Herengracht

Entrepotdok

Waterlooplein Mr. Visserplein

Plantage Kerklaan

Plantage Doklaan

24

Nieuwe

Artispark

Rembrandtplein

Plantage Middenlaan

25

Nieuwe Keizersgracht

Plantage Muidergracht

Plantage Muidergracht

Utrechtsestraat

Nieuwe Kerkstraat

Skinny Bridge 28

Amstel River

Nieuwe Prinsengracht

Weesperstraat

27

Nieuwe *Achtergracht*

Sarphatistraat

26

Falckstraat

29

Sarphatistraat

Oosterpark

Frederiksplein

Mauritskade

Singelgracht

Stadhouderskade

0 100 m
110 y

N

dining a

2nd cafes

Dutch food and
Amsterdam
restaurants are the
butt of a lot of
jokes—only some
of them deserved.
The city's cafes

are better than its eateries, the saying goes. And the truth is, Amsterdam's more than 1,400 cafes and bars—among the most atmospherically smoky, friendly, cozy, pleasantly worn in the world—are a hard act to follow. Also true is that a lot of Dutch food is heavy-going, consisting of meat and vegetable stews, sausages, potatoes and gravy, and plenty of bland cheese. Unlike Italians or French, locals dining out here *avoid* local food, favoring Indonesian, French, Italian, Asian, and other foreign specialties (there are 145 nationalities in town) or fusion mergers thereof. In the last 15 years, though, the once-dreary restaurant scene has become surprisingly dynamic roller-coastering from the sublime to the ridiculous. You really can get a good meal here at a variety of both international and home-grown restaurants—but you can also spend a lot of money on bad, silly, or contrived food. Still, it's nonsense to claim, as do other Europeans (the French in particular), that there is no such thing as "Dutch cuisine." Veteran food guru Johannes van Dam (see sidebar) has a collection of centuries-old Dutch cookbooks describing dishes that would send a modern French chef to culinary heaven. Members of the Dutch Regional Cuisine organization (Neerlands Dis) are reviving lost recipes, ingredients, wines, liquors, and cooking techniques from the various regions of the Netherlands. Dozens of flavorful finds include dishes like smoke-dried *nagelhout* beef, braised codfish with mustard sauce, and marrowfat peas with onions, bacon, and pickles. The real dynamism lies, however, with several dozen chefs—Dutch, French, and Indonesian—producing dishes at hip Amsterdam restaurants that would fit right into the foodie scene in New York, Los Angeles, San Francisco, or Sydney. For these chefs, variations on northern Italian, French, and Asian themes—sometimes mixed and matched—are all the rage. Handled by skilled practitioners, these variations can be world-class. Fusion remains the trend of the early 21st century; sometimes the results are more confused than anything else. And be warned: Service is almost universally slow and often sloppy. Everyone knows that A'dam's restaurants, with few exceptions, are "understaffed with overpaid amateurs."

Only in Amsterdam

Fish, fish, and more fish. The staggering wealth of the 17th-century Dutch Golden Age was based in large part on herrings. The Dutch eat them raw (see sidebar) and pickled in a variety of ways. Try them at one of the dozens of herring stands (*herringhuis*) scattered around town. Other Atlantic and North Sea fish are on many menus, and they're generally fresh and delicious. Among snack foods, *osseworst* is a delicious smoked beef sausage eaten cold, like salami. The beef or shrimp croquette (sometimes spelled "kroquette") is a local obsession. At their worst, these large, gooey dumplings rolled in dia-mond-hard crumbs, then deep fried, taste like instant gravy mix. They're always served scorching hot; Amsterdammers split them open, place them on a slice of white bread, then add mustard and/or fried parsley. Small, round croquettes are called *bitterballen* and are a favorite hors d'oeuvre.

Locally you can find dozens of cheeses, including the ubiquitous Edam and Gouda. You can also find deli-cious aged varieties, and others made with raw milk (*boerenkaas*), hidden treasures that aren't available abroad. These cheeses, plus various cold cuts, go into the standard Dutch lunch, which consists of small, often round sand-wiches—*broodjes*—that would be considered a mere snack or finger food in most other countries.

The most celebrated dish hereabouts is *stamppot*, a vast mound of mashed pota-toes and gravy, usually served with endive, sauerkraut, or kale, plus pork ribs and sausages. Don't forget *ertwensoep*,

Van Dam vs. Iens

Amsterdam guru of gastronomy Johannes van Dam has a mis-sion: to reward talented chefs and encourage others to improve. Improving sometimes means changing jobs. So, while the pneumatic tire man of the Michelin red guide makes chefs tremble in France, it is bearded, Bibendum-like van Dam whose reviews in the daily Het Parool can make or break an A'dam restaurant. He uses a 10-point system. There is nothing worse than being "van damned" with a low score. All-time lows have gone to the Reflet Brasserie at the Krasnapolsky (4). Enter Iens Boswijk, a rival reviewer whose "Iens Independent Index" (info@iens.nl or www.iens.nl) lists most A'dam restaurants worth a damn, rating them with Zagat-style assessments and dividing them conveniently into theme categories. Best of all, this pocket-sized guide is avail-able in English at most A'dam bookstores and newsstands. Too bad the "nonsmoking" cat-egory remains woefully inaccu-rate: There are practically no nonsmoking restaurants in town worth your patronage. Look for van Dam's reviews— often posted prominently—in the windows of A'dam restau-rants. The big man is still the city's most reliable restaurant barometer.

INTRODUCTION | DINING AND CAFES

pea soup, that perennial winter favorite; it should be thick enough to hold a spoon upright. A lighter favorite in May and June is white asparagus, eaten with local boiled ham (and sometimes sprinkled with cinnamon or nutmeg).

Dutch pancakes are the sort of comestible brick that has given Dutch food a bad name. Called *pannekoeken* when pizza-sized and *poffertjes* when smaller, they are often gooey and only half-cooked. Toppings include everything under the sun, from curried turkey to pineapple to sweet corn. The less said, the better. Indonesian food from the Netherlands' former colony, the Dutch East Indies, has been thoroughly adopted by Amsterdammers, who consider it their own. You find chicken *sate* (also spelled *sateh* and *satay*) with peanut sauce everywhere, from ethnic eateries to Dutch steakhouses and sidewalk fry shops. The celebrated Indonesian *rijsttafel* (rice table) is a colonial invention, designed to regale Dutch potentates with a mind-boggling parade of 20 or 30 dishes. Indonesia is a vast country, comprising Java, Borneo, and Sulawesi, with dozens of regional cuisines; what you get in Amsterdam is a pan-Indonesian mix of star dishes, most of them Javanese. Try spicy *babi ketjap* (pork in soya sauce) or mild *gado-gado* (vegetables and bean sprouts in peanut sauce). The true test of an Indonesian chef, however, is *rendang padang*—beef with chili and coconut sauce; it should be very spicy and of a creamy but firm consistency.

Local beers include those inexplicably world-famous brews Heineken and Amstel. There are two good microbreweries in town, Bierbrouwerij 't IJ and Brouwhuis Maximiliaan (see "Cafes and bars," below). Dutch Riesling wine, grown near Maastricht, is good but difficult to find. There is only one local producer of *genever* (Dutch gin), Cees van Wees; his products are available at De Admiraal.

Cafe Society

Cafe culture thrives here as it did 50 years ago in other European capitals, Paris in particular. A lot of Amsterdammers still start their day at their favorite cafe (usually a so-called brown cafe), have lunch there, return for drinks before dinner, and then go back for a bit of socializing, a game of snooker, and some live (or canned) music and a sing-along (see Nightlife). Of course all of this is lubricated by aperitifs, digestifs, and stirrup cups. The bartender doesn't bother to ask what to pour, and the pool cues are as ubiquitous as the bentwood chairs. Since everyone goes to these cafes, they are the ultimate democratic institutions. You, the street sweeper, drink with the CEOs and politicos and speak your mind about everything from croquettes to geopolitics.

At last count there were 1,404 cafes and bars in Amsterdam proper; in the Cafes and Bars section of this chapter, we list a small selection. Of the four basic types, the most famous are the centuries-old *Bruine Kroeg*, better known by their English name, "brown cafes." They're brown because of tobacco stains (a red flag for rabid non-smokers) and because the proprietors make a cult of never washing or painting the spectacularly fly-blown walls. How to recognize them? They are the quintessence of coziness (*gezelligheid*) and seem trapped in a time warp—anywhere from about 1600 (the Golden Age) to 1968 (Provos, hippies). They are amazingly interchangeable, whether authentically old or made to look that way—neo-browns. Standard trappings include: picturesque locals who feign surprise at the sight of a non-regular; a worn wooden or zinc bar; (empty) barrels of *genever* or beer; a snooker table; sand—not sawdust—on the floor; a sidewalk terrace; and carpets on the worn wooden tables. The carpets absorb spilled beer, are optional, and seem to be going out of fashion. Brown cafes often open in the morning (between

Still Holland's best ice cream

Back in the 1920s, Silvano Tofani's father, Peppino, emigrated to Amsterdam from Lucca, in Tuscany, with a dream: to open an ice cream parlor. As of January 2000 you can read about Peppino's ascension at the Amsterdam Historical Museum. You might reasonably ask why Peppino left Lucca for a city where it rains almost 250 days a year and there is a five-month winter. A silly question: Business boomed. Peppino's colorful carts could be seen all over town in spring and summer. The carts are no longer, but Silvano, born in Tuscany, and his wife, Anelide, took over Peppino's modest ice-cream parlor, near the Albert Cuypstraat market, several decades ago and continue the family art. Everything is homemade with fresh produce: strawberries, peaches, zucchinis, rice, and more unexpected ingredients. Silvano has perfected 100 different ice creams, all made with his own recipes. Creamy, light, flavorful—this is possibly the world's best, made with Italian skill and peerless Dutch dairy products. The frothy cappuccinos are unquestionably A'dam's most authentic. Best of all, Silvano and Anelide, like their 100 flavors, are as sweet as can be. (Gelateria Italiana Peppino; tel 020/676–4910, 1e Sweelinckstraat 16; daily 11–11, late March–Oct only).

INTRODUCTION | DINING AND CAFES

8 and 10) and close late at night (between 1 and 3). They're found all over town, with a high concentration between Spui and Centraal Station, and in the Jordaan. The standard lunch and snack menu features a selection of small bun sandwiches (*broodjes*) made with everything from *osseworst* (smoked beef sausage) to cheese, pastrami, vegetables, ham, and salami; *toost* (toasted white bread) with ham and cheese, smoked eel, or beef tartare; and a variety of simple salads. Occasionally omelets, croquettes, or quiches crop up.

The opposite of the brown cafes are the "white" or "grand" cafes: modern, spacious establishments that usually have big windows and terraces and more food on the menu (salad bar, quiches, sandwiches, daily specials, pasta, and so forth). They can be refreshingly anonymous and sunny after all those chummy, cheek-by-jowl brown-cafe conversations, though they're often just as smoky.

Falling between the extremes are the dozen or so "designer" cafes, frequented primarily by a self-consciously sophisticated crowd. They combine elements of the old (coziness, smoke patina, sand on the floor, regulars) and new (spaciousness, better food, a degree of anonymity). They're all in the center of town, and opening hours are generally 10am to 1–2am. Dozens of other cafes, tea salons, and diners don't fit into these categories; some resemble old-fashioned American bakeries or collegiate coffee shops. (The viral Planet Hollywood and the homegrown theme park, Three Sisters, a hodgepodge of mock-Americana and pseudo-Brit, continue to thrive.)

Tap Houses

It's no coincidence that tap water in Amsterdam is called "municipal beer" (*gemeente pils*)—which perhaps explains the success of those local brews Heineken and Amstel. Tap houses, *proeflokaalen*, are where *genever* and beer are swilled from noon until about 8pm, usually by middle-aged and older tipplers. Food is rarely available. The best ones are within stumbling distance of Dam Square. (See You Probably Didn't Know for more on Dutch gin and how to drink it.)

How to Dress

The Dutch are casual, but not frumpy. As long as you don't have hygiene problems, you can wear just about anything to just about any restaurant. At trendy places people wear casual-chic clothing, but no one will bat an eye if you wear a tie to a diner, or show up in jeans at a schmancy restaurant (exceptions: Vermeer, La Rive, and ultra-starchy L'Excelsior).

When to Eat

Amsterdammers like to eat a hearty breakfast (cheese, ham, bread, and more) and a light lunch at a cafe (a salad or sandwich), and they prefer to dine early (from 5:30 on). Local restaurateurs, used to tourists, joke about "national time slots"; the Dutch come first, followed by Americans and Germans (6:30), Scandinavians (7), French and Italians (8:30), and Spanish (9). Normal restaurant hours are 5:30 to 10; *eethuis* (simple restaurants and diners) serve from about 4 to 10; cafe hours vary widely, many open from 10am to 1am (see Cafes and Bars, below).

Getting the Right Table

The trick to snagging a good table is to time your reservation—reserve whenever possible—to suit the kind of restaurant. Go later (8pm on) to an authentic Dutch restaurant; early (7:30 or so) to a trendy or ethnic spot that fills up late. Once you've got your table, you can stay as long as you like; most restaurants make no attempt to "turn tables." Service is often relaxed, i.e., slow. The Dutch are proud people and are funny about tips (they hate to feel they're being coerced). Slipping the maitre d' a wad might get you a window table at a finer (or ethnic) establishment, but it won't go down well elsewhere.

Celebrity Chefs

Chef-watchers were stunned in 2001 by a series of toque transfers worthy of a quick-change artist: **Robert Kranenborg** left La Rive for his posh new place, Vossius, while his second-in-command became top dog at Vermeer; with watch synchronized, Vermeer's chef moved to La Rive to replace Kranenborg. At the same time, another Michelin-pedigree star chef, **Gertjan Hageman,** came out of mothballs to open the hotspot De Kas, in a reconverted hothouse. Meanwhile, at Blakes designer restaurant (in a reconverted 18th-century bakery), **Schilo van Coevorden** continues to number among Amsterdam's hottest culinary properties, a proficient practitioner of a number of ethnic cuisines (Thai, Italian, French). Legendary chef **Jean Beddington** sold her same-name restaurant in 2001 and retired (the place is still there but the less said about it the better). Bordewijk, serving French/Italian–inspired seasonal dishes, is the creation of two restaurateur/chefs, **Wil Demandt** and **Hans Mosterd**, but the restaurant's fame derives from the place itself—a chilling, echoing postmodern designer number, on a trendy Jordaan square. Back to La Rive, at the mega-luxury Amstel Inter-Continental Hotel. It's now under the baton of Michelin-starred chef **Edwin Kats,** who won praise for his classics at another luxury hotel-restaurant, Vermeer, at the Golden Tulip Barbizon Palace. Under its new chef **Pascal Jalhaij,** Vermeer remains straitlaced but attracts serious foodies (Jalhaij was sous-chef at La Rive under Kranenborg). Frenchman **Christophe Royer** *is* Christophe, chic Grachtengordel's perennial haven for reverent epicures. Christophe was among the first chefs in Holland to be awarded a Michelin star, and he isn't likely to let his fall from gourmet heaven. Dutch/French/Thai chef **Jos Boomgaardt** reinvented himself several years ago as the high priest of fusion (at Tom Yam Fusion Cuisine), but is now fighting a rear-guard battle for continued notoriety.

The Lowdown

Going Dutch... If you eat only one Dutch meal in Amsterdam, make **De Roode Leeuw** the place. The old-fashioned interior is what you want in a famously stuffy place like this: carved wood, red armchairs, starched white tablecloths, professional service. The raw new herring and shrimp and beef croquettes are about as good as you can get; in spring, the white asparagus and farmhouse ham are out of this world. Otherwise unfindable delicacies like dried *nagelhout* beef are a house specialty. There is even surprisingly quaffable Dutch Riesling from Maastricht on the wine list.

If your euros are low and you still haven't had a real Dutch meal, clog over to **De Blauwe Hollander** near Leidseplein. Locals, provincial Dutch, and tourists in the know will be at the worn wooden tables, scarfing down the spareribs, brown beans with apple and bacon, and mountains of meatballs, sauerkraut, and boiled veggies. To see office workers, provincials, and package tourists at their happy-hour best, hit magnificently kitschy but cozy **Haesje Claes** near Spui. Mustachioed proprietor André Duyves is a miracle worker: His jovial tourist trap actually serves decent grub (classic mashed potatoes with a pool of gravy, sauerkraut, and pork ribs, plus game in winter). But you haven't seen anything until you've buzzed over to **D' Vijff Vlieghen**, better known as the "Five Flies," an Old Dutch theme park of a place founded by flamboyant antiques dealer Nicolaas Kroese. Back in the 1950s, he raced out to the airport in a limo every time a celeb came to town, then immortalized their visits with brass plaques on his bentwood chairs. Stuffed with authentic antiques and delft tiles, the labyrinth of dark, cozy rooms spreads through five ramshackle 16th-century buildings near Spui. Through the candlelit gloom, the tourists and conventioneers probably can't see the farmhouse ham with fresh apple salad on their plates. A pity; it's not bad.

The Pancake Bakery is the place to go if you and the kids really must experience the infamous Dutch pancake. You'll soon forget you're in the basement of a converted Prinsengracht warehouse—there are American ice-cream parlor-style marble tabletops on old sewing-machine legs, laminated menus, and an old Dutch stove chugging away. Among the 70 kinds of pancakes, stick to the sweet ones. No matter what your constitution, the surreal fantasies topped with turkey in curry sauce, pineapple, apricot, and raisins will stick to you. **Piet de Leeuw Steakhouse** is the kind of joint you feel right at home in—Pete's Place. There's a cigarette machine on one wall, and the dark interior was probably last decorated circa 1955. The famous cholesterol-rich killer beefsteaks, pan-fried in margarine with onions, come with a slice of white bread. Central-casting waiters suss you out before bringing you toothpicks with tiny American flags to spear your raw herring, sweet pickles, and triangles of toast.

Dutch on the run... When you've had enough of the potentially lethal french-fry stands all over town, and the 50s-style, out-of-the-wall Febo automats (Holland's equivalent of McDonald's) selling croquettes, hamburgers, and other dubious-looking quickies on greasy trays, it's time to go fish: Amsterdammers take their herring very seriously. As British ambassador George

DINING AND CAFES | THE LOWDOWN

Downing reported in 1661, the city's Golden Age riches depended on the fact that people were better nourished—on herring—than the rest of Europe. New, young, virginal herring, called *Nieuwe haring,* comes on the market late May or early June and is best only for a few weeks, though it's sold well into the summer. There are dozens of *herringhuis* fish stands in the center of town. The best of all is **Van Altena**, a class operation across from the Rijksmuseum. Owner Pieter van Altena has spent a lot of time and money perfecting the raw herring preservation process; connoisseurs travel miles to stock up on his fresh and pickled herring and lunch on delicious salmon or crab salad. No plastic here: You use proper stainless-steel flatware and drink chilled white wine in a stemmed glass. **Van Dobben** has been *the* spot for the last 55 years to try that famous Amsterdam specialty, the croquette (though these curious lumps are no longer made in-house). Once you've burned your tongue on one and decided croquettes are a quaint curiosity, order a glass of milk at the vintage counter and try an eel or pastrami sandwich instead.

Real *Rijsttafel*... At **Tempo Doeloe**, owner Nagy Ghebrial explains to interested first-time guests how to progress through each course, moving methodically from mild (*risolles*—crêpes with beef), to spicy (*soto ajam*—chicken soup), to hot (*ajam roedjak*—chicken with chili and coconut milk), to very hot (*ikan pepesan*—poached mackerel with chili sauce). Take Nagy's advice: Even chili devotees will weep, sweat, and possibly swoon when eating the infernal "very hot" selections. The skillfully contrasting dishes, professional but laid-back service, and pleasant theatrical decor make this the best Indonesian in town. Right next door, Nagy's former business partner Thomas Hart has opened a simpler place with take-out food: **Tujuh Maret.** The food is excellent. Further competition comes from classy **Long Pura,** in the Jordaan. You are handed an orchid blossom and seated under upside-down parasols hung from the ceiling. The *daging mbe* (dried, stewed beef with onions and spices) is divine. **Sahid Jaya** is a luxury restaurant with good food, though the spice has been toned down to please Dutch tastebuds. The business and tourist clientele seem most interested in the polished service, the posh decor (apricot drapes, cream tablecloths, and Indonesian shadow puppets), and the al fresco dining in a beautiful Golden Bend backyard. **Sama Sebo** is still among the city's best-known Indonesian restaurants, possibly because it's near the Rijksmuseum and the fashion boutiques of P.C. Hooftstraat. The decor is unobtrusive—traditional dyed fabrics, reed mats—but the tables are small and pushed too close together. The food is no longer the best in town, though the Indonesian signature dish, *rendang padang* (beef with chili and coconut sauce), is excellent. For quick, cheap, and tasty dishes served until the early hours, head for **Bojo,** near Leidseplein.

Bombay on the Amstel... Amsterdam can't compete with London when it comes to Indian food, but **Memories of India**, a lavish maharajah's palace of a place near Rembrandtplein, is in the running (maybe because it's run by the owners of two distinguished Indian restaurants in London). The kind of place where you'd expect to see an Indian movie star posing under the faux palm trees, it borders on glitzy exotica. The lamb vindaloo is authentically spicy, though, the chapatis and nans fresh and flavorful, and the service polished. **Shiva,** just a few doors down, has been around longer—it's equally upscale, with starched white tablecloths and uniformed waiters, but it's smaller, considerably less showy, and the food is equally excellent. The curries range from mild to scorching, and there is moist tandoori or tikka chicken and nicely spiced madras lamb.

Thai me up, Thai me down... **Cambodia City** is the kind of nondescript, hole-in-the-wall eatery you'd walk right by on the way to the Albert Cuypstraat market, but don't miss some of the city's most authentic and flavorful Thai/Vietnamese/Cambodian food. Try the whole crispy fish with spicy Thai curry, or the *banh hoi nems* (deep-fried rolls) with sugarcane, all served without fuss and at half the price of trendy places like **Rakang Thai,** the most unusual Thai place in town: originally a tiny designer furniture boutique in the Jordaan, whose owners, seeing that business was slow, mummified the chairs in white canvas, rearranged the furnishings, and hired chef Nathapong Mungkorn in

1995. Seven years later the place is still a hit with trendy media types, artists, models, and foodies. Luckily, the chef is no slouch, and the food, though preciously presented and overpriced, is as spicy and authentic as you'd like it to be.

Asian delights... **Yoichi**, near Frederiksplein, offers plenty of sake, sukiyaki, teriyaki steaks, and other classic Japanese meat dishes on the menu, plus good fish, sushi, and veggies, of course, with bonsai trees and Buddhist calm all around. This was the first Japanese restaurant in town; now there are more luxurious ones in and around the Okura Hotel, way out on the edge of the Old South, but local Japanese still flock to Yoichi. Most non-Japanese are directed to the dreary converted Dutch cafe downstairs—make sure there are no holes in your socks, and reserve a table in the upstairs tatami room instead. New and totally different, **Wagamama** is a new-age noodle restaurant that's so Zen—no smoking, no GMOs, no reservations—you can't help wondering where they're hiding the joy. The ramen and udon noodles are great, though, and the price is right. **At Mango Bay** is a trendy Philippino restaurant in the Jordaan, with mock-Gauguin murals and a chic-bistro atmosphere. With an eye to the success of the Indonesian *rijsttafel* formula, it specializes in a festive parade of small portions of Philippino delicacies, including *lumpia* (egg rolls), *adobong manok* (chicken with coconut, laurel, and black peppercorns), and mango mousse for dessert. Local Surinamese swear by **Warung Marlon,** an outwardly unappealing cafe/take-out joint in the far-flung De Pijp neighborhood: great roasted meat and Surinamese Asian melting-pot specialties (everything from banana chips to wonton soup, from *sate* chicken in spicy peanut sauce to Peking duck). Cheap, fast, totally non-smoking too.

Utopian Ethiopian... **Kilimanjaro**, a small, chic East African restaurant not far from the Maritime Museum in eastern central Amsterdam, remains popular after six years of favorable reviews. This outpost of exotica serves such authentically good food that, with seating for only 25 or so on the ground floor of a narrow old house, you may not be able to get a table. Persist. The Dutchman who runs the place fell in love with Africa and works with an Ethiopian cook to reproduce a variety of specialties like Senegalese lamb curry, crocodile steak (very snappy), and *doro wat*, spicy Ethiopian chicken sautéed in pepper sauce and served with a spinach salad. And the simple decor—high ceilings, white walls, and colorful tablecloths designed in Africa but made in Holland—smartly manages to avoid the usual colonial jungle-cabana look.

Multi Mediterranean... There are dozens of Italian restaurants in town, most of them more Dutch than Italian, with the usual straw-wrapped flasks and vaguely Neapolitan/Tuscan dishes and pizzas. Open the Yellow Pages and take your pick. Others feature pasta and live opera singing, or people-watching over indifferent food. Pricey **Caruso**, in the Italian-owned Jolly Hotel Carlton overlooking Munt Plein, looks like a bordello, with red-velvet armchairs and carpets, huge Venetian chandeliers, and gilt plasterwork. It makes no pretense of offering anything but updated nuova cucina—the kind of nouvelle food you'd get in a swank hotel restaurant in Milan or Rome. The chef, brought in from Italy specifically to make this the best ristorante in town, hasn't succeeded yet, though he does excel with fish. Out beyond the Albert Cuypstraat market, in the multiethnic part of central A'dam, is one of the city's authentic neighborhood Italian eateries, the kind of place you'd find down a backstreet in Bari. It's called **L'Angoletto** because it sits on a corner (*un angolo*), which in terms of decor is its only distinctive feature (other than the fact that you can sit in front of the pizza oven downstairs or on a cramped mezzanine). It's run by young Italians from Taranto, in southern Italy, who serve crisp classic pizzas (napoletana, margherita), simple but tasty pasta (spaghetti with tomato sauce and hot pepperoncini), and meat such as Tuscan steaks. Meanwhile, on the Spanish front, the tapas craze—which hit Amsterdam five years later than the rest of Europe—is still going strong. So if you thought you could avoid the music, the posturing youngsters, and the endless procession of bite-sized goodies, think again. **Duende** is the quintessential Jordaan tapas bar, where self-conscious twentysomethings lounge around the cool tile-floored interior, or, in summer, hang out on the terrace. Try the tasty *calamares* (squid rings), *bacalao* (salt cod), and chorizo. **Tapas Bar Català**, near Spui, probably has better food, and will appeal to middle-aged folks looking for empanadas, mushrooms, prawns, and salads of all kinds. **Grekas Traiterie** is a Greek catering and takeout restaurant. Though its few tables are sandwiched between a cold case and the kitchen, it is modern, spotless, plays classical music, and serves perhaps the city's best stuffed bell peppers, *spanakopita* (spinach pie), and stuffed grape leaves, plus daily specials, all at reasonable prices.

The French connection... When in Amsterdam, take the appellation "French" with a truckload of *sel*. Most places serve Dutch variations on French themes, and some of the best restaurants commonly considered French actually serve something more akin to California cuisine than anything you'd find in Paris. The jury is out on **Vossius,** star chef Robert Kranenborg's new, posh-minimalist temple of gastronomy overlooking the Vandepar K. Kranenborg had two Michelin stars at La Rive but many wondered then if his food would've won such distinctions in other surroundings. Another Michelin-star pedigree chef, Gertjan Hageman, has made a comeback with his new French restaurant **De Kas,** in a reconverted hothouse in eastern Amsterdam. Hageman grows most of his own (organic) produce and the offering changes daily. There's no menu. But the soups, breads and simple roasted fish are excellent, so much so that the place gets booked up weeks or months ahead. At perennial **Bordewijk**, facing Noorderkerk in the Jordaan, the gray-and-black postmodern decor is chilling, the crowd too chic. Always inspired, the seasonal menu is at the forefront of the creative pack, with nods to France, northern Italy, and Spain. **Christophe** is chef Christophe Royer's authentically French yet creative luxury restaurant in the monied Grachtengordel neighborhood. It has a comfortable, grayscale postmodern interior, less angular and stark than Bordewijk's. Here, too, the menu changes regularly, offering variations on the theme of southwestern French and Provençal dishes (langoustine *tagine* with broadbeans; turbot with spices and puréed artichokes).

   L'Excelsior, at the Hotel de L'Europe on the Amstel River, is the kind of starchy luxury-hotel restaurant that you might as easily find in London, New York, or Paris. There are faux Louis-something armchairs, thick carpets, and a brigade of uniformed waiters, bus-boys, and sommeliers to bring you the competently pre-pared Dover sole with chanterelles, roast lamb with thyme, and mouthwatering desserts. **Café Roux**, at The Grand Hotel, is the brainchild of superstar chef Albert Roux (of three-star Le Gavroche in London). His wife came up with the art deco–inspired interior, and his lieu-tenants prepare his rather unstartling, brasserie-style dishes. Meanwhile, over at the Amstel Inter-Continental Hotel, **La Rive**, a classic French operation from the name on up, continues to wow locals. There seem to be as many waiters and busboys as diners. Thick carpets tempt you to go barefoot; the baroque flower arrange-ments are straight out of the Golden Age; and starched cloth drapes elegantly on spacious window-side tables overlooking the Amstel River. Now that Edwin Kats has taken over the kitchen, the food has a distinctly Provençal–Med flavor (monkfish with sun-dried tomato wrapped in Jabugo ham, with eggplant purée and creamy caper sauce). **Vermeer** is another corporate foodie hot spot, Kat's former fief, now in the hands of Pascal Jalhaj. His pigeon smoked on the bone with roasted pineapple and white-peach and bay leaf *jus* with salsify is ambitious (perhaps too ambitious), but there is a Calvinistic, quin-tessentially un-fun feel to the place. Housed in two restored buildings, it belongs to the luxury/business Golden Tulip Barbizon Palace Hotel. The decor features mock–Louis XIII armchairs, delft-blue plates, silver platters, and crystal. **Silveren Spiegel** is another French/Dutch luxury restaurant, a survivor despite umpteen bad reviews, in two old houses near the Singel, and has yet another interior plucked from a Golden Age canvas: Antique black-and-white tile floors, a carved spiral staircase, silver candlesticks, and crisp white table-cloths. The service can be equally stiff, and the cooking probably isn't worth the $50-a-head bill.

For that special moment... No question, *the* place to pop corks, people-watch, and applaud when the food arrives is still **Le Garage**. Flamboyant restaurateur Joop Braakhekke is a TV celebrity, and his wildly successful restaurant reminds you of New York's Le Cirque and L.A.'s Spago. The smell of garlic hits the socialites and jet-setters smack in the face as they enter. The menu shuttles between a Parisian brasserie and a Tuscan trattoria, with stopovers in Tokyo and Bombay. The decor would be a hit in Vegas—mirrors, red vinyl banquettes, and black, wraparound wooden chairs. You'll be thankful for the basket of garlic bread because the atmosphere is so festive it can take an hour to get food on the table. At Gertjan Hageman's new restaurant **De Kas** you sit in an immense reconverted hothouse with 40-foot ceilings, but the festive mood at dinner (lunch is quiet) fills the space, spilling into the chef's organic plantings and out into the surrounding park. If you dress up in black to celebrate, and I don't mean a tux, then head for ultra-hip and hyper-pricey **Blakes,** in the hotel of the same name, where the disarmingly affable chef Schilo van Coeverden is cooking up Thai/Italian/French–inspired delicacies (foie gras soup with sweet Thai basil and lime; chicken with gingko-nut curry) in a reconverted landmark bakery decorated by Anouska Hempel (aka Lady Weinberg, if you please).

Forget about the food at the **Café Americain,** and you'll have a grand time drinking, people-watching, and gazing at the gorgeous art nouveau–cum–art deco landmark interior. The chandeliers are right out of the *War of the Worlds* set design; ceiling fans create a pleasant haze of smoke that accents the Gatsbyesque atmosphere. This is where locals come for Sunday brunch, before or after the theater, or to celebrate everything from weddings and golden anniversaries to divorces. The French brasserie–style dishes—like smoked rabbit salad with walnut-raspberry dressing or duck breast with caramelized mango sauce and red peppercorns—are perfectly edible, if overly ambitious. **Long Pura** is the place to go for a swanky Indonesian feast amid neo-colonial decor, served by costumed waiters. Happily the food is spicy, authentic, and delicious. **Lucius,** the city's liveliest fish restaurant, is always packed (with locals and tourists), noisy, and fun, and longtime owners George and Marleen Lodewijks do all they can to keep the Parisian brasserie atmosphere frenzied. It's a miracle the fish stay so fresh; it's as if they'd just leapt out of the huge aquarium in the dining room (except that those are tropical fish, in case you're wondering).

Overrated... Silveren Spiegel, a luxurious French/Dutch

restaurant near Singel in a gorgeous Old Dutch setting—
centuries-old step-gable facade, creaking spiral staircase,
antique tables—serves okay food, and the service can be
starchy indeed. The clientele is distinctly business- and
tourist-oriented, and the staff may think that, what with
the antique black-and-white tile floors and the polished
silver candlesticks, no extra effort is required. A lot of
people used to refer to Tom Yam as the best Thai restaurant in town, confusing luxury with authenticity. Now
that it's been reinvented as **Tom Yam Fusion Cuisine,**
guess what? The more things change, the more they stay
the same. The service is still excellent, the food very
good indeed, but let's be honest: Chef Jos Boomgaardt
tailors his fusion delicacies to please tame Dutch palates.
Sama Sebo, near the Rijksmuseum, used to serve some
of the best Indonesian food in town, but fatigue has
apparently gained the upper hand. The food is okay but
nothing more, though visitors continue to flock here,
paying premium prices. **Le Pecheur** has fine-quality fish
and the setting is swell—a pleasant dining room or
lovely outdoor terrace—but the prices are high, the pre-
tensiousness-factor on the rise, and the fussy herb sauces
just possibly unnecessary.

See-and-be-scenes... In June 2001 chef Robert Kranenborg left his cushy two-star hotel restaurant at the
Amstel Inter-Continental (see below) to start his own
restaurant, **Vossius,** overlooking Vondelpark. The jury is
still out—but in the meantime suits, fashion models, and
the gastro-chic foodie crowd are fighting for a place in
the toney blue-minimalist formal dining room (the
smaller, less formal bistro area is uncrowded). Another
A'dam veteran with a Michelin-star pedigree, Gertjan
Hageman, draws the same self-consciously sophisticated
crowd to his new organic, market-menu hot spot, **De
Kas,** in a former hothouse reconverted to the tune of
$1.5 million. At **Le Garage** you still have to beg to get a
reservation. The service is a circus act, and you can wait
hours to get fed, but the fusion-fare is worth it (cubed
tuna tartare with curry and a crisp spinach pancake and
flaming-hot Thai chicken with green chili sauce).
Blakes, in the new ultra-chic designer hotel of the same
name, is where neo-millionaires, jet-setters, and media
tycoons go to check out each other's black duds while

feeding on skate fillet with squid ink sauce or chicken Fabergé with lobster and ginger. **Amsterdam**, on the western edge of town in a former water-pumping plant, is where young trendies mix with the middle-aged TV and media crowd from the broadcasting studios next door. The menu is eclectic, the food edible (smoked halibut with horseradish; minty lamb stew). Despite a change of toques in the kitchen, **La Rive** is still *the* place to show off your diamonds, Savile Row suit, or designer leather pants. You never know—one of the Amstel Inter-continental Hotel's dozens of celebrity regulars might stroll in, and chef Edwin Kats is no slouch: He had a star at Vermeer before taking over from Robert Kranenborg. Across town in the Jordaan, land of converted warehouses, you'll find the hip loft set displayed like rough diamonds on **Bordewijk**'s black-and-red tables. You may wonder whether your 30-ish neighbor has come to eat the superb, French/Italian–inspired cuisine or just to see what the competition is up to. Move over a few streets in the Jordaan and shave off a decade from the average age of the clients and you'll find **Rakang Thai**, an exotic design restaurant, featured regularly in trendy magazines. This is still *the* place to show off your crazy club-wear and establish your credentials as an eater of hot ethnic food.

Landmarks... Once upon a time, **L'Excelsior**, in the 1896 Hotel de L'Europe, was the top French restaurant in town. The Michelin stars may have departed, but this is still a luxury establishment, its dining room overlooking the Amstel River at Munt Plein. Some of the waiters seem like they've been around since the place was built, and the food, though traditional, is rather good. The early 1900s **Café Americain** at Leidseplein is a place architecture students seek out for the landmark Jungenstil (Dutch art-nouveau) decor, with art-deco additions. Hanging from the high, vaulted ceiling are huge bronze and stained-glass lamps that look like they might take wing. The wall clock with gold letters and symbolist murals recalls the opulence of West Egg. It's a delight to have a drink or an undemanding French-Dutch meal here and people-watch. **Amsterdam**, a trendy restaurant favored by TV types and wannabes, is in a magnificent 19th-century water-pumping plant, with 100-foot ceilings. Ornamental iron and brickwork, huge pumps, and engines surround the hundreds of wooden tables. **De Roode Leeuw**, in a peculiar turn-of-the-century building, has the city's oldest enclosed (and heated) sidewalk terrace. The old-fashioned paneled dining room is decorated with wonderfully hideous carved wooden wagons hanging from the ceiling on otherworldly sleds. Despite having two strikes against it—it's on neon-lit Damrak and it's Dutch—the place hits a home run for the homey atmosphere and food.

Cheap eats... If you're hankering for copious servings of Dutch *stamppot* (mashed spuds, gravy, ham, sausages, sauerkraut...) or spareribs, head for **De Blauwe Hollander**, a neighborhood eatery near Leidseplein, with clogs on the walls and paper place mats on the wooden tables. **Van Dobben** is great for sandwiches and croquettes. Several good bets are near the Albert Cuypstraat market. Order carefully at **Cambodia City**, an unprepossessing *eethuis*, and you can get some of the city's best Thai/Vietnamese/Cambodian food for a song. Nearby, in the De Pijp neighborhood, **Warung Marlon** is a favorite for cheap, fast, and lip-smacking Surinamese (rice topped with chicken in peanut sauce, wonton soup, Peking duck, and banana chips) and it's totally non-smoking. One of the cheapest Indonesian restaurants in town is **Bojo,** near Leidseplein. All the usual favorites are served until 4am on Friday and Saturday nights. **Grekas Traiterie**, on Singel near Spui, is more a caterer's shop than a restaurant, but the Greek food—grape leaves, moussaka, and eggplant and chickpea dips—is tops. Nearby **Haesje Claes** has a cheap tourist menu with all the rib-sticking Dutch goodies, including *stamppot*. **The Pancake Bakery**, in the basement of a Prinsengracht warehouse, offers 70 kinds of meal-in-one pancakes, each guaranteed to fill you to bursting for a relative pittance.

Isn't it romantic?... In Amsterdam, you pay for romance and atmosphere. **Le Pecheur** is at its best when the lights are low and the elegant decor—white tablecloths, nautical prints—becomes a mere backdrop. Better still is a table in the flower-filled backyard, tucked between the 17th-century mansions of the Golden Bend; there is no more gorgeous a place to feast on fish—some of the city's best. Try the saffron and fennel soup with sautéed Dutch shrimp, or the thyme-perfumed brill fillet with tagliatelle. When you feel like singing a love duet, **Caruso** may be just the place for you—along with the tasty, updated Italian food, you get a setting worthy of La Scala and a deliciously obsequious staff who will whisper to you in Italian if you like (it's remarkably more romantic-sounding than Dutch).

Tempo Doeloe may have the best Indonesian food in town, but it's also romantic in a spunky, exotic way. The theatrical lighting makes everyone seem to have bedroom eyes. **Long Pura**, the other top Indonesian, has a spiffy neo-colonial decor and soft lighting: An orchid blossom greets you at the table, but the rest is up to you. **Moko,** under the spreading trees of Amstelveld Square, must be the prettiest restaurant in town for besotted intellectual couples wearing existentialist black. The warm-weather terrace is best, but even the discreet designer interior, in the basement of old Amstelkerk, has big windows, aquariums, and uncomfy designer furniture to encourage intellectual intercourse. The kitchen does a fairly competent job with the eclectic menu, offering Asian-Med fusion food. **Pier 10** can't help being romantic, perched as it is on an old pier behind Centraal Station. Candlelight softens the increasingly funky diner decor, and the fanciful international-eclectic food—salads of all kinds, new herring, steak, and fish—ebbs and flows like the River IJ, largely unremarked, as trendy youth stare into each other's mauve makeup, caress each other's designer club-wear labels, and wonder if romance will bloom later on the dance floor of More, Sinners in Heaven, or IT (see Nightlife).

Tourist traps... D'Vijff Vlieghen, better known to English speakers as The Five Flies, is the mother of all themed tourist traps and a must for anyone interested in the genre. It was founded after World War II by flamboyant antiques dealer Nicolaas Kroese, whose motto ran, "You haven't been to Amsterdam if you haven't been to the Five Flies." The instant-ancient decor alone is worth a detour. To top it all, the French/Dutch fare isn't that bad (lots of updated ham and apple dishes, plus game and fish). **Haesje Claes** has become The Five

Flies' direct competitor. Owner André Duyves, too, has an instant-old pedigree: The restaurant has been around since 1970, but he touts the date 1520 prominently because that's when Lady Haesje Claes was born nearby ("The spirit and period atmosphere linger," Duyves likes to say through his impressive moustache.) The place is marvelously kitsch, with mock everything, except the authentically old buildings (totally rebuilt, of course). Luckily, it's all good fun, and the traditional Dutch food is good enough, as long as you stick to things like *stamppot* or salad with herring and smoked eel. **The Pancake Bakery** is something altogether different, designed especially for Americans, it seems, and for kids who've just gotta have a *pannekoek*. Don't bother to ask your fellow diners what's what—they're not Dutch.

Something fishy... For reasons beyond the ken of a non-Dutch person, all Amsterdam's best fish restaurants are landlocked and about as far from the rivers or canals as possible in this floating city. The Atlantic and North Sea fish at **Albatros** have the great virtue of being grilled, poached, and fried in the simplest manner possible, then served in ship-ahoy decor by friendly old-timers in a relaxed Jordaan neighborhood atmosphere (there's even a nonsmoking section). Try the mixed seafood salad, the raw herring, and the sea bass (they make a mean tiramisu, too). No quaint fishermen's nets adorn **Le Pecheur**, a stylish restaurant on Reguliersdwarsstraat. The canal isn't in view, but you can admire the backsides and gardens of 17th-century mansions as you dine on elaborate fish dishes, skillfully prepared. You'll marvel—or gasp—at the chef's use of herbs and sauces (sea bass with taragon-mustard sauce; prawns with a garlicky fennel sauce). At lively and fun **Lucius**, the herring, plaice, sole, and bream are equally tasty raw, grilled, poached, or baked. The seafood's so fresh you almost wish you'd ordered it without that delicious, flavorful, but superfluous cayenne or green pepper sauce.

Can you put that out, please?... Amsterdam is a nonsmoker's hell—the opposite of California—so eat outside or pick an uncrowded time and ask the waiter or host to make an effort to seat nonsmokers near you. Call ahead and explain your request in detail—then prepare to be smoked like a local eel. The only totally smoke-free eateries I've found in town are cheap, cheery, and delicious Surinamese **Warung Marlon** and the hip new Japanese noodle bar **Wagamama. De Vrolijke Abrikoos,** a vegetarian restaurant, reserves half of its one big room for non-puffers (weekdays only). **Cafe in de Wildeman**—a beer joint—has an entire room for non-smokers. **Café Americain** has a small section in the bar/cafe area (not in the brasserie). **Albatros,** a friendly seafood eatery, has a big, bona fide nonsmoking area and a staff that'll defend your air space. The managers of **Haesje Claes** (Dutch classics) and **Memories of India** are sympathetic to the anti-tobacco crowd, but there's only so much they can do to convince other patrons to stump out those cigs and—ever popular—cigars. Tolerance! And good—cough—luck.

When the play's the thing... The Dutch eat dinner very early indeed, and most restaurants stop serving by 11pm, so post-theater meals in restaurants are hard to manage: It's as if Calvin wouldn't approve if you enjoyed two forms of entertainment on a single night. **Café Americain** specializes in feeding the concert and theater crowds of the Stadsschouwburg across the street in Leidseplein and the Lido casino and cabaret around the corner on Singelgracht; it serves dinner until midnight, and light meals and snacks until 1am. So what if the stunning art-nouveau interior and ambience are more interesting than the French-inspired food? **Le Pecheur**, a swanky fish restaurant on Reguliersdwarsstraat near Rembrandtplein, is within striking distance of all the city's venues, especially the Muziektheater and Carré, nearby on the Amstel River. The well-heeled international clientele is used to late dining; and if you come in too late for the main menu, after around 11pm, there's a variety of classy snacks served until 1am—caviar, cold lobster, oysters, smoked salmon, and more. One of the wildest, hottest restaurant in town, **Le Garage**, is not a late-night place per se, but the kitchen will serve until about midnight, and the tables are still crowded well after the witching hour. At **Amsterdam**, another hip eatery, the kitchen stays open until 11:30pm, and you can get snacks and light meals until 1am (till 2am on Fri and Sat). On weekends, you can get a pan-fried steak or a plate of herring until midnight at homey **Piet de Leeuw Steakhouse**. **Bojo,** a cheap and cheery Indonesian eatery near Leidseplein, that serves until 1am (4am Friday and Saturday nights). Other after-11 eats are found at: **Lucius** (fish), **Memories of India, Pier 10, Tapas Bar Català, Tempo Doeloe, Van Dobben,** and **D' Vijff Vlieghen.** Beyond these, your best bet for a late-night hangout is a cafe (see Cafes and Bars).

Kid pleasers... The Dutch are very tolerant of rambunctious youngsters. You can take them almost anywhere (at least anywhere not strictly for elitist trendies), as long as you can afford to pay for them. One spot they're sure to love is **Haesje Claes,** a roistering Dutch place with Old Dutch decor. Host André Duyves seems right out of Walt Disney, and his food will remind the kiddies of school lunches—the house specialty, *stamppot*, is none other than mashed potatoes with a ladle of dark gravy, sausages, ribs, sauerkraut, and more. Kids love the croquettes and milk at **Van Dobben.** At **The Pancake Bakery**, you might be back home at a demented IHOP. The kids can splash and spill corn and sugar syrup (no maple syrup in view) without danger, since the tabletops are marble and the menus laminated. They're sure to find something they like among the omelets and 70 kinds of pancakes topped with everything from fried chicken to sweet corn. Since few kids can resist a good pizza, you might also try the straightforward trattoria **L'Angoletto.** Surprisingly, hip **Amsterdam** is very brat-friendly; the eclectic food and industrial decor (an old water-pumping plant) appeal to budding trendies.

For a quiet tête-à-tête... Vermeer, the Golden Tulip Barbizon Palace's luxury Dutch/French restaurant, is synonymous with discretion. There's enough room between the tables for rafts of waiters and busboys to glide by; the thick carpets absorb unpleasant sounds, and the mock–Louis XIII armchairs are as upright as the diners in them. Classically French **La Rive** and **L'Excelsior** have some of the highest prices in town, which keeps the number of diners to a minimum. An added plus at La Rive is the pianist, who produces soothing background music. **De Roode Leeuw**, a serious Dutch restaurant, has the kind of old-fashioned paneled decor, big tables, and professional waiters that perfectly complement intimate conversations.

Vegging out... The anti-meat crowd is well served in Amsterdam, since most menus feature salads and fish. There really is no need to seek out the dozens of joyless, mediocre vegetarian-only eateries where the owners and clients are likely to snarl at anyone wearing leather shoes. However, if that's your bag, and you can stomach the name, try **De Vrolijke Abrikoos**, considered by those in the know the very best veggie eatery in Amsterdam—good for succulent tofu and satisfying salads. Everything is biodynamically grown and respectfully consumed. There's a big nonsmoking section (weekdays), and the walls are a comforting shade of edible apricot. Described by its owners as a "non-destinational food station," **Wagamama,** a Zen-style Japanese noodle restaurant, has dozens of great veg combos (it's nonsmoking and the food is GMO—and humor—free). Most other Asian restaurants, and all the Indonesian places in town, offer a variety of vegetable-only dishes and vegetarian fixed-price menus. **Tempo Doeloe** has two vegetarian menus (plus up to five courses à la carte) that are out of this world, featuring a variety of veggies and bean sprouts with mild or spicy peanut sauce (*gado-gado* and *sajoer lodeh*) and sweet and sour *petjel* sauce, plus saffron-perfumed rice, vegetable pancakes, and fruit desserts.

When the boss is paying... **Silveren Spiegel**, which sits across the street from the Amsterdam Renaissance Hotel in two handsome old buildings, is the kind of place food-challenged businesspeople and upscale conventioneers head to when they don't have to spend their own money. The fancy French/Dutch food fits the candlelit, antiques-crammed setting. At **Vermeer**, another architectural gem in two landmark houses, the Golden Age atmosphere accompanies excellent French-inspired cuisine. **Vossius,** the new hot spot opened by star chef Robert Kranenborg, may just be the most expensive place in town. Across the center of town at **L'Excelsior**, the tables are generously distanced, the wine list is long on three-digit vintages from la belle France, and the punctilious waiters know when to light the candles and stop hovering. Timing the removal of the dishes with amazing grace, they may glide up to your table with a succulent roast lamb or Dover sole with chanterelles. **La Rive**'s comfortable armchairs are never sullied by wallets (they are worn inside suit pockets or carried in diamond-spangled handbags); it's the quintessential place to spend lots of money on classic, Michelin-starred French food. **De Kas,** in a reconverted hothouse, is a hip goldmine: There's no menu, just the chef's picks of the day, and the drinks, dessert, and coffee push the tab through the glass roof. **Bordewijk**, near Noorderkerk in the Jordaan, attracts a similarly chic clientele with its stellar French/Italian food. Nearby **Christophe**, a French restaurant favored by A'dam's beau monde, is a great place to squander the company's euros on tempting French regional dishes. At designer-chic **Blakes,** feast on Thai/Italian/French delicacies prepared by celeb chef Schilo van Coevorden; the prices are breathtaking.

Al fresco... **Moko** must be the most attractive spot in town for fine-weather dining. Its wide terrace spreads under the big old trees on Amstelveld Square, bordering Prinsengracht. There is no traffic; lovers stroll along the canal; kids play soccer in the cobbled square; and behind is the old wooden Amstelkerk (the restaurant's dining room is actually in the church's basement). The fusion-Med food on the menu is competent, but then you really didn't come for the food, anyway. **Albatros**, a friendly, simple fish restaurant, has a narrow terrace on the sidewalk where in summer you can watch the seagulls and albatrosses flying overhead. Soak up the atmospheric Jordaan, where there's little traffic and locals chatting on stoops. Trendy **Pier 10** has great riverside views of the IJ from its big outdoor terrace on a pier behind Centraal Station, set back far enough that you won't be bothered by the noise. In summer at **Le Pecheur**, you can dine on fresh fish in a lovely, flower-filled backyard; a few doors down is **Sahid Jaya**, probably the most luxurious and pricey of Amsterdam's Indonesian restaurants, which also has a pleasant backyard terrace amid Golden Bend mansions.

Take me to the river... For a city built on dozens of canals and two big rivers—the Amstel and the IJ—it's amazing how few restaurants take advantage of the waterfront real estate; you can count them on the claws of one paw. Some of the well-heeled diners at **L'Excelsior** arrive by boat at the Hotel de L'Europe's private dock on the Amstel, ready to dine on classic French food. Down the river a half mile or so, with its own private dock, is another formal French choice, **La Rive**, the Amstel Inter-Continental's posh and much-touted dining room. When you disembark from your saloon boat and settle into the dining room, which sits almost at water level, you feel like you're on a luxury liner, with canal-boats and yachts cruising past the windows. When those same boats and ships decide to head to sea, they sail down the IJ within view of trendy **Pier 10**, practically the only restaurant in town where you're aware of the sea and port traffic—once A'dam's lifeblood.

Cafes and bars

Vintage brown cafes... **Cafe Chris** is the oldest of them all (1624), a Jordaan institution with beer mugs hanging from the ceiling, a pool table, and an old chain-pull toilet which you actually flush from the main room. (Now *there's* atmosphere for you.) **Cafe Karpershoek**, across from Centraal Station, comes second (1629) and attracts a blue-collar crowd to its smoky, darkwood interior and sandy floor, while **Cafe de Druif**, the third-oldest (1631), out east near the Maritime Museum, claims to be older than them all. It's the archetypal neighborhood hangout, with old *genever* and beer barrels piled high behind the bar, and a mezzanine where the regulars perch like voluble old parrots. **Cafe Papeneiland**, from 1642, is a Jordaan hangout near Noorderkerk, with beautiful delft tiles and a cast-iron stove. **Cafe Hegeraad**, another vintage Jordaan place, is especially lively on market days. **Cafe Hoppe** is favored by well-heeled locals and the Spui literary set; it's great for studying the human comedy from a lively terrace. **Cafe Mulder**, on the southern edge of central A'dam on Weteringlaan, has a gorgeous interior with etched glass, a hummy barkeep, and carpets on the tables. **Cafe de Sluyswacht** has a nondescript interior but panoramic terraces overlooking a lock on the Oude Schans canal; boats glide under your table. **Cafe 't Smalle**, a relative newcomer (founded in 1786), is among the Jordaan's most popular spots, with a tiny dock terrace under trees, packed with trendies and locals.

Neo-browns... **Cafe Ruk & Pluk** is run by a famous gay couple of the same names; it's wild, festive, campy, and located way out east of Oosterpark. **Schaak Cafe Het Hok** is a smoky, friendly place near Leidseplein where fans of Amsterdam's soccer team, Ajax, play chess—there are stop clocks hung from the rafters. **Cafe Thijssen**, on the Jordaan's northern edge, could be in Paris, and so could the pretentiously hip clientele. **Cafe Daalder**, also in the Jordaan, has great apple pie, a nice terrace, and attracts a less self-important crowd. **Het Molenpad**, a Grachtengordel hangout, has a clubby, chummy feel inside, plus a wonderful canal-side summer terrace. **Engelbewaarder**, full of cig and dope smoke, is a self-styled "literary cafe" east of the red-light district where self-styled intellectuals listen to jazz on Sunday afternoons. **De IJsbreker**, with a big tree-shaded terrace on the east bank of the Amstel River, is the trendy, neo-brown section of the celebrated music club of the same name.

White cafes... **Dantzig** is a spacious place attached to City Hall and the Muziektheater complex, with a library corner and a wraparound Amstel River terrace that's great for poseurs. **Cafe de Jaren**, on the Amstel 100 yards north, is another big, sunny spot, with a panoramic upper-floor terrace where the young and hip survey the city in sweet, smoky anonymity.

Designer cafes... **De Kroon** is where media culture-vultures gather, either at the yard-wide zinc bar (flanked by bizarre displays of butterflies, bugs, and dusty bones) or on the enclosed, second-story terrace overlooking the rabble below on Rembrandtplein. **Cafe Luxembourg**, at Spui, draws much the same crowd (plus white collars) to its mock-old interior and enclosed terrace. **In de Waag,** inside a medieval tower, is a hip Internet cafe/restaurant near Centraal Station. **Cafe Wildschut**, near the Concertgebouw, features designer 25- to 35-year-olds in an early-1900s Amsterdam School building with stained-glass, booths, armchairs, and a wrap-around banquette. At **Gambit**—one of a contingent of so-called "chess cafes"—regulars, and the occasional visitor, play chess, dominoes, and other board games in a cozy, smoky setting in the Jordaan.

Tap houses (proeflokalen)... **De Admiraal**, a recently opened upscale place in the Grachtengordel neighborhood, has sofas for those who've indulged in too much *genever*. **De Drie Fleschjes** is the mother of all tap houses, a crowded place in an alley behind Dam Square where red-nosed regulars tipple out of their own private barrels. Ditto **Wijnand Fockink**, founded in 1679 in an alley between Dam and the red-light district. Be careful how you pronounce the name. **Cafe Hooghoudt**, a friendly instant-retro spot near Rembrandtplein, is stuffed with enough Ye Olde Decor—jars, vats, barrels, and farm implements—to stock a flea market. **Proeflokaal André Lacroix**, near Vondelpark, is redolent of strong tobacco and alcohol and is probably the darkest, most authentic, and utterly un-touristed of all A'dam's tap houses.

For suds... **Cafe in de Wildeman** is a venerable brown cafe and beer bar in the heart of Old Amsterdam, serving about 180 bottled brews and 20 on tap. It has what may be the city's only cafe nonsmoking room. **Bierbrouwerij 't IJ** is the city's top microbrewery, on the eastern edge of central A'dam, where a distinctly young crowd guzzles suds on the terrace under the authentically old De Gooyer windmill. **Brouwhuis Maximiliaan**, near Nieuwemarkt, is another microbrewery, with a brown cafe atmosphere.

Best cafe food... **Dantzig**, a big, bright white cafe attached to City Hall, serves great *bitterballen*, croquettes, egg rolls, sate chicken, and daily specials; it's a good place for a pre- or post-theater snack. **Cafe Luxembourg**, a designer cafe at Spui, gets a lot of its food from top restaurants and has the best croquettes (from Holtkamp, see Shopping), dim sum, chicken *sate*, salads, and sandwiches of all the city's cafes. **Cafe Papeneiland**, a 1642 brown near Noorderkerk, serves the best hot-pastrami sandwich in town, plus a tasty onion soup. **Cafe Daalder**, a neo-brown in the Jordaan, makes some of the best apple pie and sandwiches in town. **Het Molenpad**, another neo-brown, has great sandwiches and daily specials to match its chummy atmosphere and classic jazz tapes. **De IJsbreker**, part of the music club of the same name, serves Sunday breakfast, plus good soups and sandwiches. **Cafe de Jaren** is a sunny white on the Amstel with a great salad bar, soups, and good daily quiches; the regular restaurant here features unnecessarily complicated dishes.

The Index

Note: 1 euro=$.88-.95 U.S.

$$$$$	over $60
$$$$	$40–$60
$$$	$26–$40
$$40	$18–$26
$	under $18

(Per person for a meal—3-course dinner or full lunch—without wine or beverages.)

Albatros. Flipping fresh Atlantic and North Sea fish grilled, poached, and fried is the specialty at this Jordaan neighborhood restaurant.... *Tel 020/627-9932. Westerstraat 264, tram 10 to Marnixbad. Reservations recommended. Dinner only. Closed Sun. $$$$* **(see pp. 69, 70, 73)**

Amsterdam. A hip new cafe and restaurant in a reconverted 19th-century waterpumping plant on the western edge of town. Authentic industrial decor, 100-foot ceilings, and machinery. The menu ranges from tomato soup to foie gras, calf's brain with sage, minty lamb stew—all of it astoundingly edible.... *Tel 020/682-2666. Watefforenplein 6, tram 10 to terminus at Watertorenplein. Open daily 11–1am (2 on Fri–Sat); meals served 11am–11:30pm. $$* **(see pp. 66, 70, 71)**

At Mango Bay. This Philippino bistro with faux-Gauguin murals (hmmm, wasn't he in Tahiti?), tall mirrors, and white tablecloths pulls in the hip Jordaan youngish set for its classic *lumpia* (egg rolls) and tasty specialties like *adobong manok* (chicken with coconut, laurel, and black peppercorns).... *Tel 020/638-1039. Westerstraat 91, trams 13, 14, 17 to Westerkerk. Dinner only.* $$

(see p. 60)

Bierbrouwerij 't IJ. Quintessential Dutch—the city's best microbrewery, with a vast terrace in the shadow of a windmill northeast of Artis Zoo.... *Tel 020/622-8325. Funenkade 7, trams 6, 10 to Zeeburgerdikj, buses 22, 32 to Oostenburgergracht.* **(see p. 76)**

Blakes. Chic-est of all Amsterdam's new designer restaurants, located in Blakes Hotel. Presided over by affable celeb chef Schilo van Coevorden, master of Thai/Italian/French–inspired wonders.... *Tel 020/530-2010. Keizersgracht 384, trams 13, 14, 17 to Westerkerk. Chic dress. Reserve far in advance.* $$$$$ **(see pp. 64, 65, 73)**

Bojo. Amsterdam's long-established cheap and late-night Indonesian restaurant, near Leidseplein.... *Tel 020/622-7434. Lange Leidsedwarsstraat 51, trams 1, 2, 5, 6, 7, 10 to Leidseplein. No credit cards. Open 4pm–1am (4am Fri/Sat).* $ **(see pp. 59, 67, 71)**

Bordewijk. The French/Italian–inspired menu is among the city's best, the postmodern Jordaan setting endlessly hip.... *Tel 020/624-3899. Noordermarkt 7, tram 3 to Nieuwe Willemstraat. Reservations essential. Casual-chic dress. Dinner only. Closed Mon.* $$$$

(see pp. 62, 66, 73)

Brouwhuis Maximiliaan. A microbrewery on the edge of the red-light district at Nieuwemarkt with 5 house-brewed beers, tours, tastings.... *Tel 020/626-6280, www.maximiliaan.nl. Kloveniersburgwal 6–8, Metro to Nieuwemarkt, all trams and buses to Centraal Station.*

(see p. 76)

Café Americain. This landmark cafe's stunning art-nouveau and art-deco interior eclipses the overly ambitious, though perfectly edible, French-inspired food. Special theater menus, brunch, and high tea.... *Tel 020/623-4813. Leid-*

seplein 28, trams 1, 2, 5, 6, 7, 10 to Leidseplein. Reservations recommended. $$$ **(see pp. 64, 66, 70)**

Cafe Chris. The oldest of the old browns, founded in 1624, and a Jordaan institution. Famous for Sunday afternoon opera tapes.... *Tel 020/624-5942. Bloemstraat 42, trams 13, 14, 17 to Westerkerk.* **(see p. 74)**

Cafe Daalder. A neo-brown in the Jordaan—go on market days for the view.... *Tel 020/624-8864. Lindengracht 90, tram 3 to Nieuwe Willemsstraat.* **(see pp. 75, 76)**

Cafe de Druif. Though it claims an even earlier pedigree, Druif is the 3rd-oldest brown, dating to 1631. Far flung, near the Maritime Museum, and probably the friendliest, most authentic of them all.... *Tel 020/624-4530. Rapenburg 83, buses 22, 32 to Kadijksplein.* **(see p. 74)**

Cafe de Jaren. A postmodern, big, and sunny white cafe overlooking the Amstel near Munt Plein, where beautiful young A'dammers lounge on the terrace.... *Tel 020/625-5771, www.cafe-de-jaren.nl. Nieuwe Doelenstraat 20, trams 4, 9, 14, 16, 24, 25 to Munt Plein.*
(see pp. 75, 77)

Cafe de Sluyswacht. A 1695 brown with canal-side terraces, bordering the Jewish quarter.... *Tel 020/625-7611. Jodenbreestraat 1, trams 9, 14 to Muziektheatre.* **(see p. 74)**

Cafe Hegeraad. A vintage brown behind Noorderkerk, with carpets on the tables.... *Tel 020/624-5565. Noordermarkt 34, trams 13, 14, 17 to Westerkerk.* **(see p. 74)**

Cafe Hooghoudt. A spacious *proeflokaal* and bar that's only a few years old but has a bogus "old Amsterdam" aura. Just south of Rembrandtplein.... *Tel 020/420-4041. Reguliersgracht 11, tram 4 to Keizersgracht.*
(see p. 76)

Cafe Hoppe. A vintage brown, from 1670, that's a great place to people-watch.... *Tel 020/420-4420. Spui 18–20, trams 1, 2, 5 to Spui.* **(see p. 74)**

Cafe in de Wildeman. This beer bar, down an Old A'dam alley,

DINING AND CAFES | THE INDEX

started life in 1690 as a distillery; it serves more than 200 beers. Nonsmoking room.... *Tel 020/638-2348. Kolksteeg 3, trams 4, 9, 14, 24, 25 to Korte Kolkstraat.***(see pp. 70, 76)**

Cafe Karpershoek. The 2nd-oldest brown, from 1629. Prototypical, and within shouting distance of Centraal Station.... *Tel 020/624-7886. Martelaarsgracht 2, trams 1, 2, 5, 13, 17 to Martelaarsgracht.* **(see p. 74)**

Cafe Luxembourg. A slick crowd blends into the designer decor.... *Tel 020/620-6264. Spui 22–24, trams 1, 2, 5, to Spui.* **(see pp. 75, 76)**

Cafe Mulder. A handsome old brown on the southern edge of central A'dam.... *Tel 020/623-7874. Weteringschans 163, trams 6, 7, 10, 16, 24, 25 to Weteringlaan.* **(see p. 74)**

Cafe Papeneiland. A vintage Jordaan brown (1642) near Noorderkerk.... *Tel 020/624-1989. Prinsengracht 2, buses 18, 22 to Buiten Browersstraat.* **(see pp. 74, 76)**

Café Roux. Albert Roux's brasserie in The Grand Hotel serves updated French classics with the occasional nod to the locals.... *Tel 020/555-3111. Oudezijds Voorburgwal 193, trams 16, 24, 25 to Spui. Reservations essential. Jacket and tie recommended. $$$$* **(see p. 63)**

Cafe Ruk & Pluk. One-of-a-kind neo-brown way out east of Oosterpark, with a *Cage aux Folles* carnival spirit. Crowd and decor to match.... *Tel 020/665-3248. Linnaeusstraat 48, tram 9, buses 59, 61, 120, 126 to Linnaeusplantsoen.* **(see p. 75)**

Cafe Thijssen. This hip neo-brown on the Jordaan's northern edge is best on Lindengracht market days.... *Tel 020/623-8994, www.cafethijssen.com. Brouwersgracht 107, buses 18, 22 to Buiten Browersstraat.* **(see p. 75)**

Cafe 't Smalle. Founded as a distillery in 1786, this popular Jordaan brown is near Westerkerk.... *Tel 020/623-9617. Egelantiersgracht 12, trams 13, 14, 17 to Westerkerk.* **(see p. 74)**

Cafe Wildschut. A designer cafe in an Amsterdam School building near the Concertgebouw.... *Tel 020/676-8220.*

Roelof Hartplein 1–3, trams 3, 5, 12, 24 to Roelof Hartplein.
(see p. 75)

Cambodia City. A surprising little *eethuis* with the usual red papier-mâché lions, serving some of the city's best Thai/Vietnamese/Cambodian food.... *Tel 020/671-4930. Albert Cuypstraat 58–60, trams 16, 24, 25 to Albert Cuypstraat. Open 5–10pm, closed Mon. $$* **(see pp. 59, 67)**

Caruso. Italian nuova cucina served in an operatic bordello setting—some of the city's best Italian (and fish) dishes are here.... *Tel 020/623-8320. Singel 550, trams 4, 9, 14, 16, 24, 25 to Munt Plein. Reservations recommended. Jacket and tie recommended. $$$$* **(see pp. 61, 68)**

Christophe. Chef Jean Christophe Royer's eponymous restaurant—*très* French, superb.... *Tel 020/625-0807. Leliegracht 46, trams 1, 2, 5, to Westerkerk. Reservations essential. Casual-chic dress. Dinner only. Closed Sun. $$$$*
(see pp. 62, 73)

Dantzig. A spacious white cafe with a river terrace, at City Hall; tasty food.... *Tel 020/620-9039. Zwanenburgwal 15, trams 9, 14 to Muziektheatre.* **(see pp. 75, 76)**

De Admiraal. A *proeflokaal* in the Grachtengordel neighborhood, pouring Cees van Wees' famous spirits (see Shopping).... *Tel 020/625-4334. Herengracht 319, trams 1, 2, 5 to Raadhuisstraat or Spui.* **(see p. 76)**

De Blauwe Hollander. Authentic and cheap Dutch fare in a cozy setting.... *Tel 020/623-3014. Leidsekruisstraat 28, trams 6, 7, 10 to Leidseplein. No reservations. Dinner only. Open daily 5–10pm. No credit cards or large bills. $$*
(see pp. 56, 67)

De Drie Fleschjes. Vintage *proeflokaal*, just behind Dam Square, where regulars have their own barrels of *genever*.... *Tel 020/624-8443. Gravenstraat 18, all trams to either Dam or Raadhuisstraat.* **(see p. 76)**

De IJsbreker. A neo-brown on the east bank of the river, attached to the celebrated music club of the same name (see Entertainment and Nightlife). Great Amstelside terrace.... *Tel 020/665-3014. Weesperzijde 23,*

tram 3 to Ruyschstraat, 7, 10 to Weepersplein
.   **(see pp. 75, 77)**

De Kas. Hip new restaurant, owned by celeb chef Gertjan Hageman, in a reconverted hothouse in eastern A'dam. The French-Dutch specialties change daily. No menu: It's the chef's call. Book way ahead.... *Tel 020/462-4562, www.restaurantdekas.nl. Kamerlingh Onneslaan 3, tram 9 to Hugo de Vrieslaan. $$$$*
(see pp. 62, 64, 65, 73)

De Kroon. A vast designer cafe with extraordinary curiosity cases. The media crowd hangs out here.... *Tel 020/625-2011, juan@escape.nl. Rembrandtplein 17, trams 4, 9, 14.* **(see p. 75)**

De Roode Leeuw. Great Dutch regional cuisine served in a cozily kitsch, old-fashioned interior. Try the dried *nagelhout* beef or braised codfish with mustard sauce.... *Tel 020/555-0666, www.hotelamsterdam.nl. Damrak 93–94, trams 4, 9, 16, 24, 25 to Dam Square. $$$* **(see pp. 56, 67, 71)**

De Vrolijke Abrikoos. The biodynamically grown veggie goodies taste better than the name sounds. Big nonsmoking section weekdays only.... *Tel 020/624-4672. Weteringschaus 76, trams 6, 7, 10 to Spiegelgracht/Weteringschaus. Open daily from 5:30pm. Reservations recommended.* **(see pp. 70, 72)**

Duende. This hip tapas bar in the Jordaan has tile floors, wooden tables, and a summer terrace out front.... *Tel 020/420-6692. Lindengracht 62, tram 3 to Nieuwe Willemstraat. No reservations. No credit cards. $* **(see p. 61)**

D' Vijff Vlieghen. A must for the decor alone: dark wood paneling and a labyrinth of timbered rooms. The Dutch-continental fare is surprisingly edible.... *Tel 020/624-8369. Spuistraat 294–302, trams 1, 2, 5 to Spui or Paleisstraat. Reservations recommended. Dinner only. $$$$* **(see pp. 57, 68, 71)**

Engelbewaarder. A literary neo-brown east of the red-light district—wonderfully pretentious, surprisingly seedy.... *Tel 020/625-3772. Kloveniersburgwal 59, Metro to Nieuwemarkt.*
(see p. 75)

Gambit. One of Amsterdam's most competitive "chess cafes," located in the Jordaan.... *Tel 020/622-1801, m.gold berg@cable.a200.nl. Bloemgracht 20, trams 13, 14, 17 to Westerkerk.* **(see p. 75)**

Grekas Traiterie. This spotlessly clean takeout joint with just a few tables serves the city's tastiest Greek food.... *Tel 020/ 620-3590. Singel 311, trams 1, 2, 5 to Spui. No reservations. Open 5–10pm. Closed Mon–Tue. No credit cards. $* **(see pp. 62, 67)**

Haesje Claes. This quintessential but endearingly *gezellig* tourist trap actually serves excellent *stamppot* (mashed potatoes with sauerkraut and pork ribs) and salad with herring and smoked eel.... *Tel 020/624-9998, www.haes-jeclaes.nl. Spuistraat 275, trams 1, 2, 5 to Spui or Paleisstraat. Reservations recommended. $$* **(see pp. 57, 67, 68, 70, 71)**

Het Molenpad. Neo-brown neighborhood cafe with clubby atmosphere, jazz tapes, and some of the best cafe food in town day and night (sandwiches, daily specials). Canal-side terrace.... *Tel 020/625-9680. Prinsengracht 653, trams 1, 2, 5 to Prinsengracht.* **(see pp. 75, 76)**

In de Waag. Trendy cafe in a centuries-old tower.... *Tel 020/422-7772. Nieuwarkt 4, all trains to Centraal Station. $$* **(see p. 75)**

Kilimanjaro. This chic African restaurant with only 7 tables is run by a Dutchman, but the Ethiopian cook makes a variety of East African specialties.... *Tel 020/622-3485. Rapenburgerplein 6, bus 22 to Prins Hendrikkade and Kadijksplein. Reservations essential. Dinner only. Closed Mon. 4% surcharge on credit cards. $$* **(see p. 60)**

L'Angoletto. Utterly unpretentious, it's run by young Italians who make good classic pizzas, pasta dishes, and meat.... *Tel 020/676-4182. Hemonystraat 18, tram 3 to Amsteldijk or 4 to Sarphatipark. Reservations recommended; dinner only. Closed Sat. No credit cards. $$* **(see pp. 61, 71)**

La Rive. Dutch-French food by celeb chef Edwin Kats at ultra-luxe restaurant.... *Tel 020/622-6060. Professor Tulpplein*

1, trams 6, 7, 10 to Sarphatistraat. Reservations essential. Jacket and tie recommended. $$$$$
(see pp. 63, 66, 71, 73, 74)

Le Garage. It's a cross between a Parisian brasserie, a Tuscan trattoria, and a noisy Las Vegas nightclub. Nonetheless, the wildly creative food is virtuoso stuff.... *Tel 020/679-7176. Ruysdaelstraat 54–56, trams 3, 5, 12 to Roelof Hartplein. Reservations essential. Chic dress. No lunch weekends. $$$$* **(see pp. 63, 65, 70)**

Le Pecheur. This upscale fish restaurant run by Rien van Santen has a flower-filled backyard on the Golden Bend and fresh, highest-quality seafood.... *Tel 020/624-3121. Reguliersdwarsstraat 32, trams 1, 2, 5 to Koningsplein. Lunch weekdays only. Closed Sun. MC not accepted. $$$$*
(see pp. 65, 67, 69, 70, 73)

L'Excelsior. Michelin stars come and go, but this perennial French restaurant at the Hotel de L'Europe stays.... *Tel 020/531-1778. Nieuwe Doelenstraat 2–8, trams 4, 9, 16, 24, 25 to Spui. Reservations recommended. Jacket and tie required. $$$$$* **(see pp. 62, 66, 71, 72, 74)**

Long Pura. Swank Indonesian restaurant in the Jordaan. Costumed waiters, neo-colonial decor, fresh orchids to put behind your ears. Happily, the food is great—some of the best *sambal goreng udang petjel* (shrimp and petjel beans with spicy coconut milk sauce) in town. Steep prices but worth it.... *Tel 020/623-8950, longpura@x54all.nl. Rozengracht 46–48, trams 13, 14, 17 to Westerkerk. Dinner only. $$$* **(see pp. 58, 64, 68)**

Lucius. Run by friendly George and Marleen Lodewijks, this is among the city's liveliest fish restaurants.... *Tel 020/624-1831. Spuistraat 247, trams 1, 2, 5 to Spui or Paleisstraat. Dinner only. Closed Sun. $$$$***(see pp. 64, 69, 71)**

Memories of India. Upscale, authentic Indian food. Don't miss the perfumed chapatis and nans, spicy lamb vindaloo, and tender tandoori chicken.... *Tel 020/623-5710. Reguliersdwarsstraat 88, trams 4, 9, 14, 16, 24, 25 to Munt Plein or Rembrandtplein. Dinner only. $$$*
(see pp. 59, 70, 71)

Moko. Formerly Kort, this is still among the prettiest, friendliest cafe/restaurant combos in town. The food is fusion-Med.... *Tel 020/626-1199, www.moko.nl. Amstelveld 12, tram 4 to Prinsengracht. Reservations recommended. $$$*
(see pp. 68, 73)

The Pancake Bakery. In the basement of a converted Prinsengracht warehouse. Of the 70 pancakes offered, first on the list is the "American Pancake," which boasts fried chicken, sweet corn, paprika, carrots, and spicy Cajun sauce.... *Tel 020/625-1333, www.pancake.nl. Prinsengracht 191, trams 13, 14, 17 to Westerkerk. $*
(see pp. 57, 67, 69, 71)

Pier 10. Set on a pier behind Centraal Station, this trendy spot serves an international menu. Great harbor views from the "serre" (glassed-in) room at the end of the pier.... *Tel 020/624-8276. De Ruyerkade Steiger 10, all transport to Centraal Station. Reservations recommended. Dinner only. $$$*
(see pp. 68, 71, 73, 74)

Piet de Leeuw Steakhouse. Back in the States it would be called "Pete's Place" or "The Lion," with a dark, cozy interior that smells slightly of beer. The famous (and delicious) artery-clogging beefsteak with onions is fantastic.... *Tel 020/623-7181. Noorderstraat 11, trams 16, 24, 25 to Prinsengracht. Dinner only on weekends. $$*
(see pp. 57, 71)

Proeflokaal André Lacroix. Dark, atmospheric, 19th-century tap house one block from Vondelpark. Serves *genever* only.... *Tel 020/618-1072. Overtoom 219–221, trams 1, 6 to C. Huygensstraat. $*
(see p. 76)

Rakang Thai. A stylish Jordaan restaurant packed with trendies. Try the squid or chicken with lemongrass and coriander, sticky rice, or beef with peppers and basil.... *Tel 020/627-5012. Elandsgracht 29, trams 7, 10 to Elandsgracht. Dinner only. $$*
(see pp. 59, 66)

Sahid Jaya. Al fresco dining and the sumptuous, if inauthentic, rice tables (dozens of dishes, from chicken *sate* in peanut sauce to *rendang padang*—beef with chili and coconut sauce) help alleviate the pain of the bill. Tasteful Indonesian luxury interior, polished service.... *Tel 020/626-3727. Reguliersdwarsstraat 26, trams 1, 2, 5, to Koningsplein. Dinner only. $$$$* **(see pp. 58, 73)**

Sama Sebo. Among the city's least-undiscovered Indonesian spots, with lots of small tables where you eat increasingly overrated *rijsttafel* elbow-to-elbow with connoisseurs and crowds of bemused tourists.... *Tel 020/662-8146. P.C. Hooftstraat 27, trams 2, 5 to Pieter Vossiusstraat. Reservations required. Closed Sun. $$$***(see pp. 59, 65)**

Schaak Cafe Het Hok. A brown cafe favored by soccer fans and chess players, just east of Leidseplein.... *Tel 020/624-3133. Lange Leidsedwarsstraat 134, trams 1, 2, 5, to Leidseplein. $* **(see p. 75)**

Shiva. This small, refined Indian restaurant serves flavorful curries, possibly A'dam's best.... *Tel 020/624-8713. Reguliersdwarsstraat 72, trams 4, 9, 14, 16, 24, 25 to Munt Plein or Rembrandtplein. Dinner only. $$* **(see p. 59)**

Silveren Spiegel. A top-dollar French/Dutch restaurant. You'll pay dearly for delicious dishes like duck breast on a bed of leeks with tiny corn pancakes or leg and fillet of guinea fowl with wild mushrooms.... *Tel 020/624-6589. Kattengat 4, trams 1, 2, 5, 13, 17 to Korte Kolkstraat or Martelaarsgracht. Reservations required. Jacket and tie recommended. Dinner only. Closed Sun. $$$$$*
(see pp. 63, 64, 72)

Tapas Bar Català. Belly, shout, and elbow your way through the cocktail-lounge interior to the best tapas bar in town.... *Tel 020/623-1141. Spuistraat 299, trams 1, 2, 5 to Spui. No reservations. Lunch weekends only. Closed Tue. No credit cards. $$* **(see pp. 61, 71)**

Tempo Doeloe. If you're eating just one Indonesian meal in town, this is probably still the place to go. Try the succulent *oedang madoera* (prawns in a gentle macadamia-nut sauce).... *Tel 020/625-6718. Utrechtstraat 75, tram 4 to Keizersgracht or Prinsengracht. Reservations essential. Dinner only. $$$* **(see pp. 58, 68, 71, 72)**

Tom Yam Fusion Cuisine. Former Michelin-starred Dutch/ French chef Jos Boomgaardt now cooks fusion food (puff pastry with guinea fowl, sauerkraut, and mashed potatoes) in this upscale Dutch/Thai restaurant, where the dishes are beautifully presented but overpriced and under-spiced.... *Tel 020/622-9533, fusion@tomyam.nl or www.tomyam.nl. Staalstraat 22, trams 9, 14 to Muziektheater. Reservations required. Dinner only. Closed Sun–Mon.* $$$$ **(see p. 65)**

Tujuh Maret. Small, welcoming new Indonesian restaurant (eat in or take out) run by veteran restaurateur Thomas Hart.... *Tel 020/427-9865. Utrechtsestraat 73, tram 4 to Keizersgracht or Prinsengracht. Closed Mon.* $$. **(see p. 58)**

Van Altena. The city's premier herring stand. A very serious operation where master fishhandler Pieter van Altena serves raw and pickled herring, salmon or crab salad, and a dozen other fishy delights on warm whole-grain buns.... *Tel 020/676-9139. Stadhouderskade, trams 2, 5, 6, 7, 10 to Rijksmuseum. No reservations. Open 11am–7pm. Closed Mon. No credit cards.* $ **(see p. 58)**

Van Dobben. Time has stood still since June 1945, when this wonderful milk-and-soda diner served its first scorching-hot croquette and smoked-eel sandwich. A must.... *Tel 020/624-4200. Korte Reguliersdwarsstraat 5, trams 4, 9, 14 to Rembrandtplein. No reservations. No credit cards.* $ **(see pp. 58, 67, 71)**

Vermeer. The old-fashioned interior is a setting for new celeb chef Pascal Jalhaij's French-Dutch cuisine (smoked pigeon with roasted pineapple or braised calves cheeks on sauerkraut).... *Tel 020/556-4885. Prins Hendrikkade 59–72, all trams and buses to Centraal Station or Prins Hendrikkade. Reservations essential. Jacket and tie recommended.* $$$$$ **(see pp. 63, 71, 72)**

Vossius. Star chef Robert Kranenborg's new temple of French-Dutch gastronomy.... *Tel 020/577-4100. www.restaurantvossius.com. Hobbemastraat 2, tram 2 to Vondelpark. Reservations essential.* $$$$$ **(see pp. 62, 65, 72)**

Wagamama. New, ultra-clean, Zen-style Japanese noodle bar (ramen, kare, gyoza, udon, and other noodle or rice combos). Totally non-smoking, veg and kiddie-friendly.... *Tel 020/528-7778, www.wagamama.com. Max Euweplein 10, trams 1,*

THE INDEX | DINING AND CAFES

2, 5 to Leidgeplein. No reservations. Open daily noon–11pm. $ **(see pp. 60, 70, 72)**

Warung Marlon. Amsterdam's most authentic, if spartan, Surinamese eatery. Great roasted meats and rice or banana-based specialties. Totally non-smoking.... *Tel 020/671-1526. Le Van der Helstraat 55, trams 16, 24, 25 to Albert Cuypstraat. 11am–8pm only. No credit cards. $* **(see pp. 60, 67, 70)**

Wijnand Fockink. The darkest of all *proeflokaalen*, in an alley between Dam and the red-light district.... *Tel 020/624-9649. Pijlsteeg 31, trams 4, 9, 14, 16, 24 to Dam Square. $* **(see p. 76)**

Yoichi. The *sashimi-tako* (octopus), charcoal-grilled teriyaki steak, and sukiyaki beef with veggies still rank with the best.... *Tel 020/622-6829. Weteringschans 128, trams 6, 7, 10 to Weteringplein or Frederiksplein. Reservations recommended. Dinner only. Closed Wed. $$$* **(see p. 60)**

DINING AND CAFES | THE INDEX

Dining in the
Museumplein Area & Amsterdam South

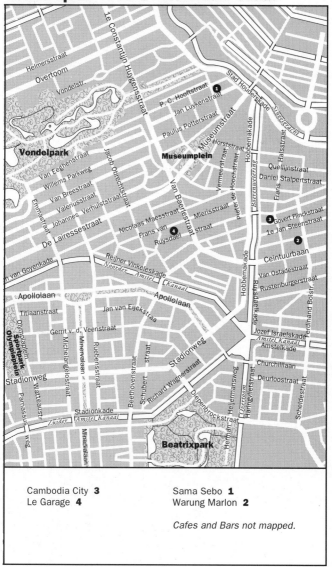

Cambodia City **3**

Le Garage **4**

Sama Sebo **1**

Warung Marlon **2**

Cafes and Bars not mapped.

Dining in Central Amsterdam

Cafes and Bars not mapped.

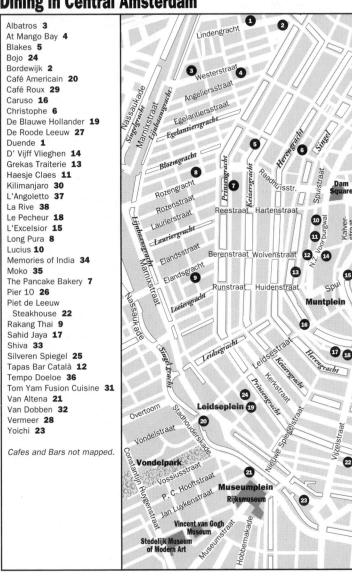

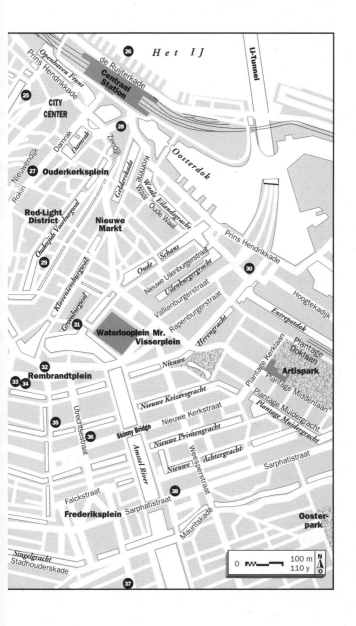

Het IJ

IJ-Tunnel

de Ruijterkade

26 Centraal Station

Openhaven Front

Prins Hendrikkade

25 CITY CENTER

Damrak

Damrak

Nieuwendijk

Rokin

Zeedijk

28

Oosterdok

27 Ouderkerksplein

Gelderskade

Krommme Waal

Waals Eilandsgracht

Oude Waal

Red-Light District

Nieuwe Markt

Prins Hendrikkade

Oudezijds Voorburgwal

29

Oude Schans

Nieuwe Uilenburgerstraat

Uilenburgergracht

30

Kloveniersburgwal

Valkenburgerstraat

Rapenburgerstraat

Hoogtekadijk

Entrepotdok

Groenburgwal

31

Herengracht

Waterlooplein Mr. Visserplein

Plantage Kerklaan

Plantage Doklaan

32 Rembrandtplein

Nieuwe

Artispark

33 34

Plantage Middenlaan

Nieuwe Keizersgracht

Plantage Muidergracht

35

Nieuwe Kerkstraat

Plantage Muidergracht

Utrechtsestraat

36

Skinny Bridge

Nieuwe Prinsengracht

Amstel River

Nieuwe

Weesperstraat

Achtergracht

Sarphatistraat

Falckstraat

38

Frederiksplein

Sarphatistraat

Mauritskade

Ooster-park

Singelgracht

Stadhouderskade

0   100 m
    110 y

N

37

3

sions

Everyone seems
to tell the same
standard story
about a first trip
to Amsterdam.
First you go to
the appropriate

cafe to either eat hash brownies or drink *genever*, then you get lost in the canals, roam the red-light district, see a live sex show "by mistake," and finally end up at the Van Gogh Museum.

If you want to come home with more than the same standard story, you have to know how to approach this city. The whole of central A'dam, within the semicircular Singelgracht canal, could fit on the tip of Manhattan. Add in the 19th-century Old West, Old South, and East neighborhoods, with the main museums, Vondelpark, and Artis Zoo, and you've got a mid-sized town. But don't let the size fool you: The number and quality of attractions is very high indeed. It takes time to discover and explore them. So do like the locals and bring clothes in which you can comfortably pedal one of the city's 500,000 old-fashioned *fiets* (bikes), and most important, a pair of sturdy walking shoes. Amsterdam is not just a stroller's city. It is *the* stroller's city.

Amsterdammers are very proud of their doll's house of a capital, and do their sightseeing and cultural accounts like CPAs. Within this densely populated cosmopolis of 720,493 inhabitants are about 7,000 landmark buildings (from the 16th through the 18th centuries), 2,400 houseboats (probably closer to 5,000, with half docked illegally), and 1,404 cafes and bars. Not to mention the 1,281 bridges (eight of them wooden drawbridges) spanning 165 canals and rivers, or the 28 parks and 42 museums. These numbers are important—everyone knows them. In fact, philomegamaximania—an obsession with the huge, the minuscule, and all other manner of impressive statistic—is rampant. For instance, passersby gleefully point out the world's narrowest house (Singel 7) and boast about the world's tiniest diamond (.24 milligrams, cut by Van Moppes). The fact that the Royal Palace sits on exactly 13,659 wooden pilings thrills school kids and tourism officials, as does the knowledge that there are 22 paintings by Rembrandt in town and 206 by mad Vincent van Gogh—guaranteed tourist draws. I might add that there are probably 1,001 pool tables where you can challenge local sharps. And 9,999 places to sit under one of the city's 220,000 trees and take in the view—of quaint old houses, boats, and tree-lined canals, or of sizzling neon winking meretriciously on Damrak or in the red-light district.

You don't have to work hard to enjoy all this. For example, half of the historic buildings have dates engraved on them; exactly 726 of them bear brightly colored plaques called "gablestones" that, before street numbering was introduced by Napoleon, explained pictorially who had the house built and what it was used for—a sailing ship for a sea captain, beer barrels for a brewer, fish for a fisherman, and so forth. The past is easy to read. The city is an open book, a cracked nut, a picnic, whatever.

Getting Your Bearings

Attractions are spread fairly evenly throughout the center of town, though the big three museums—Rijksmuseum, Van Gogh, and Stedelijk— are within a few hundred yards of each other on Museumplein in the **Old South** neighborhood, just beyond Singelgracht. So too is the most popular city park, Vondelpark (pronounced "fondlepark," appropriately, since it's a steamy pick-up spot by night). If crowds are what you want, cross the Singelgracht and head for **Leidseplein**, two lively squares near the Vondelpark, or for **Rembrandtplein** a bit farther east, near the Amstel River. Between these lie the three concentric, semicircular 17th-century grand canals of the **Grachtengordel** (moving inward, the Prinsengracht, the Keizersgracht, and the Heren-gracht), where all the canal-house museums are. Cupped within them lies the Singel (not to be confused with Sin-gelgracht), the curving canal that defines the border of the old **city center**—the focal point of which is tacky, crowded Dam Square. Between Dam Square and

King of the Culture Vultures

"My guides are interesting people, not faceless tour oper-ators," says René Dessing, a suave, bespectacled art historian–turned–tour operator. "And please stop calling me a vulture!" If you're finicky about your culture, Dessing is the man to go to for everything from architectural walks to painting classes on canal boats, restaurant or cafe tours, hotel bookings, and private dining in canal mansions. The list of VIPs who have bought Dessing's pitch—at dizzying rates of 275 euros per day, 186 euros per half-day plus 19% VAT—includes heads of state, corporate bigwigs, and aristocrats. Why bother? Access. Dessing's multilingual freelance guides—trained art historians—can get you into private collections, the Royal Palace (even when it's closed to the public), and almost any-where else you want. Trips to clog-makers or tulip fields— though heavily discouraged— are given a highbrow spin. Some clients wind up spending half their day in a cozy brown cafe. "The idea," says Dessing, "is to make new friends." His company, Artifex Travel (tel 020/620–8112, fax 020/ 620–6908; Herengracht 342, 1016 CG Amsterdam. E-mail: info@artifex-travel.nl or www.artifex-travel.nl), can plan your entire trip to Amsterdam, from airfare on.

Nieuwemarkt, to the east, lies the city's historic **red-light district**, usually packed with tourists and gawkers at night. The **former Jewish district**, rich with historical and cultural landmarks, lies south of the red-light district, just east of Waterlooplein. Though it has few mainstream draws, the **Jordaan** neighborhood, west of Centraal Station and just beyond the Grachtengordel, is an atmospheric part of town for a stroll, a bike ride, or a game of pool at a brown cafe. Ditto the **Westerdok** and **Western Islands**, up-and-coming areas to the west with a Greenwich Village feel. To the east is the Java-Borneo island development, with daringly eclectic architecture. The Amstel cuts across the city's canals from the southeast; a complicated series of locks feeds water from the Amstel into the canals. The IJ (pronounced Ay) used to be a bay in the Zuiderzee (just to confuse you, it's now called the IJsselmeer), but over the centuries has been dammed, harnessed, dredged, and turned into a wide canal. Maps never seem to indicate street numbers, and if you set out from Centraal Station to, say, Prinsengracht, looking for number 400, you can walk for several miles if you start on the wrong end. Just remember that house numbers always start from the west and run counterclockwise on the concentric, semicircular canals (the Grachtengordel). For example, if you step out of the train station, turn right, and walk to the canal ring, you'll find number 1. On radial arteries, numbers begin at Centraal Station and increase as you move away from the center of town.

The Lowdown

Where the tourists go... One of Amsterdam's prime industries is tourism—more than 17.5 million visitors swim through in a good year, most of them in spring and summer. As in Venice, many stick to well-trod canals and gathering places in the small historic center of town. Unlike many other Europeans, most Amsterdammers actually seem to enjoy their company, which cranks up the energy level of the tourist areas even more. Authentic touristy Amsterdam can be a supremely kitschy experience—don't skip it entirely. Most visitors' first experience of Amsterdam is a stroll from Centraal Station down the Damrak, a living Pop Art installation with fast-food eateries, souvenir shops, and bumper-to-bumper traffic. At its end is **Dam Square**, the historic heart of town overlooked by the gaudy Koninklijk Paleis—**Royal Palace**. Today the area is noisy, tacky, and a prime spot for pickpockets, so stay alert. The view from Dam Square back up the Damrak is an unforgettable 21st-century cityscape. If you're allergic to crowds and noise, avoid the L-shaped **Leidseplein** and its surroundings on the southwest side of town (not far from the teeming Rijksmuseum). In summer, swarms of trinket hawkers and street musicians besiege the Leidseplein's chaotic sidewalk cafes. **Rembrandtplein**, south of the red-light district, is a handsome, though frowzy, square ringed by a mix of cafes, touristy restaurants, and sleazy coffee shops frequented by dope smokers and lager louts. While most of the Rembrandtplein's cafes cater to the theme-park crowd, a few attract hip locals (the De Kroon—see Dining and Cafes); literati hang out at the bar in the Schiller-Hotel (see Accommodations). Other tourist magnets are the dozen or so big diamond factories scattered throughout town, especially **Van Moppes'** (sparkling with busloads of gawkers who've seemingly never seen a real gemstone; see Shopping) and the no-longer-brewing-but-still-serving **Heineken Brewery**, a favorite place to get drunk on free beer shipped in from the suburban brewery. When the tour buses from Germany roll

The city of the 7,000 gables

Before Napoleon imposed a rational numbering system on Amsterdam in the 1790s, gablestones indicated who owned the building and what went on there. Walls in the Begijnhof and on Sint Lucien-steeg at the Amsterdam Historical Museum have some good gablestones, including the oldest known stone, from 1603, showing a milkmaid balancing her buckets. That goes partway to explaining why most of Amsterdam's seven thousand landmark buildings have gables. Gables also hide the pitched roofs (like the false fronts of a town center in the American Old West) and demonstrate the architect's vertical showmanship in a city where tax laws encouraged thin buildings. If you can pick out Amsterdam's various gable styles without developing Sistine Chapel Neck Syndrome, you can date the buildings fairly accurately. The neck gable, for example (about 1660–1790), looks like a headless neck, with curlicues on the shoulders—see the first one at Herengracht 168 (the Netherlands Theater Institute), a 1638 mansion. The earliest is the wooden, triangular gable (circa 1250–1550). Only two remain—in the Begijnhof and at Zeedijk 1.

DIVERSIONS | THE LOWDOWN

in, it's Oktoberfest on the Amstel. **Holland Experience** is the kind of "multidimensional film and theater show" (their words) that draws the coach crowds, couch potatoes, tulip-and-clog lovers, and their bawling brats. Here's how the tourist office's monthly newsletter describes the show: "Seated on a moving platform, in the comfort of an aircraft seat, come with us on a trip through the many different faces of Holland. It's all there, the waterland, the agricultural areas, all the tourist-sites, the culture and even the high-tech industry." Gee, maybe we could just buy the video and save on airfare? The **newMetropolis** (yes, all one word, "n" lowercase) science and technology center is a cut above, mobbed by virtual-reality fiends and their nerdy offspring. Forget Amsterdam and become a mechanic, doctor, ballet dancer, explorer....

Don't believe the brochures... The must-see sights in Amsterdam are not as advertised—most of them come with disclaimers. The celebrated "Skinny" Bridge isn't skinny; the Heineken "Brewery" stopped brewing beer in 1988; most of the "floating" flower market doesn't float; Queen Beatrix and Prince Claus don't live in the Royal Palace (see "Lifestyles of the rich and deceased," below); and much of Van Gogh's best work is in New York and Paris, not the Van Gogh Museum (see "For culture vultures," below). That doesn't mean these sights aren't appealing, though. The Skinny Bridge is broad but handsome; the Heineken Brewery is swell for beer guzzlers; the sidewalk flower market is gorgeous; the Royal Palace is appropriately palatial; and the Van Gogh Museum is heaven for Van Gogh fanatics.

The most quintessentially Dutch non-attraction in town is the **Skinny Bridge** (Magere Brug—on the Amstel River at Kerkstraat). It's the same kind of white drawbridge Van Gogh (and a thousand others) painted as emblematic of Holland. Here's the tale: Two rich sisters named Mager, living on opposite sides of the Amstel at Kerkstraat, had the bridge built in 1672 so they could visit each other with ease. Well, maybe, but the original bridge—which was authentically narrow—more likely got its name from the Dutch word for skinny (*magere*). At any rate, it was replaced with this overfed one in the 18th century, but the brochure writers haven't heard about it yet.

The **Heineken Brewery** brewed its last lager in

1988, but the name hasn't been changed to "museum" yet. If you take a tour and are disappointed to learn that the beer you are offered after visiting the antique vats is brewed in the suburbs, well—let the boozer beware. Don't forget that for centuries Amsterdammers couldn't drink the local water, and brewing it into beer was simply a sanitary precaution. (Tap water is still called *gemeente pils*— "municipal beer.")

How about the "oldest house in Amsterdam?" The brochures say it's in the **Begijnhof** (see "Everybody's favorite getaway," below), and indeed there is a wooden house there, dated 1475, but it was taken down from its original location and moved there and totally rebuilt. I suppose it all depends on how you define "old." At **Zeedijk 1** you'll find a similar wooden house, from about 1550, though heavily remodeled; at least it wasn't moved, and it's not in the brochures. As to the "narrowest house in the world," the local misinformation bureau claims it is **Singel 7**, not far from Centraal Station. It looks like it's just over a yard wide, but actually only the front door is narrow; the house, built on an irregular lot, widens behind it. The house at **Oude Hoogstraat 22** is wider—2.02 meters (6.5 feet)—but it's small all the way back, running only 6 meters (21 feet) deep. This makes it, according to the A'dam tourist office, the narrowest house in Europe, at least—no cheating. And as for the "floating" **Flower Market (Bloemenmarkt),** well, Bangkok has a real floating market, on boats and rafts. Amsterdam's market is on the sidewalk of Singel; some of the shops are built on piers, a few on rusting, permanently moored barges. You can get everything from apricot trees to zinnias, including marijuana seeds and starter kits, but the only things you'll be able to take home—if you live in America—are phytosanitary-certified bulbs (see Shopping).

For culture vultures... Culture vultures and coach tourists alike seem to think the **Rijksmuseum** is synonymous with Amsterdam; they simply must see Rembrandt's *Nightwatch*. Luckily, the painting is larger than the Louvre's embattled *Mona Lisa*, so you stand a better chance of seeing it over hundreds of heads. But don't get too close: A security guard hovers nearby. If you're lucky enough to view it in silence, this painting will take possession of you: Irresistibly, one face after another in the civic guards company of Captain Frans Banning Cocq and Lieutenant Willem van Ruytenburch draws your eye in. Like the Metropolitan or the Louvre, the Rijks-museum can be extraordinarily enriching or utterly exhausting. To navigate it successfully, buy a detailed guidebook at the museum shop. And bear in mind that there is life beyond Rembrandt and Vermeer, which are best viewed out of season or at lunchtime. There are 150 or so rooms to explore, plus the newly refurbished south wing, if you've got the stamina. The print room (Rijksprentenkabinet) has rotating shows of engravings and etchings; the east wing has interesting exhibitions on Dutch history. You can also take a breather in the museum's architectural garden out back. Note that sections of the museum will be closed for remodeling starting September 2002.

No one in Holland would touch Van Gogh's wild, tortured paintings when he was alive, but the **Van Gogh Museum** is now a national treasure. The painter's tragic life and times are traced from rural Dutch roots in Nuenen, via Paris, Arles, the asylum of St. Remy (he'd snipped off part of his ear), to suicide at age 37 in Auvers-sur-Oise. Among the 200 or so Van Gogh oils in the permanent collection are *The Potato Eaters*, *Sunflowers*, and *Wheatfield with Crows*. You can also see letters written betweeen Vincent and his brother Theo, hundreds of sketches, drawings, and watercolors, as well as paintings by Van Gogh contemporaries Emile Bernard, Toulouse-Lautrec, Gauguin, Monticelli, and Koning. The collection is housed in a rather aggressively minimalistic, concrete building designed by Gerrit Rietveld in his senescence and opened (after he died) in 1973. The muse-um's new wing (added in 1999), is a jumble of rounds and rectangles that appears to land on Museumplein, a flying saucer poised on a cracker box. Unfortunately, almost since it opened it's been ringed by metal fencing to keep graffiti aficionados and stray dogs at bay. Inside, huge win-dows catch the city's rarefied light. The building's relent-lessly sculptural shapes provide a challenging venue for temporary Van Gogh–related exhibitions. Be prepared for crowds in high season.

One of the world's great modern-art collections is at the **Stedelijk Museum (Modern Art Museum),** a refreshing break after acres of Van Gogh or Dutch mas-ters. So vast are the holdings—works from the sublime (Malevich's *Suprematism*) to the ridiculous (Koons' *Ush-*

ering in Banality)—that you'll never see the museum hung in the same way twice. Post–World War II art is the strongest suit, but samplings from 1850 through the present are within the museum's scope, including Manet, Monet, Cézanne, Picasso, and Chagall on the pre-war timeline. Abstract and De Stijl practitioners Malevich, Mondrian, and Kandinsky are well represented, as are Expressionists like Kirchner, Polke, and Dix. There are also works you'll never see elsewhere by CoBrA (Copenhagen/Brussels/Amsterdam) group painter Karel Appel—he decorated parts of the museum, including the Appelbar and former cafeteria. (A new-wing project on hold for several years due to public outcry over plans to demolish parts of the museum will go ahead as of September 2002, so expect chaos and a major re-shuffle.)

Picture perfect... Inaugurated in 1999, **Huis Marseille** is the city's top international photography venue, a nonprofit foundation based in a stunning 1665 canal-house mansion (called "Marseille House" by the French merchant who built it). Vast display rooms on four floors showcase rotating exhibitions. Even if you're not a shutterbug, the house alone is worth the visit.

Courting privacy... Hidden between center-city blocks, and especially in the Jordaan (see "Walking the Jordaan," below), are scores of courtyard housing complexes called *hofjes*. Built as almshouses for pious lay sisters, widows, the elderly, and the disabled, they were the "projects" of their day, underwritten by religious orders or, more commonly, wealthy merchants embarrassed by their riches. Most have become normal apartment complexes now, with a common courtyard and stairwells that you can poke around in, as long as you enter and leave quietly. The biggest, most spectacular, and most visited is the **Begijnhof**, just off Spui (there's no number, but the name is chiseled above the door). Built in the 14th century around an oblong courtyard, this complex of buildings housed devout (sometimes fallen, and often poor) women who couldn't quite convince themselves to take religious vows, but wanted to be left in pious peace. All of the original houses are gone (they were rebuilt in the 17th century and later), and few lay nuns still live here. Nonetheless, the Begijnhof is marvelous, one of the loveliest spots in the city. Go at off-hours (the door is open until 10pm May to

DIVERSIONS | THE LOWDOWN

September, from 10–5 the rest of the year), or out of season, and you'll be able to muse among the lawns and flowers and the horse-chestnut trees towering over humpback buildings. Among several churches in the compound, the De Engelse Kerk (English Reformed Church), at number 48, has a remarkable wooden barrel-vaulted ceiling with delicate blue decorations. The church was built in 1392 (and doubtless rebuilt since), has been English-speaking since 1607, and offers a rousing Sunday worship at 10:30 precisely. An extraordinarily discreet Roman Catholic church, at number 29, has a U-shaped balcony and a series of paintings and stained-glass windows showing the bizarre Amsterdam Miracle of the Host (it was vomited up by a dying man; see "Fabulous festivals," below). The houses lining the grassy courtyard are from the 17th and 18th centuries, including the so-called oldest house in Amsterdam, from the late 1400s (it was moved here and rebuilt).

Ladies with a past... The nuns of the Begijnhof didn't have a monopoly on institutionalized pious living. For further insight into the Dutch mind, keep an eye out for the **Spinhuis** when you're in the red-light district. This 1597 landmark was long used as a women's penitentiary or labor camp, where the unlucky ladies generated considerable income for the managers of the establishment. The women doubled as wool spinners and *Scarlet Letter*–style performers—upright citizens actually paid an admission price to watch the sinners at work. A plaque over the door reads: "Don't cry, I take no vengeance for wrongdoing, but force you to be good. Stern is my hand, kind is my heart." I'll bet. The building is no longer open to the public, but the surrounding neighborhood is full of places where you can pay to watch women plying another trade.

Looking down on it all... Amsterdam is flat as a *pannekoek*, and has no skyscrapers. The best way to get a perspective is to scale the various church towers in town (call ahead to make sure they're open—admissions policies are in flux). The highest, and most spectacular, is **Westertoren**, that leaning, 260-foot Golden Age masterpiece. You'll be panting by the time you reach its imperial crown, the only thing between you and heaven. Below are the roofs, canals, and spreading trees of the Grachtengordel and Jordaan. On a clear day you can see the whole of old A'dam. Southeast, just beyond the red-light district, is the lower **Zuidertoren**, from which you see the medieval section of town, from the alleys and narrow canals around Oude Zijds Voorburgwal to the Amstel River. In the center of the red-light district, the onion-domed, 16th-century bell tower of **Oude Kerk** rears its head. Below twinkle the neon lights of Sodom and Gomorrah, with particularly detailed, bird's-eye views into the transvestite/prostitutes' area just north of the church. Get another perspective altogether from the top-floor, panoramic cafe of **Metz & Co.**, an upscale department store at the junction of swank Keizersgracht and Leidsestraat, where you can spy on the canal-house mansions of Grachtengordel millionaires. The city's newest tower, in the **Kalvertoren** shopping mall, rises to a staggering 100 feet and is located in the center of the tacky Kalverstraat shopping district, and gives you a new perspective on bulging wallets and old A'dam rooms. Among my favorite views is from the **Beurs van Berlage** tower, a tough climb but worth it for the aerial perspective of the red-light district and Damrak. The roof of **newMetropolis**, in the harbor, offers a great waterfront panorama, as do the showrooms and bug-box cafe-restaurant at **Pakhuis**, a reconverted Eastern Docklands warehouse now used as an interior design center.

Lifestyles of the rich and deceased... Amsterdam, unburnt since the 15th century and largely spared by world wars and real estate speculators, is lousy with historic buildings, particularly 17th-century landmarks that express the parvenu tastes of Dutch merchants of the Golden Age. The vast, imposing (and ugly) **Royal Palace** on Dam Square is the queen mother of them all. "Piling it on" is the operative phrase: Schoolchildren know it was built in 1648 by Jacob van Campen to replace an earlier city hall and sits on precisely 13,659 wooden pilings (take 365, as in the number of days in a year; add a "1" in front and a "9" afterward...). It's been the royal palace since 1808, but of course the royal family no longer lives here. In the 17th century, this was the zenith of nouveau riche taste—witness the acres of white-marble floors and staircases and the colossal proportions. Stride across the Citizen's Hall and you cross heaven and earth: It's paved with inlaid marble and bronze maps of the hemispheres formerly under Holland's control. Less ostentatious, but far more instrumental in Amsterdam's ascension, is the **East India House**, a currently politically incorrect totem of Dutch colonialism in what's now the red-light district (Oude Hoogstraat at Kloveniersburgwal). For centuries, starting in 1603, it was the headquarters of the Verenigde Oost Indische Compagnie (East India Company), the mighty trading company that maintained its own army and navy and brought to heel Indonesia, Ceylon, and other Asian countries. You can't enter this late-1500s landmark (because the University of Amsterdam has offices in it), but step into its courtyard and you can almost feel the filthy old lucre holding the bricks together. Around the corner on Kloveniersburgwal are the remarkably wide **Trippenhuis** and remarkably narrow **Kleine Trippenhuis** (the Trip House and the Trip Coachman's House, neither of which is open to visitors). The former is one of Amsterdam's most striking statements of Golden Age taste. It was built in the neoclassical style in 1660–1664 for the Trip brothers, Hendrick and Louis, fabulously rich arms manufacturers who had their chimneys sculpted like cannons and their Corinthian colonnade decorated with a gun. Right across the canal is the yard-wide servants' house built to shut up the Trips' upstart coachman—envious of his masters' double-wide, he said he'd be glad to have a place as wide as the mansion's front door. (Guess what he got.) Another significant neoclassical mansion from that era is **De Pinto House**, now a public library in the former Jewish district. Isaac de Pinto, co-founder of the East India Company, was one of the Portuguese Jewish community's leading lights. He bought this house in 1651 and spent a fortune remodeling it in the Italian Renaissance style (100 years after it had gone out of fashion in Italy). Only some painted ceilings and paneling have survived, but it's enough to show that ostentation and glitz were *not* first invented in the late 20th century.

Many of Amsterdam's Golden Age landmarks are the work of Hendrick de Keyser (1565–1621), who, as the city's official architect during the early 1600s, was largely responsible for the design of the Grachtengordel grand canals. **Bartolotti House**, built in 1618 north of the Golden Bend on Herengracht, is one of de Keyser's most ambitious mansions. Wide, tall, ornate, and distinctly red, it was commissioned by a rich brewer and banker, a Mr. Van den Heuvel, who, to satisfy his mother-in-law, changed his name to Bartolotti. (Talk about henpecked.) You can visit a series of sumptuous rooms via the next-door **Netherlands Theater Institute Museum**, itself a 1638 canal house, built by Philip Vingboons and remarkable for having the city's first "neck gable." Look up to see its ceilings painted with mythological scenes by Jacob de Witte in 1729. The place was restored top to bottom in 1999, and its formal Renaissance gardens are now open to humble visitors. The so-called **House of Heads** is not a pothead's crash pad—it's a 1624 de Keyser mansion, one canal over at Keizersgracht 121. Its name comes from the row of six huge classical heads across the facade, representing Diana, Bacchus, Athena, Mars, Ceres, and Apollo.

Okay, if you've gotta see windmills... Once upon a time, when Amsterdammers clomped around in clogs, there were hundreds of windmills right in town. Now there are only half a dozen, two of which are worth visiting. The **De Gooyer Windmill**, a former corn mill built in 1725, still towers over the Nieuwevaart canal northeast of Artis Zoo. In it is Bierbrouwerij 't IJ (see Dining and Cafes), a terrific microbrewery. A century older, but a total rebuild job, is the thatched **De Rieker Windmill**, moved to a site way out on the banks of the Amstel River at Amstelpark. Now an elegant private house, it was originally built to drain the Rieker *polder*, a tract of low, reclaimed land a few miles south of Amsterdam. You've doubtless seen this mill in all those Rembrandt paintings and engravings you know by heart; just to make sure you don't miss the connection, there's a statue here of Rembrandt at work.

For history buffs... Spend a few days soaking up the city's atmosphere before exploring the totally rejiggered and immensely improved **Amsterdam Historical Museum**, so you can properly appreciate the hundreds of new displays ranging from antique delftware to bits of demolished houses (carved beam consoles, gablestones), from medieval sculptures to a re-created smoking coffee shop and an entire A'dam brown cafe (with a fascinating interview on tape of the cafe's last owner, a piss-and-vinegar dame). The museum building itself is intriguing; it started life as an orphanage in the Middle Ages and was rebuilt

DIVERSIONS | THE LOWDOWN

around cloistered courtyards in the 17th century. There's a mesmerizing computerized map that shows how the Golden Age boomtown doubled and trebled in size in a matter of decades. Rembrandt's gruesome *The Anatomy Lecture* now hangs here. The immense **Maritime Museum**, housed in the 1655 Admiralty Building in the Eastern Docklands, has rooms so huge that full-sized boats have been lugged into them—dig the dazzlingly kitschy royal barge, so encrusted with gold it's a miracle it ever floated. On the wharf out front bob several historic ships, including the reconstructed *Amsterdam*, a three-master from 1749 where kids can play pirates with costumed performers, and the brand-new (and gorgeous) clipper ship *Stad Amsterdam* (hey, that's original). The **Jewish Historical Museum** offers little such lighthearted entertainment. Skillfully set in four former Ashkenazi synagogues from the 17th and 18th centuries, the modern, airy exhibition hall is a serious—though not downbeat—devotion to Jewish history, religion, and culture in the Netherlands, up to and including the Jewish community's near annihilation during the Nazi occupation. Pre–World War II photos of everyday life in the former Jewish district, where the museum sits, are downright mesmerizing.

Moments in time... First gorge yourself on the Rembrandts at the Rijksmuseum, then head to the **Rembrandt House Museum,** on the edge of A'dam's former Jewish district and lavishly restored and expanded in late 1999. The artist's colorful life and times are captured in the house he owned from 1639 to 58 (a bon vivant, his extravagance bankrupted him, and he died, not in this house, in destitution). Poke around its dark, atmospheric rooms (leaded windows, creaky floors). The new Cabinet Room replicates Rembrandt's personal collection of artworks and objects such as Chinese porcelain, bizarre woven baskets, celestial globes, Venetian glass, busts of Roman emperors, weapons, and shells. Some of these turn up in his paintings, making for a highbrow treasure hunt. The glinting high-tech new wing, conceived to display etchings, also hosts temporary exhibitions.

The celebrated **Anne Frank House**—"restored" and expanded in 1999, with a huge new wing—is a Prinsengracht canal house with secret back rooms where the gifted Jewish teenager hid from Nazi occupiers with her family from 1942 to 1944. But there's little in the house except a few snapshots of English royalty and movie stars Anne had cherished—you'd love to stand here and reflect on the unquenchable love of life that made Anne's diary so great, but forget it. Expect long lines, crowded rooms, and an all-too-commercial boutique at the exit, plus a new cafe-restaurant. At the **Van Loon Museum**, an imposing 1671 mansion on Keizersgracht, you ring the bell and a curator ushers you straight into the Golden Age. White-haired, affable Maurits van Loon, scion of the family that owns the mansion, may join your tour as you wander down the marble halls admiring the stucco work and the family portraits. One canal away on Herengracht's Golden Bend is the recently renovated **Willet-Holthuysen Museum**, in an even bigger mansion, this one built in 1687. Its downstairs kitchen has remarkable antique delft tiles, and Jacob de Wit painted the mezzanine room's rococo ceiling. There are also d'Aubusson tapestries, family portraits, and countless intriguing knickknacks. The **Amstelkring Museum**, known in English as "Our Lord in the Attic," is the city's only surviving Roman Catholic "attic" church, built in 1663 into the upper floors of three canal and back houses in an era when Roman Catholics were forced to worship in secret. Navigate the maze of stairways to stumble onto a startlingly beautiful chapel, and a Golden Age kitchen, bed-nook, and dining room.

Sacred sights… Across Dam Square from the Royal Palace is the **Nieuwe Kerk** (New Church), which is in fact one of the oldest churches in town. (But gee, it was new when it was built—six centuries ago—and they just never thought to change the name afterward….) When Golden Age architect Jacob van Campen wasn't gilding the lilies at the Royal Palace, he turned his hand to this Protestant monument to faith, which now doubles efficiently as a church and exhibition space. (The Dutch never let sacredness get in the way of a good real estate deal.) The wooden pulpit—about 35 feet tall—must be the most elaborate outside Italy, with hundreds of figures, and angels sliding down the banister (it took Albert Janszoon Vinckernbrinck 19 years, from 1645 to 1664, to carve it). Beatrix was crowned here in 1980; her mother, Juliana, in 1948; and so forth down the centuries. In 2002 Prince Willem Alexander and his bride Maxima tied the knot here. Where there's a New

Church that's really old, there must be an old church that's even older. **Oude Kerk** is as old as Amsterdam, and must have been built right after the first dam and the first tavern. We're talking about the early 13th century, though most of the building dates from the 14th to the 16th centuries. Your sense of religious awe may be somewhat spoiled by the ticket booth at the entrance, but no matter. The stained-glass and painted wooden ceiling are lovely; the tombstones (Rembrandt's wife Saskia was once under number 29) and choir stalls are masterfully carved; the organ is sonorous and grand.

Prominent Golden Age architect Hendrick de Keyser built the **Zuiderkerk** and **Zuidertoren** (Southern Church and Southern Tower), and when he died in 1621 he was buried here. Built from 1602 to 1611 on the edge of the former Jewish district, it's among the earliest churches erected specifically for a Calvinist congregation and has one of the finest carillons (played each Thursday at noon) in town. Climb the tower for a panorama of Old Amsterdam. Arguably de Keyser's masterpiece is the **Westerkerk** (Western Church) and its bell tower, the **Westertoren**, which he found time to design the year before he died. The 260-foot tower, topped with Maximilian of Austria's rather obscenely plump imperial crown, leans forward over Prinsengracht, providing see-forever views. Records show that Rembrandt was buried in 1669 in an unmarked rental grave somewhere in or around the church, and the whereabouts of his bones is still hotly debated. In the heart of the former Jewish district, the 1675 **Portuguese Synagogue**, long the world's biggest synagogue, proves how wealthy the Sephardic Jewish community here was, having helped Amsterdam to become Europe's richest city during the Golden Age. Despite savagery during the Nazi occupation, its tall, elegant windows, 12 marble columns, and giant brass chandeliers have survived intact.

Turrets syndrome... Though Golden Age Amsterdam burst outward beyond its medieval boundaries, a handful of landmarks still standing define the old city's outer limits. You can visit two of them, and stroll by others, to reconstruct a view of Old Amsterdam. The red-light district's eastern boundary is Nieuwemarkt, an oblong square in whose center stands **De Waagebouw** (The Weigh House, Nieuwemarkt 4), originally the Sint Antonies-

poort city gate, built in 1487 (now a trendy Internet cafe—
see Dining and Cafes). Bristling with seven mismatched
turrets, the fearsome fortress was rebuilt in the early 1600s
as a public weighing house, with trade guilds housed on
the upper floors. Another tower built in the seaward walls
in 1487, on what is now Prins Hendrikkade at Geldersekade, near Centraal Station, is where sailors' wives
would come to see their husbands off. That's how it got its
name, the **Schreierstoren** (The Weeping Tower, Prins
Hendrikkade at Geldersekade), and a 1569 gablestone
shows just such a sobbing wife. In 1609, Henry Hudson
embarked here on a misguided adventure that resulted in
the founding of New Amsterdam—New York (this tower,
too, houses a cafe). Just down the quay from the Schreierstoren is a relic of a much later era, the 1912–1916
Scheepvaarthuis (The Shipping Building, Prins Hendrikkade 108). This magnificent, turreted fantasy,
crawling with bas-reliefs recounting the city's naval history, houses Amsterdam's port authority administrative
offices. It is the inspired work of Amsterdam School archi-
tects Michel de Klerk, Pieter L. Kramer, and J. M. van der
Mey. A few hundred yards east, overlooking the Oude
Schans canal, is the **Montelbaanstoren** (Oude Schans at
Waals Eilandsgracht), a fortified tower from 1512 that
protected what was the city's main shipyard. By now you'll
recognize the tiered crown, added in 1606, as the work of
the ubiquitous Hendrick de Keyser. At Munt Plein, and
the juncture of Singel and Rokin, the **Munttoren**, another
piece of the 1487 city walls, was transformed by de Keyser
in 1620, who topped it with one of his signature crowns.
Amsterdam was forced to mint its own money here during
a war with France and England in 1672, and the name
munt has been used ever since for this part of town.

Row, row, row your boat... There are more canals here
than you'd care to count, and viewing the city from water
level shows you a whole different town. The Dutch call
pedalos (*waterfiets*) **canal bikes**; no local would be caught
dead using one, but who cares? Rent one and splash across
the murky brown water to your favorite sights (see Getting Outside for more details). Cruises, in special low and
narrow boats built to get under bridges and navigate
turns, are the conventional way to go, and make you feel
like a bona fide tourist. They run day and night, and even
offer lunch, dinner, and wine-and-cheese cruises. For the

full ultra-touristy effect, take one in combination with a diamond workshop or Heineken Brewery tour. **The Museumboot** is a cut above. The tour groups don't usually use it, and the high-tone name puts some people off. It offers hop-on, hop-off service all day, just like the more generically named **Canal Bus**, except that you also get negligible reductions on museum entry fees. **Monne de Miranda, Aquadam,** and **Classic Boat World** are the posh way to cruise around and cost a small fortune. You get a gorgeous antique boat with a liquor cabinet, a captain and hostesses in snazzy uniforms, and privacy.

Diamonds in the rough... Diamond-polishing workshops are an Amsterdam specialty, and though the city isn't on a par with Antwerp, New York, or Tel Aviv, it does have a centuries-old tradition in the trade. Paradoxically, the tours (nearly always free, available daily) are better taken in groups; most operators act like it's a bother to explain to individual visitors the process of extracting, studying, cutting, and evaluating these mesmerizing rocks. There are two dozen workshops; if you're going to buy a sparkler at the end of the tour—the object of the exercise for your hosts—you should probably stick to the biggies, who have a reputation to uphold. Their tours are pretty much interchangeable, though **Gassan**, in the old Jewish district, is particularly, well, polished. **Van Moppes Diamonds** is probably the biggest of them all, and draws the busloads; glitzy **Coster Diamonds** is also firmly on the package-tour route (the Tourist Tram—see below—stops there). **Stoeltie Diamonds** is smaller but reliable, and the tours are particularly informative. The **Amsterdam Diamond Center** seems like a sales outlet (and Rolex repair shop), but you can still view workers turning roughs into brilliants within striking distance of the cash register. (See Shopping for details on all five dealers.)

Sex, drugs, and torture museums... Keen on the seamy, steamy side of town? The **Sex Museum**, on suitably sleazy Damrak, and the interchangeable **Erotic Museum** in the heart of the red-light district, are favorites for guys and gals—straight and gay—who get off on rental flesh, porn videos, live sex on stage, S&M, and so forth. You might recognize the guy with the raincoat from your local porno cinema. Actually, these titillating museums full of dildoes and lewd photos of bumping uglies are both rather harmless; you'll see plenty of more shocking stuff in the shops, bars, and neon-lit windows of the red-light district itself. That is where **The Hash, Marijuana, and Hemp Museum** is found, within stumbling distance of countless smoking coffee shops, whores, and S&M bars for the skintight-jeans set. Lovers of the pungent weed—and anyone curious about its origins and myriad uses—will be fascinated, I'm sure. Softer drug addicts will want to wake up and smell the coffee at the **Geels & Co. Coffee and Tea Museum** (see Shopping), also in the red-light district. The shop has been around for more than a century, sells great stuff, and has a formidable collection of grinders, roasters, tea canisters, and all sorts of brewing paraphernalia in its small, upstairs museum, open only Saturday afternoons. You have to be something of a masochist to enjoy the **Torture Museum**, a commercial cabinet of horrors on Singel, near the Flower Market, where eternal adolescents stare slack-jawed at the centuries-old instruments of torture, from the seat of nails and rack to the guillotine and various charming cages. The Amnesty International blurb rightly reminds visitors that torture is still going on today, and gives this grotesquerie a patina of respectability.

Museums that won't bore the kids... Watch your sprout become a mechanic, doctor, ballet dancer, or explorer before your boggled eyes in the **newMetropolis** science and technology center in the harbor, between Centraal Station and the Maritime Museum. Designed by Renzo Piano (aka Mr. Pompidou Center in Paris), the newMetropolis may look like a beached supertanker but manages to ship kiddies into various unknown worlds of virtual reality (real reality just ain't good enough these days). While your young'uns play pirate at the **Maritime Museum** on the three-masted sailing ship from 1749, you can relax in the panoramic cafeteria (with a non-smoking area that actually lives up to the name, unlike most in town). Kids go hog-wild over all the real boats on the wharf as well as those indoors (including the royal barge, which drips with gold). There are 500 or so antique scale models of ships, too. Across the Nieuwevaart canal is the **Kromhout Shipyard Museum**. Budding mariners and old salts can see historic vessels being repaired in this 19th-century working shipyard. Several leaky old tubs are always on hand, and the warehouse is redolent with the fumes of early internal-combustion marine engines, including the celebrated 12-horsepower Kromhout. The place has seen better days, and that's precisely why it's so charming. The **Houseboat Museum** is in a 1914 former cargo barge, the Hendrika Maria, transformed decades ago into a houseboat, and in 1997 into a house museum. Devised to teach kids 6 to 12 about other cultures, the **Kindermuseum** section of the **Tropenmuseum** (Tropical Museum) is really a fairly adult affair. Youngsters seem perfectly capable of appreciating instead the fascinating, grown-up ethnographic exhibits—reconstructed African, Indian, or East Asian villages and bazaars, complete with rickshaws—in the main museum, whose primary purpose, in less politically correct days, was to glorify Dutch colonialism.

More kidding around... If you're in town with family, the **Artis Zoo** is going to be on your list. This is the oldest zoo in the country, founded in 1838, and about 6,000 animals from around the world live in it. The park setting is a bonus, and when they've had their eyeful of zebras, pythons, and orangutans and tire of petting them at the animal farm, kids can stargaze in the planetarium. If that doesn't send everyone back to the hotel for a nap, take them to the tiny **Petting Zoo** (Kinderboerderig De Dierencapel) in the Western Islands neighborhood, where exotic-looking piglets, banal chickens, fragrant goats, and woolly sheep nibble, root, and peck along the banks of the Bickersgracht canal. The Punch 'n' Judy show—called "Pantijn"—at the open market at Nooder-markt (in the Jordaan, bordering Prinsengracht), on Saturday mornings may be in Dutch, but kids will love it anyway. The Waterlooplein flea market is always entertaining, and you can avoid spending your euros by pointing out that most of the junk isn't worth shipping home to the rumpus room.

The **Tram Museum** (Elektrische Museumtramlijn) is in fact a streetcar ride, but all the better: Kids love it. The museum has several old trolleys and trams once used in other European cities, and they rattle down special tracks from Haarlemmermeerstation through the Amsteldamsebos (a wooded park with tons of family amusements; see Getting Outdoors) to suburban Amstelveen and back. The same kind of ride is offered by **The Tourist Tram**, a nifty 1920s streetcar that zips from the top of Damrak all over town. They *might* like **The Tourist Ferry**, an old ferry boat that plies the IJ River to suburban Nieuwendam and back, an old-fashioned attraction strictly for tourists, as the name implies: Skip it unless you like old boats and suburban scenery.

People-watching... Leidseplein is a prime spot to study the fauna, local and imported, and the Café Americain (see Dining and Cafes) is the best place for it. There's a terrace outside, where you'll see the square's inevitable fire eaters, clowns, and sidewalk musicians. Over in the Vondelpark, at the **Netherlands Film Museum**, hardly anyone seems to go into the resource center for cinematographers. They're all hanging out on the wide, shaded terraces of the Cafe Vertigo overlooking the park where people picnic, blade, cycle, and fornicate in plain view. Two postmodern white cafes on the Amstel River, the Cafe de Jaren and Dantzig (see Dining and Cafes), have become the ultimate see-and-be-seen venues. Both have riverside terraces; both have big, airy interiors where locals and visitors pose. Over on Damrak—among the winking plastic signs of peep shows and souvenir shops— is the De Roode Leeuw restaurant and cafe (see Dining and Cafes), with the oldest heated terrace in town, a comfy spot from which to watch dazed tourists and pickpockets in action. Half a mile away, at Spui, the bibliophiles, media types, and fashionable Grachtengordel residents sit on the terrace or crowd onto the sidewalk at Cafe Hoppe and Cafe Luxembourg next door (see Dining and Cafes), an old brown cafe and a designer newish one, known as A'dam's most sophisticated people-watching venues.

Behind the eight ball... About the most active sports locals go in for are beer guzzling and getting snookered at carambole, a devilishly complicated game played on pool tables without pockets. Get them to explain it to you; I can't. Pool-table games are an obsession among the brown cafe contingent, and it's as easy to pick up a game as a flea. Scores of places have tables, but Cafe Chris (see Dining and Cafes) in the Jordaan, the oldest brown in town (1624), is a particularly atmospheric, if cramped, spot to chalk a stick with regulars. Cafe Ruk & Pluk (see Dining and Cafes), a crazy joint run by a famous gay couple, is a modern brown cafe east of Oosterpark, with a pocketless table under the Brazilian carnival decor. Serious players should check out the **Bavaria Pool-Snookercentrum,** out on Van Ostadestraat, south of the Singelgracht and not too far from the Heineken Brewery, where sharps bring their own cues and reserve a table on one of four floors. For pick-up games, you'd better be good. The rival club, **De Keizer Snooker Club**, on Keizersgracht, near Westerkerk, has individual rooms where titans battle it out on the felt.

Chess cafes... Chess is another local favorite, since chess pieces can be moved with a minimum of effort and within reach of liquid refreshment. Countless cafes have chess sets for their customers, and anyone can play; a handful, called "*schaak* cafes," are frequented almost exclusively by the *schaak*-obsessed. Gambit is possibly the most competitive, a Jordaan hangout where you have to cut away at the smoke to see what the queen and king are up to. At Schaak Cafe Het Hok, also near Leidseplein, regulars sit in the fog under Ajax soccer posters, sip tea, and reach for the suspended timers. (See Dining and Cafes for details on both.)

Where to escape the crowds... There are times when even the most gregarious traveler feels like being alone. You'll find no crowds at the **Trade Union Museum** perusing the yellowed newspaper clippings, warped black-and-white photos, and lengthy documents (in Dutch) recounting the struggle of organized labor in the Netherlands. Sounds like a total yawn—and it is. But lo and behold, the early-1900s Dutch art-nouveau architecture is stunning stuff, and no one seems to know about it. Hendrick Petrus van Berlage (as in the Beurs van Berlage; see "Art nouveau to go" below) designed the vaulted, tiled building—with stained glass and sculpted bas-reliefs— for the Diamond Workers' Union. Another beautiful building where you'll never be bustled, the quiet **Bijbels Museum,** is a real treat, whether or not you're a religious scholar. It houses rather astounding scale models of biblical archeology, and the architecture is a revelation: twin 1662 canal houses with an elliptical wooden staircase, and a coffered ceiling with mythological scenes painted in 1717 by Jacob de Wit. Around the turn of the century, witty A'dammers used to quip that if you wanted to meet your mistress in private, the **Willet-Holthuysen Museum** was the place to go. Recently restored, this 1687 Golden Bend canal-house museum is still quiet. Polite visitors can peek at the downstairs antique kitchen, the mezzanine room with a rococo, painted ceiling, the d'Aubusson tapestries, and the family portraits of stern ancestors. Probably the quietest museum of them all, though, is dedicated to the memory of 19th-century satirical writer Eduard Douwes-Dekker, aka Multatuli, a legend for the Dutch but largely unknown outside the Netherlands (remember his incomparable *Max Havelaar,* set on a coffee plantation?). Despite international adoption of a "Max Havelaar" logo by fair trade activists (for coffee grown by fairly paid peasants), utter stillness reigns in the **Multatuli Museum**, where a solicitous (and surprised) curator will explain, in English, about the photos, first-edition books, documents, and old furniture in this one-room memorial. Another pure-Dutch treat, of another kind, is the **Pianola Museum**, surely the most *gezellig* museum in town. Player-piano aficionado Kasper Janse has about three dozen old pianolas in his private collection. There's a front-room brown cafe, where local Jordaaners and rare, lost tourists sip coffee and sing along to old tunes.

Art nouveau to go... Art nouveau aficionados won't want to miss the **Beurs van Berlage**, formerly the Stock Exchange, now a conference center, art exhibition space, museum, and concert hall. Built in 1896 by architect Hendrik Petrus van Berlage, it's a transition between the heavy, eclectic architecture of the late 1800s and the modernity of the Amsterdam School that followed. The complex covers an entire city block—make sure you go inside to see the best of it (the official guides are Artiflex Travel, see page 95). There are tiled arches and columns; ornate ironwork; stained glass; sinuous lights that seem straight out of a jungle; and a stunning cafe with murals. The tower offers breathtaking views—literally (there's no elevator). Another Dutch art-nouveau landmark, with art-deco additions, is the American Hotel and its Café Americain (Leidsekade 97; see Dining and Cafes, Accommodations), built in 1900. Its Emerald City–style tower rises over Leidseplein. The cafe's wall clock and the symbolist murals hark back to *Great Gatsby* times. Hanging like bats from the high, vaulted ceiling are huge bronze and stained-glass lamps that look like they might take wing. Another van Berlage treasure is the rarely visited **Trade Union Museum**, near the Artis Zoo in Eastern Central Amsterdam (see "Where to escape the crowds," above).

When you're down to your last euro... An only-in-Amsterdam musical freebie is provided by the oh-so-quaint jingle-bell carillons strategically distributed around the four corners of the oldest part of town. There are actually nine historic carillons (four date from the 17th century), but only four of them ring out classical tunes (and the occasional pop hit) once a week from the tops of their church towers. Tuesdays, go to the **Westertoren**; Thursdays, the **Zuidertoren**; and Fridays, the **Munttoren**, all at noon. On Saturdays from 4pm to 5pm it's the **Oude Kerkstoren**'s turn. Even if you can't manage to get right under the towers, the sweet-and-sour melodies turn each neighborhood into a music box. The **Zuiderkerk** has one of the nicest carillons, and also offers a free, permanent exhibition on Amsterdam's development and planning down the centuries, featuring drawings, photographs, slide shows, and scale models. You can see how the city grew and consult new urban planning schemes to see where it's stumbling next.

From October to June, both the **Muziektheater** and the celebrated Concertgebouw (see Entertainment) offer free lunchtime concerts. Head for the Boekmanzaal (part of the Muziektheater) for chamber-music performances by the Choir of the Netherlands Opera, the Netherlands Philharmonic, or the Netherlands Ballet Orchestra (times vary—check at the Muziektheater's info desk). The Royal Concertgebouw Orchestra kicks in on Wednesdays at the same time with public rehearsals of the works they'll be performing that night. Get to both when the doors open at 12:15, or you might not find a seat. **De Engelse Kerk** (English Reformed Church) at the **Begijnhof** offers its own lunchtime classical concerts on Tuesdays at 1:10pm, precisely. The Pulitzer Concert, usually held the last Saturday in August, features classical music, performed on pontoons built in front of the Pulitzer Hotel (see Accommodations; call the hotel for info).

While water taxis and canal buses can be pricey, there is one way to get onto the water without spending a euro.

The city operates a free ferry service from the docks immediately behind Centraal Station to the north bank of the IJ
River. It takes only about five minutes to get across, and
isn't exactly thrilling, but you do get a whiff of the sea and
a nice view of bustling river traffic. One ferry, the ***Buikersloterwegveer***, leaves from pier 7 and operates daily,
around the clock. The other, the ***IJ-Veer***, is smaller, easier
to pronounce, leaves from pier 8, and runs weekdays only,
from early morning to dinnertime. Whichever one you
take, the ferry is the most pleasant way to get to the dull
suburb of Amsterdam Noord—and the outdoorsy plea-
sures just beyond it. Within 15 minutes on foot or by bike
from the ferry terminal, you can explore the centuries-old
suburb of Nieuwendam, cycle through the Florapark, or
catch the bike and hiking trails leading to nearby villages
like Broek in Waterland, Monnickendam, and Zaanse
Schans (see Getting Outside for details). Also leaving pier
8 is the ***IJ-Veer 35***; a 20-minute free ride takes you to Java
Island and its novel architecture, a postmodern mix of
Lego and faux Manhattan Beach styles.

   Here's a two-in-one: If you don't feel like going into
the Amsterdam Historical Museum but are craving some
historic art and architecture, stroll through the **Schuttersgallerij**, a passageway linking Kalverstraat to Spui, via the
Begijnhof, that famously hidden courtyard. Under the
Schuttersgallerij's glass roof, you'll see 15 bigger-is-better,
17th-century paintings showing the city's heroic Civic
Guards. These paintings are in the same tradition if not
quite the same league as Rembrandt's *Nightwatch*, but
then you don't have to line up and pay to view them,
either. And seen in this relaxed context, without crowds,
they are well worth the detour. Lovers of romantic ruins
should try the **Rijksmuseum**'s architectural garden, open
and free during museum hours. Scattered among the
fountains and flower beds are weather-worn garden stat-
uary and a hodgepodge of columns, gables, festoons, and
fragments from monuments and houses destroyed over
the last century. It provides a sort of whirlwind tour of
Dutch architecture since the Middle Ages and even
includes 17th-century city gates from the cities of
Deventer and Groningen.

The red-light district... To sample the red-light district's
past and prurience, start at Centraal Station and take busy
Prins Hendrikkade east a few hundred yards to the

Schreierstoren (the Weeping Tower). Oude Zijds Kolk alley leads to the Oude Zijds Voorburgwal canal and **Oude Kerk**, the oldest church in Amsterdam. Climb the onion-dome belfry for views of the red-light district; then go inside for the stained glass, carved choir stalls, and painted wooden ceiling. There are gables and gablestones galore up and down this canal and surrounding streets and alleys. One canal east, on Oudezijds Achterburgwal, is **Spinhuis**, a 1597 Hendrick de Keyser building long used as a prison for wayward women. Walk down Oude Hoogstraat and you'll see narrow **Oude Hoogstraat 22**, the narrowest house in Europe, measuring only 6 feet 6 inches wide and 21 feet deep. Nearby is the landmark **East India House**, formerly the nerve center of the Dutch colonial empire; nip into its courtyard, then head down Kloveniersburgwal to the nearby **Trippenhuis**, possibly the most spectacular parvenu building of the Golden Age, and **Kleine Trippenhuis**, the yard-wide house built to shut up the Trips' pushy coachman. **De Waagebouw** is just down the way at Nieuwemarkt; it started out seven-turreted as the Sint Antoniespoort city gate and became a weigh house in the early 1600s (it now houses a trendy Internet cafe). Take Koningstraat to the Oude Schans canal and picturesque 1512 **Montel-baanstoren**, a fortress that protected the city's main ship-yard. Cross the Waals Eilandsgracht canal, go west toward Centraal Station, and you'll run into the immense **Scheepvaarthuis**, a turreted, 1912–1916 Amsterdam School fantasy with incredible bas-reliefs.

The old Jewish district... Start a tour of former Jewish Amsterdam at the **De Pinto House** on St. Antoniesbree-straat, once home of Isaac de Pinto, a Portuguese Jew who co-founded the East India Company. Nearby, just off the same street, is Hendrick de Keyser's **Zuiderkerk** and **Zuidertoren**, built from 1602 to 1611 for a Calvinist con-gregation. Climb the tower for views of the area. A hun-dred yards southeast, on Jodenbreestraat, is the **Rembrandt House Museum**, where the artist lived from 1639 to 1658. Follow Zwanenburgwal to the Amstel River and you'll come upon the **Jewish Memorial**, a megalith bearing witness to the Nazi atrocities that claimed 75,000 Jewish lives and destroyed Amsterdam's Jewish district. Loop around the hideous, modern city hall Stopera complex, aka the **Muziektheater**, also

known by the derisive nickname "false teeth." (Look at it
from the river and you'll see why.) Behind Mr. Visserplein,
a busy traffic circle, is the **Jewish Historical Museum**;
next door is the enormous 1675 **Portuguese Synagogue**.
A few hundred yards farther east is the **Hortus Botanicus**—a gorgeous 17th-century botanical garden. Follow
Plantage Middenlaan to the **Hollandse Schouwbrug**,
once a turn-of-the-century comedy theater, now a gutted
and roofless wreck. This is probably the most moving of
Amsterdam's memorials, a site where an estimated 60,000
Jews crossed the threshold en route to Nazi death camps.

Hofje-hopping in the Jordaan... Uncontrolled real
estate speculation at the end of the Golden Age gave
birth to the Jordaan's eccentric layout, a maze of narrow
alleys and canals and tiny, teetering old buildings. Art
galleries, hundreds of boutiques, and countless cafes
have sprouted up here now. The most atmospheric section is north of Elandsgracht, and the best scenery of all
is on the Bloemgracht, Egelantiersgracht, Brouwersgracht, and Prinsengracht canals. There are several open
markets around **Noorderkerk**, a landmark 1623 church.
Hofje-hopping—exploring the hidden courtyards of
former Jordaan almshouses—is one way to discover the
neighborhood. Start in the north on Palmgracht (28–38)
at the tiny **Raepenhofje**, marked with a gablestone
showing a beet and filled with flowers. Walk south, then
right on Lindengracht (147–165) to the **Suykerhofje**,
built in 1667 for Protestant women, with steep tile roofs
and dormers and a wonderfully overgrown garden.
Around the corner to the south is the **Huyszitten
Weduwenhof of Karthuizerhof**, on Karthuizerstraat
(21–131), a large complex whose 80 houses surround a
quad and date to 1650; it was built for widows with children. A big old water pump is home to cats, and there's
a brightly painted gablestone with a sailing ship. Continue south to narrow Egelantiersdwarsstraat (26–50)
and the **Claes Claeszhofje**, a small double courtyard
with an unusual wooden tower, wisteria, and hawthorn.
Around the corner on Egelantiersgracht (105–141) is
the **Sint Andrieshofje**, twice the size and with a restored
garden that's spectacular in spring. A 15-minute walk
south takes you to Elandsgracht (104–142) and the
Hofje Venetia of Maarloopshofje, a large courtyard
with a gorgeous garden.

The Grachtengordel mansions... To understand why this neighborhood has come to mean "monied" in Dutch, stroll along Herengracht's Golden Bend, between Leidsestraat and Vijzelstraat, with shoulder-to-shoulder mansions. Or, if you have a whole afternoon to tackle the Grachtengordel, start at the top of Prinsengracht, west of Centraal Station, walk along it as far as the Amstel River, then double back on Keizersgracht and Herengracht, weaving between them via Reguliersgracht (lots of bridges, plus handsome **Amstelveld** square), Nieuwe Spiegelstraat (the antiques dealers' quarter), and the small side streets and canals north of Leidsegracht. Along the early stretch of Prinsengracht (89–133) you'll find the **Van Brienen Hofje of de Star**—a hidden courtyard with a clock tower, water pump, and spectacular golden chain tree—and **Zon's Hofje** (157–171), an intimate, shaded courtyard with cats and picnic benches. The easily recognizable **Westerkerk**, an imposing 1620–1638 Protestant church, and its tall, leaning **Westertoren** tower, are prime examples of architect Hendrick de Keyser's handiwork, and the tower provides a terrific panorama. Behind it, on Keizersgracht, is the pink-granite **Homomonument**, a 1987 memorial to persecuted gay men and lesbians. Nearby on Keizersgracht (121) is the celebrated **House of Heads** (Huis met de Hoofden), a 1624 mansion with large, sculpted heads of Diana, Bacchus, Athena, Mars, Ceres, and Apollo. A few blocks down on the same canal (324) is **Felix Meritis**, an aesthetically challenged neoclassical theater from the 1780s that was long renowned for its acoustics (it's now used for classical musical concerts; see Entertainment). Five minutes away on the same canal is **Huis Marseille**, a 1665 mansion now housing a photography foundation. A few blocks north on Herengracht (168–170) is the **Netherlands Theater Institute Museum**, a resource center for performance-arts students housed in a remarkable 1638 mansion with the city's first neck gable and ceilings painted by Jacob de Witt. Two ground-floor rooms actually belong to the next-door **Bartolotti House**, a 1618 landmark with an exceptionally ornate red-brick facade.

A Singel–minded stroll... The medieval moat Singel—the outermost ring surrounding the city before the Golden Age boom—starts with what is supposed to be the narrowest house in the world (**Singel 7**). A few bridges down is the **Torensluis**, a 17th-century bridge with a charming downstairs dungeon that was flooded daily, to the horror of "lazy" prisoners who drowned if they didn't pump the water out fast enough. The canal ends with a flourish at the fragrant **Flower Market**, between Koningsplein and Muntplein.

Haarlem days... It's no coincidence that the distance from Centraal Station to Haarlem (12 miles) is about the same as the distance from the tip of Manhattan to Harlem (which were known in the 17th century as Nieuw Amsterdam and Nieuw Haarlem)—15 minutes on the train (trains run from dawn to midnight). Founded a thousand years ago, the city of Haarlem is older than Amsterdam, and is thoroughly provincial, prosperous, and conservative (no red-light district here). Wander its narrow streets from the Grote Markt main square to the 15th-century Amsterdamse Poort city gates, pretending you've stepped into a Dutch Master's painting. One of Haarlem's main draws is the Grote Sint Bavokerk, right on the main square, a 500-year-old Gothic mountain of stone with a 250-foot lantern tower visible from miles away. The nave itself has lofty vaults and remarkable wrought-iron grilles and woodwork. Handel, Mozart, Schubert, and Liszt supposedly tickled the keys of its 5,000-pipe Christian Muller rococo organ (you can hear it played on Tuesday evenings from mid-May to mid-September and on Thursday afternoons from April to October; tel 023/532–4399 for info), and the Golden Age painter Frans Hals (c. 1580–1666) is buried here. Hals, the most renowned of the School of Haarlem painters, spent much of his active life in Haarlem; he died in the city's 1608 Oudemannenhuis almshouse, now the biggest attraction in town—the **Frans Hals Museum**. His paintings fill the rooms of handsome, gabled cottages arranged around a main courtyard. Hals earned his reputation as a portraitist and, like Rembrandt, a painter of Civic Guards groups. Somewhat more politic than his fellow artists, he made every figure in his group portraits equally intense—that way everyone was satisfied, and each subscriber paid his share of the artist's fee. Among Hals' most famous works of this type is the *Officers of the Saint George Militia Company*; see it here. Also worth a look—if only for the architecture and curious old-fashioned displays—is the **Teylers Museum,** the country's oldest.

The Index

Amstelkring Museum (Our Lord in the Attic Museum). This is the city's only surviving clandestine or "attic" Roman Catholic church, a baroque bijou built in 1663 into the upper floors of 3 houses, now on the edge of the red-light district.... *Tel 020/624-6604. Oudezijds Voorburgwal 40, all trams and buses to Centraal Station. Open Mon–Sat 10–5, Sun 1–5. Closed Jan 1–April 30. Admission charged.* **(see p. 107)**

Amsterdam Historical Museum. Housed in a medieval-era orphanage, this is the repository for jewelry, porcelain, maps, and paintings telling the story of Amsterdam from its birth in the 13th century.... *Tel 020/523-1822, www.ahm.nl. Kalverstraat 92, trams 1, 2, 4, 5, 9, 14, 16, 24, 25 to Spui. Open Mon–Fri 10–5, weekends 11–5. Admission charged.* **(see p. 105)**

Anne Frank House. Too popular for its own good (it's been called "the Volendam of the Holocaust," i.e., a commercial exploitation of guilt), this little canal house is where Anne Frank wrote her celebrated diary when hiding with her family during the Nazi occupation. It was massively expanded in 1999 and now has a cafe-restaurant to go with the souvenir boutique and bookstore.... *Tel 020/556-7100, www.annefrank.nl. Prinsengracht 263, trams 13, 14, 17 to Westerkerk. Open Mon–Sat 9–5, until 7 daily June–Aug. Admission charged.***(see p. 106)**

Aquadam. Luxury saloon boats.... *Tel 020/344-9434. Bickersgracht 1, tram 3 to terminus at Westerkanaal.* **(see p. 110)**

Artis Zoo (Natura Artis). Founded in 1838, the oldest zoo in Europe has about 6,000 animals from around the world.

And what would a 19th-century temple of the natural sciences be without a planetarium and museums of geology and zoology?... *Tel 020/523-3400. Plantage Kerklaan 40, trams 7, 9, 14 to Artis Zoo. Open April–Oct daily 9–6, Nov–March daily 9–5. Admission charged.* **(see p. 112)**

Bartolotti House. Built in 1618, this patrician mansion north of the Golden Bend is an architectural landmark but not open for comprehensive tours.... *Tel 020/551-3300. Herengracht 170–172, trams 13, 14, 17 to Westerkerk. Open Tue–Fri, 11–5, Sat–Sun 1–5. Admission charged.* **(see pp. 104, 120)**

Bavaria Pool-Snookercentrum. Probably the city's hottest spot to chalk a cue, with 4 floors of tables, including billiards, carambole, snooker, and pool. Call ahead to reserve. Rates are about Dfl 10–15 per hour.... *Tel 020/676-7903. Van Ostadestraat 97, trams 3, 12, 24, 25 to Ceintuurbaan/Ferdinand Bolstraat. Open daily 11–1am, Fri–Sat until 2am.* **(see p. 114)**

Begijnhof. This gorgeous 14th-century *hofje*, built around an oblong courtyard, is home to the oldest house in Amsterdam, the English Reformed Church (believed to have been built in 1392), and many other historic treasures.... *No telephone. Spui, north side (no number), trams 1, 2, 5 to Spui. Open Oct–April daily 10–5, May–Sept until 10pm. Admission free.* **(see pp. 99, 101, 116)**

Beurs van Berlage (Former Stock Exchange). This 1896 Dutch art-nouveau pile is an intriguing piece of architecture, covering an entire city block; it's now a conference center, museum, and art exhibition and concert hall. It also houses a stunning cafe, open only during exhibitions. For guided tours contact Artifex Travel (see page 95).... *Tel 020/530-4141. Damrak 277, all trams and buses to Centraal Station. Open Tue–Sun 10–4. Admission charged.* **(see pp. 103, 115)**

Bijbels Museum (Biblical Museum). A quiet museum for religious scholars in a fascinating building—twin 1662 canal houses with mythological scenes painted by Jacob de Witt.... *Tel 020/624-2436. Herengracht 366, trams 1, 2, 5 to Koningsplein. Open Mon–Sat 10–5, Sun 1–5. Admission charged.* **(see p. 114)**

Buikersloterwegveer. 1 of 2 free city-operated ferries that crosses the IJ River from docks directly behind Centraal Station to Amsterdam Noord.... *No telephone. Departs from pier 7. Operates daily around the clock; 6:30am–9pm every 15 minutes, 9pm–6:30am every half hour.* **(see p. 117)**

Canal bikes. The Dutch call pedalos "canal bikes." Rent them and get splashed with brown water.... *Tel 020/626-5574. Available 10am–7pm (July–Aug 10–10) at docks at: Rijksmuseum, Leidseplein, Keizersgracht (at Leidsestraat), and the Anne Frank House. Rates Dfl 12.50 per hour per person.* **(see p. 109)**

Canal Bus. Amsterdam's answer to Venice's vaporetti, though locals don't use it.... *Tel 020/623-9886. Boat-buses stop about every 30 minutes at docks at the Rijksmuseum, Leidseplein, Keizersgracht (at Raadhuisstraat), Westerkerk (at the Anne Frank House), Centraal Station, and City Hall. A day pass costs Dfl 22; hop on and off from 10–6:30 daily. Tickets required.* **(see p. 110)**

Classic Boat World. Classy and expensive, with luxury-vintage saloon boats.... *Tel 065/371-1858. Singel 309/A, trams 1, 2, 5 to Paleisstraat.* **(see p. 110)**

De Keizer Snooker Club (Snooker Club de Keizer). A classy pool hall for serious players not interested in socializing.... *Tel 020/623-1586. Keizersgracht 256, trams 13, 14, 17 to Westerkerk. Open daily 1pm–1am, Fri–Sat until 2am. Rates about Dfl 8.50–15 depending on time slot.* **(see p. 114)**

De Pinto House (Pintohuis). Bought and remodeled in 1651 by Isaac de Pinto, a Portuguese Jew who fled persecution and cofounded the East India Company, this early-1600s mansion is now a public library.... *No telephone. St. Antoniebreestraat 69, trams 9, 14 to Mr. Visserplein. Open Mon–Fri 9:30–5. Admission free.* **(see pp. 104, 118)**

De Rieker Windmill. In the far-flung Amstelpark, detour to the riverbank for this 1636 thatched windmill, now a private home.... *No telephone. Amsteldijk at De Borcht in the Amstelpark, bus 148. Not open to the public.* **(see p. 105)**

De Waagebouw. The original, and still impressive, turretted city

gate—now home to a multimedia center and trendy cafes....
*Tel 020/557-9898. Neiuwemarkt 4, metro to Neiuwemarkt.
Open Sun–Thurs 10–1am, Fri–Sat until 2am. Admission
charged to exhibitions.* **(see p. 108, 118)**

East India House (Oostindischehuis). The University of Ams-
terdam now has offices in what was the nerve center of the
Dutch commercial empire from 1603 until recent times....
*No telephone. Oude Hoogstraat corner Kloveniersburgwal.
Not open to the public. You can visit the courtyard.*
(see pp. 104, 118)

Erotic Museum. Run by the same charmers who own the
Bananenbar and Casa Rosso, this porno haven is filled with
books, films, vibrators, S&M accessories, and customers
with sweaty palms.... *Tel 020/624-7303,
office@casarosso.com or www.casarosso.com. Oudezijds
Achterburgwal 54, trams 4, 9, 14, 16, 24, 25 to Dam.
Open daily 8–2am. Admission charged.* **(see p. 110)**

Flower Market (Bloemenmarkt). The famous flower market
that "floats" on the sidewalk, piers, and a few old barges
anchored to the Singel. Gorgeous plants and cut flowers,
plus bulbs and seeds.... *No telephone. Singel between
Muntplein and Koningsplein. Open Mon–Sat 9–5 or 6.*
(see pp. 99, 121)

Frans Hals Museum. The almshouse where the great painter
died, now the biggest museum attraction in Haarlem.... *Tel
023/516-4200. Groot Heiligland 62, Haarlem. Trains to
Haarlem run from Centraal Station. Open Mon–Sat 11–5,
Sun 1–5. Admission charged.* **(see p. 121)**

Geels & Co. Coffee and Tea Museum. See Shopping

De Gooyer Windmill. A 1725 former corn mill, northeast of
Artis Zoo, it now houses Bierbrouwerij 't IJ, the city's best
microbrewery, with a vast summer terrace (see Cafes and
Bars).... *Tel 020/622-8325. Funenkade 7, trams 6, 10 to
Zeeburgerdikj, buses 22, 32 to Oostenburgergracht.*
(see p. 105)

The Hash, Marijuana, and Hemp Museum. Everything you
ever wanted to know about the pungent weed is explained
and displayed at this private museum in the red-light dis-

trict.... *Tel 020/623-5961. Oudezijds Achterburgwal 148, trams 4, 9, 14, 16, 24, 25 to Dam. Open daily 11–10. Admission charged.* **(see p. 111)**

Heineken Brewery. Actually the last can left the brewery in 1988; most of the plant has been demolished to make way for upscale apartments and shops. You and several hundred other visitors tour the atmospheric beer museum and learn about hops and grain and water; then you swill as much of the stuff as you like, free, with all the foreseeable consequences.... *Tel 020/523-9666, www.heineken.com. Stadhouderskade 78, trams 6, 7, 10 to Weteringplein, 16, 24, 25 to Stadhouderskade. Open year-round. Tours on weekdays at 9:30 and 11; June–Sept 15: weekdays 9:30, 11, 1, and 2:30; July–Aug: also Sat 11, 1, and 2. Visitors must be 18 or over. Admission charged.* **(see pp. 97, 98)**

Holland Experience. A new multidimensional film and theater show. *What's On*, the tourist office monthly, describes it: "Seated on a moving platform, in the comfort of an aircraft seat, come with us on a trip through the many different faces of Holland. It's all there, the waterland, the agricultural areas, all the tourist sites, the culture and even the high-tech industry."... *Tel 020/422-2233. Waterlooplein 17, trams 9, 14 to Waterlooplein. Open daily 10–9. Tickets required.* **(see p. 98)**

Hollandse Schouwbrug. An estimated 60,000 Jews crossed the threshold of this turn-of-the-century comedy theater (now gutted and roofless) for "processing" before being sent by train to Westerbork, and on to the Nazi death camps.... *No telephone. Plantage Middenlaan 24, trams 9, 14 to Lepellaan. Open Mon–Fri 10–4, weekends 11–4. Admission free.* **(see p. 119)**

Homomonument. Erected in 1987, this unique monument commemorates gay men and lesbians persecuted down the centuries worldwide. It is a rallying point for the gay community.... *No telephone. Westermarkt, trams 13, 14, 17 to Westerkerk.* **(see p. 120)**

Hortus Botanicus. The lovely 17th-century park and greenhouses of this botanical garden display 6,000 or so specimens in a quiet haven.... *Tel 020/625-9021. Plantage Middenlaan 2, trams 9, 14 to Hortus Botanicus. Open* *daily April–Sept Mon–Fri 9–5, weekends 11–5, Oct–March until 4. Admission charged.* **(see p. 119)**

House of Heads (Huis met de Hoofden). This 1624 mansion, built by Hendrick de Keyser, is celebrated for the six large heads on the facade.... *No telephone. Keizersgracht 121, trams 13, 14, 17 to Westerkerk. Not open to the public.*
(see pp. 105, 120)

Houseboat Museum. In the 1914 former cargo barge "Hendrika Maria," a houseboat for decades, and since 1997 a house museum. Discover what life's like on the A'dam canal.... *Tel 020/427-0750. Prinsengracht, moored opposite #473, trams 1, 2, 5 to Koningsplein. Open Mar–Oct Tue–Sun 10–5, closed Mon. Admission charged.*
(see p. 112)

Huis Marseille. A'dam's new and impressive photography foundation, in a 1665 canal house, has rotating shows of work by international talents.... *Tel 020/531-8989, www.huismarseille.nl. Keizersgracht 401, trams 1, 2, 5, 11 to Keizersgracht. Open Tue–Sun 11–5. Admission charged.*
(see pp. 101, 120)

***IJ-Veer* 35.** Free city-run ferry that crosses the IJ River from docks directly behind Centraal Station to Amsterdam Noord.... *Leaves pier 8 every 15 minutes, Mon–Fri 6:35am–6:05pm.*
(see p. 117)

Jewish Historical Museum. This vast museum, housed in 4 ancient synagogues, displays photos, paintings, documents, and other objects relating to Jewish culture in the Netherlands. Museum cafe and shop.... *Tel 020/626-9945, www.jhm.nl. J.D. Meijerplein 2–4, trams 9, 14 to Mr. Visserplein. Open daily 11–5. Closed on Yom Kippur. Admission charged.* **(see pp. 106, 119)**

Jewish Memorial. Commemorating the estimated 75,000 Amsterdam Jews killed by Nazi atrocities during World War II.... *Tel 020/626-9945. Waterlooplein at Zwanenburgwal, trams 9, 14 to Waterlooplein.* **(see p. 118)**

Kindermuseum. See **Tropenmuseum.**

Kromhout Shipyard Museum. This small working shipyard in eastern Amsterdam, where historic boats are still repaired, has two magnificent ironwork sheds plus a handful of old ships and scores of early ship engines.... *Tel 020/627-6777. Hoogte Kadijk 147, buses 22, 28 to Oosterkerk. Open Mon–Fri 10–4. Admission charged.* **(see p. 111)**

Maritime Museum. Everything Dutch relating to the sea.... *Tel 020/523--2222, www.generali.nl/scheepvaartmuseum. Kattenburgerplein 1, buses 22, 28 to Kattenburgerplein. Open Tue–Sat 10–5, Sun 12–5. Closed Mon (except June 14–Sept 13). Admission charged.* **(see pp. 106, 111)**

Metz & Co. The panoramic, top-floor cafe of this upscale department store at the junction of Keizersgracht and Leidsestraat has lovely views over canal houses and mansions.... *Tel 020/624-8810. Keizersgracht 455, trams 1, 2, 5. Open Mon 11–6, Tue–Fri 9:30–6, Thur 9:30–9, Sat 10–5 Sun 12–5.* **(see p. 103)**

Monne de Miranda. Vintage saloon-boat rentals include captain, crew, and well-stocked liquor cabinet.... *Tel 020/330-1234, rstalman@xs4all.nl. Recht Boomssloot 47c, all trams/buses to Centraal Station. Rates vary widely.*
(see p. 103)

Multatuli Museum. Photos, first-edition books, and old furniture in this 1-room house-museum dedicated to the 19th-century satirical writer Eduard Douwes-Dekker.... *Tel 020/638-1938. Korsjespoortsteeg 20, trams 1, 2, 5, 13, 17 to Korte Kolkstraat. Open Tue 10–5, Sat noon–5, and by appointment. Admission free.* **(see p. 115)**

The Museumboot. Hop-on, hop-off service to 20 museums for Dfl 27.50 per day, with 10–15% reductions on museum entry fees. Stops at Centraal Station, the Anne Frank House, the Rijksmuseum, Leidsegracht (at Herengracht), Muziektheater Kwartier, and Nautisch Kwartier.... *Tel 020/622-2181. Boats run every 45 minutes 10–6 daily. Tickets required.* **(see p. 110)**

Muziektheater/Stadhuis. This vast, modern complex on the Amstel River at Zwanenburgwal houses both the city hall (stadhuis) and the Muziektheater opera/concert house.... *Tel 020/625-5455. Waterlooplein 22 or Amstel 1, trams 9, 14 to*

Muziektheater. Box office open Mon–Sat 10–6, Sun 11:30–6. Admission free Tue at 12:15. **(see pp. 116, 118)**

Netherlands Film Museum. A resource center for cinematographers and film buffs, this movie museum has a 2-screen theater that shows Dutch and other films to members.... *Tel 020/589-1400, info@tin.nl or www.tin.nl. Vondelpark 3, trams 1, 3, 6, 12 to Vondelpark. Cafe open daily. Tickets required for screenings (hours vary).* **(see p. 113)**

Netherlands Theater Institute Museum. This rather dry resource center for performance-arts students is in a gorgeous, newly restored 1638 canal house with a Golden Age garden.... *Tel 020/551-3300, www.tin.nl. Herengracht 168, trams 13, 14, 17 to Westerkerk. Open Tue–Fri 11–5, weekends 1–5. Closed Mon. Admission charged.*
(see pp. 105, 120)

newMetropolis. This new, harborside science and technology center features state-of-the-art virtual reality. Designed by Renzo Piano, it looks like a supertanker; great waterfront views from the roof.... *Tel 0900/9191-100. Oosterdok 2, all trams to Centraal Station. Open Sun–Thur 10–6, Fri–Sat (and daily July–Aug) until 9. Admission charged.*
(see pp. 98, 103, 111)

Nieuwe Kerk (New Church). Venerable Protestant church on Dam Square.... *Tel 020/638-6909, www.nieuwekerk.nl. Dam Square, trams 1, 2, 4, 5, 9, 13, 14, 16, 17, 24, 25 to Dam. Open daily 11–5. Admission charged during exhibitions.* **(see p. 107)**

Noorderkerk. Another marvel by the ubiquitous Hendrick de Keyser. Built in 1623, it stands at the edge of the Jordaan and is surrounded several times a week by lively open markets.... *No telephone. Noordermarkt, buses 18, 22 to Binnenoranjestraat. Opening hours vary due to ongoing restoration.* **(see p. 119)**

Oude Kerk/Oude Kerkstoren (Old Church and Tower). Ancient church (parts of it date to the early 13th century), in the heart of the red-light district.... *Tel 020/625-8284, www.oudekerk.nl. Oudekerksplein 23, all trams and buses to Centraal Station. Open Mon–Sat 11–5, Sun 1–5. Tower* open June–Sept Wed–Sun 2–4, Sept–April daily 1–5, Sat 11–5. Admission charged.**(see pp. 103, 108, 116, 118)**

Pakhuis Amsterdam. International interior design center in a reconverted warehouse east of Centraal Station; great views of city and harbor.... Tel 020/421–1033. Oostelijke Handelskade 14–17, buses 28, 32 to Pakhuis. Open Mon–Sat 10–5. **(see p. 103)**

Petting Zoo (Kinderboerderig De Dierencapel). Piglets, chickens, goats, sheep, and various other animals roam along the banks of a canal, near houseboats and shipyards, in the atmospheric Western Islands.... Tel 020/420-6855. Bickersgracht 207, buses 18, 22 to Binnenoranjestraat. Open Tue–Sun 9:30–4. Closed Mon. Donations accepted.

(see p. 112)

Pianola Museum. Player-piano lovers congregate to listen to— and sing along with—vintage tunes played on 35 old pianolas.... Tel 020/627-9624. Westerstraat 106, trams 3, 10 to Marnixbad. Open Sun 1–5 and by appointment. Admission charged. **(see p. 115)**

Portuguese Synagogue. Long the world's largest synagogue, this 1675 edifice miraculously survived the Nazi occupation.... Tel 020/622-6188 or 625–3509, www.esnoga.com. Mr. Visserplein 3, trams 9, 14 to Mr. Visserplein. Open Sun–Fri 10–12:30, 1–4. Closed Sat and Yom Kippur. Admission charged. **(see pp. 108, 119)**

Rembrandt House Museum. The artist lived and worked here from 1639 to 1658.... Tel 020/520-0400, www.rembrandthuis.nl. Jodenbreestraat 4–6, trams 9, 14 Mr. Visserplein. Open Mon–Sat 10–5, Sun 1–5. Admission charged.

(see pp. 106, 118)

Rijksmuseum. Amsterdam's answer to the Louvre. The architectural garden is open during museum hours.... Tel 020/674-7000, www.rijksmuseum.nl. Stadhouderskade 42, trams 2, 5, 6, 7, 10 to Rijksmuseum. Open daily 10–5. Admission charged. **(see pp. 99, 117)**

Royal Palace (Koninklijk Paleis). The quintessential Golden Age architectural statement, designed in the mid-17th century to replace an earlier city hall.... Tel 020/620-4060,

www.kon-paleis.amsterdam.nl. Dam Square, trams 4, 9, 14, 16, 24, 25 to Dam. Open June–Sept daily 12:30–5, Oct–May hours vary widely. Admission charged.
(see pp. 97, 103)

Schuttersgallerij (Civic Guards Gallery). Difficult to find but worth it, this covered passageway houses 15 large 17th-century paintings showing the city's heroic Civic Guards.... *No telephone. Open Mon–Fri 10–5, weekends 11–5. Admission free.* **(see p. 117)**

Sex Museum. A 1-stop emporium of carnality. While many of the displays are flaccid, the voyeurs pour in by the thousands.... *Tel 020/622-8376. Damrak 18, all trams and buses to Centraal Station. Open daily 10–11:30. Admission charged.* **(see p. 110)**

Spinhuis. A landmark 1597 building in the red-light district used for centuries as a correctional facility, i.e., labor camp, for wayward women.... *No telephone. Oudezijds Achterburgwal 28, all trams and buses to Centraal Station. Not open to the public.*
(see pp. 102, 118)

Stedelijk Museum (Modern Art Museum). A world-class modern and contemporary art museum.... *Tel 020/573-2911, www.stedelijk.nl. Paulus Potterstraat 13, trams 2, 3, 5, 12, 16 to Stedelijk Museum. Open daily 11–5. Admission charged.* **(see p. 100)**

Teylers Museum. An eclectic museum featuring everything from fossils to Michaelangelo.... *Tel 023/531-9010. Spaarne 16, Haarlem. Trains to Haarlem run from Centraal Station. Open Tue–Sat 10–5, Sun 1–5. Admission charged.*
(see p. 121)

Torture Museum. This highly commercial "museum" is little more than a cabinet of titillating horrors stuffed with scores of centuries-old instruments of torture.... *Tel 020/320-6642. Singel 449, trams 4, 9, 14, 16, 24, 25 to Munt Plein. Open daily 10–11. Admission charged.*
(see p. 111)

The Tourist Ferry. This old ferry plies the IJ River to Nieuwendam.... *Call or visit the VVV city tourist office for tickets and info: 0900/400-4040 (see Hotlines and Other Basics).*

THE INDEX | DIVERSIONS

Leaves from Pier 8 behind Centraal Station, all trams and buses to Centraal Station. Open daily, mid-April–mid-Oct. Ferries leave at noon, 2pm, and 4pm. Tickets: 4 euros adults, 2.50 euros children. (see p. 113)

The Tourist Tram. The name says it all: This 1920s streetcar runs from the top of Damrak (opposite the Victoria Hotel) around town, with stops at various museums and at Coster Diamonds, on Sundays and on Ascension Day.... *Call or visit the VVV city tourist office for tickets and info: 0900/400-4040 (see Hotlines and Other Basics). Operates March 30–Sept 15 only. Tickets: 4 euros adults, 3 euros children.* (see p. 112)

Trade Union Museum (De Burcht Vakbondsmuseum). Exhibits on the struggle of organized labor in the Netherlands; the art-nouveau building by Hendrick Petrus van Berlage is worth a trip.... *Tel 020/624-1166, www.deburcht-vakbondsmuseum.nl. Henri Polaklaan 9, trams 7, 9, 14 to Plantage Middenlaan or Henri Polaklaan. Open Tue–Fri 11–5, Sun 1–5. Closed Sat, Mon. Admission charged.* (see pp. 114, 116)

Tram Museum (Elektrische Museumtramlijn). A free-wheeling collection of old streetcars, trolleys, and trams rattles from the edge of town through the Amsteldamsebos to suburban Amstelveen.... *Tel 020/673-7538. Amstelveenseweg 264, trams 6, 16 to Haarlemmermeerstation. Call ahead for precise departure times. Tickets required, kids under 4 travel free.* (see p. 112)

Trippenhuis and Kleine Trippenhuis (Trip House and Trip Coachman's House). A 1660s neoclassical mansion and narrow coachman's house.... *No telephone. Kloveniersburgwal 29 and 26, respectively, Metro to Nieuwemarkt, all trams and buses to Centraal Station. Not open to the public.* (see pp. 104, 118)

Tropenmuseum and Kindermuseum (Tropical and Children's museums). Established early this century, the permanent collection here was devised specifically to teach kids aged 6–12 about foreign cultures.... *Tel 020/ 568-8215, www.kit.nl/tropenmuseum. Linnaeusstraat 2, trams 9, 10, 14 to Tropenmuseum-Oosterpark. Open Mon–Fri 10–5, weekends and holidays noon–5; Kindermu-*

seum by appointment only at tel 020/568–8300. Admission charged. **(see p. 112)**

Van Gogh Museum. Herein discover the tragic life and times of the mad, peripatetic Dutch genius, told in 200 of his oil paintings, hundreds of sketches, drawings, watercolors, and letters. Recently expanded with a new exhibition wing.... *Tel 020/570-5200, info@vangoghmuseum.nl or www.vangoghmuseum.nl. Paulus Potterstraat 7, trams 2, 3, 5, 12, 16 to Museumplein. Open daily 10–6. Admission charged.* **(see p. 100)**

Van Loon Museum. If you visit only 1 canal-house museum, make this it. You ring the bell of an imposing 1671 mansion (built by Adriaen Dortsman) and are admitted to a showcase of life in the Golden Age.... *Tel 020/624-5255, mvl@box.nl or www.musvloon.box.nl. Keizersgracht 672, trams 16, 24, 25 to Keizersgracht. Open Fri–Mon 11–5. Closed Tue–Thur. Admission charged.* **(see p. 107)**

Westerkerk/Westertoren (Western Church and Tower). Arguably the masterpiece of the prolific Golden Age architect Hendrick de Keyser, this airy Protestant church is a city landmark.... *Tel 020/624-7766. Prinsengracht 281, trams 13, 14, 17 to Westerkerk. Church open Mon–Sat 10–4, open Sun for worship only at 10:30; tower open June–Sept only Wed–Sat 10–4. Church free; admission charged to climb tower.* **(see pp. 102, 108, 116, 120)**

Willet-Holthuysen Museum. An atmospheric 1687 Golden Bend canal-house museum. Opened in 1889, restored during 1996–1997.... *Tel 020/523-1870. Herengracht 605, trams 4, 9, 14 to Herengracht or Rembrandtplein. Open Mon–Fri 10–5, weekends 11–5. Admission charged.* **(see pp. 107, 115)**

Zuiderkerk/Zuidertoren (South Church and Tower). This 17th-century church has one of the finest carillons in town; houses a free, permanent exhibition on Amsterdam's development and planning down the centuries.... *Tel 020/ 622-2962, vdl@dro.amsterdam.nl. Zuiderkerkhof 72, Metro to Nieuwemarkt, trams 9, 14 to Mr. Visserplein. Open June–Oct 15 Wed–Thur 2–5, Fri 11–2, Sat 11–4, Oct 16–May Mon, Wed, Fri noon–5, Thur noon–8. Church free; admission charged to climb tower.* **(see pp. 103, 108, 116, 118)**

Diversions in Central Amsterdam

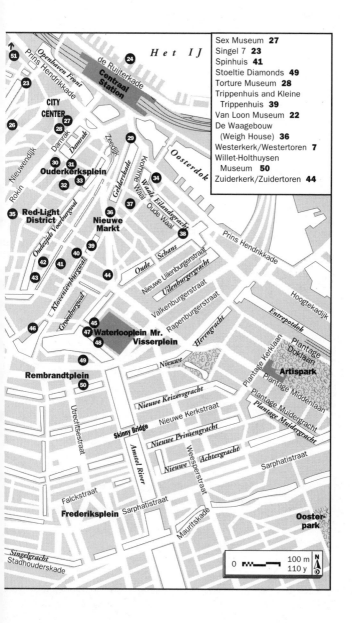

Het IJ

Sex Museum **27**
Singel 7 **23**
Spinhuis **41**
Stoeltie Diamonds **49**
Torture Museum **28**
Trippenhuis and Kleine
  Trippenhuis **39**
Van Loon Museum **22**
De Waagebouw
  (Weigh House) **36**
Westerkerk/Westertoren **7**
Willet-Holthuysen
  Museum **50**
Zuiderkerk/Zuidertoren **44**

Openhaven Front
Prins Hendrikkade
de Ruijterkade
Centraal Station

CITY CENTER

Nieuwendijk
Damrak
Damrak
Zeedijk
Gelderskade

Ouderkerksplein

Rokin

Red-Light District
Oudezijds Voorburgwal

Kromme Waal
Oude Waal
Eilandsgracht

Oosterdok

Nieuwe Markt

Prins Hendrikkade

Oude Schans

Nieuwe Uilenburgerstraat
Uilenburgergracht
Valkenburgerstraat

Kloveniersburgwal
Groenburgwal

Rapenburgerstraat

Hoogtekadijk
Entrepotdok

Waterlooplein Mr. Visserplein

Herengracht

Plantage Kerklaan
Plantage Doklaan

Artispark

Plantage Middenlaan

Rembrandtplein

Nieuwe

Nieuwe Keizersgracht
Nieuwe Kerkstraat

Plantage Muidergracht
Plantage Muidergracht

Skinny Bridge

Nieuwe Prinsengracht

Amstel River

Nieuwe Achtergracht
Nieuwe Weesperstraat

Sarphatistraat

Utrechtsestraat

Falckstraat
Sarphatistraat

Frederiksplein

Mauritskade

Ooster-park

Singelgracht
Stadhouderskade

0   100 m
    110 y

N

Diversions in the
Museumplein Area & Amsterdam South

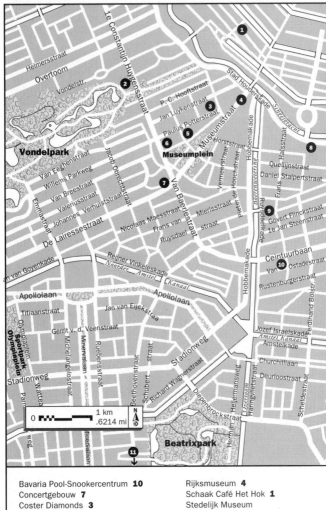

Bavaria Pool-Snookercentrum **10**
Concertgebouw **7**
Coster Diamonds **3**
Heineken Brewery **8**
Netherlands Film Museum **2**
De Rieker Windmill **11**

Rijksmuseum **4**
Schaak Café Het Hok **1**
Stedelijk Museum
  (Modern Art Museum) **6**
Van Moppes & Zoon **9**
Van Gogh Museum **5**

Diversions in Amsterdam East

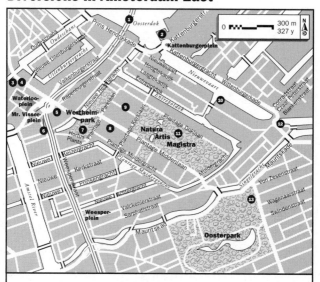

Artis Zoo (Natura Artis) **11**

De Gooyer Windmill **12**

Holland Experience **4**

Hollandse Schouwburg **8**

Hortus Botanicus **7**

Jewish Historical Museum **6**

Kromhout Shipyard Museum **10**

Maritime Museum **2**

newMetropolis **1**

Portuguese Synagogue **5**

Rembrandt House Museum **3**

Trade Union Museum
   (De Burcht Vakbondsmuseum) **9**

Tropenmuseum & Kindermuseum **13**

getting

4
outside

In Amsterdam, drinking beer and socializing at a brown cafe qualify as sports and rec-reation. Playing pool, snooker, carambole, or chess, or picnicking in the Vondelpark seem downright active. Like many Europeans, Amsterdammers just aren't sports fanatics. Locals are particularly baffled by joggers; biking is a form of transport, little more; canal bikes (as pedal boats, or pedalos, are known in Amsterdam) are strictly for tourists; roller-blading is for the trendy (and only in good weather, i.e., almost never). Amsterdammers consider golf a game for British snobs, so playing a round here is like ordering champagne at Oktoberfest. As for the seaside, the only readily accessible beach from Amsterdam is Zandvoort, and its scenery (high-rise apartments) and water (seaweed, jellyfish) are about as appetizing as the name. In short, don't come to Amsterdam looking for a resort experience: This is a northern European city-like city.

The Lowdown

Green spaces... Believe it or not, the tourist office has actually counted 28 parks, 220,000 trees, and 600,000 "bulb flowers" (tulips among them) in Amsterdam. Everything is green, including many houses, which often have a patina of moss and lichen. But everyone's favorite city park for picnics, cycling, and musical and carnal improvisation is **Vondelpark** in the Old South neighborhood, just beyond the Singelgracht and near the big museums. Its landscaping is mid-1800s English Romantic, with meandering paths, ponds, and bridges, and it takes its name from Joost van den Vondel, a lighthearted poet of the Golden Age who lived too long for convenience (1587–1679) and died a pauper. His surname, pronounced "fondle," is certainly apropos for this park, given certain activities that go on under its bridges, particularly at night. **Hortus Botanicus** in eastern Amsterdam near Artis Zoo sounds terribly Latin and scientific, but it's a wonderful botanical garden that's been around since the 17th century. Sensitive souls love the quiet, old greenhouses, and vegetarian visitors can enjoy a perverse thrill by cheering on the carnivorous botanical specimens (take that, flesh-eaters!). Houseplant aficionados should ask to see the celebrated potted cycad, a palm that's about 400 years old. **Sarphatipark** (near the Heineken Brewery and Albertcuypmarkt); **Beatrixpark** (south of the New

South); and **Oosterpark** (east of Artis Zoo) are all smallish, landscaped gardens with the usual ponds, paths, and kiddie play areas. They're fine if you're in the neighborhood, but not really worth a detour unless you're visiting during the spectacular tulip season (April–May). You'll need a bike to make the trip to **Amstelpark** worth it, but this vast park on the Amstel River a few miles south of central Amsterdam has a remarkable rose garden and rhododendron dell. On its edge is the thatched 1636 De Rieker windmill that marks one of Rembrandt's favorite bucolic views (see Diversions). When the Great Depression hit in the early 1930s, the city decided to put thousands of folks to work reclaiming land and foresting what is now the 2,200-acre **Amsteldamsebos** (buses 170, 171, 172 to Bosbaan). It's a wild and woolly place south of the city in suburban Amstelveen. But if you're hankering for seriously long walks, or bike, pony, and horse rides along miles of waterways, through deep, dark forests, this is the place. The **Bosmuseum**, at the eastern edge of the park, tells the (not exactly riveting) story of the park; pick up a map of the park there or study the one at the main entrance. There's also a goat farm, where you can buy goat-milk cheese, ice cream, and fresh milk, animal reserves for deer and buffalo, a miniature golf course (A'dammers call it "midgetgolf"), and a children's play pool. Too bad the jets to and from Schiphol Airport roar overhead every few minutes.

Two-wheeling it... Locals bike everywhere to get around, not for recreation. There are probably as many bikes as inhabitants (the official number is 500,000, but tens of thousands are fished from the canals or pried off lampposts every year). Bike lanes abound so *use them* because Dutch drivers can be amazingly aggressive. Contrary to what you'd expect, the most awkward and frustrating areas to ride in are the Grachtengordel of grand canals and the red-light district. Neither has bike lanes, the streets are cobbled, uneven, and narrow, and there are so many landmark buildings that you'll be constantly stopping for a look. You're better off walking. The same goes for the center of town, between Spui and Centraal Station. The best places to cruise undisturbed include the atmospheric Jordaan, where there is little traffic; big parks like Vondelpark, Amstelpark, and Amsteldam-sebos; the quiet Western Islands and sprawling Eastern Docklands (including the new architecturally aston-ishing Java and Borneo islands); the residential Old South and New South; and across the IJ River in Nieuwendam. Locals snicker at tourists with bikes bearing the rental company's name. If that sort of thing matters to you, rent an unmarked bike from friendly **Frederic Rent A Bike** (Brouwersgracht 78, tel 020/624-5509, www.frederic.nl) or **Bike City** (Bloemgracht 68–70, tel 020/626-3721); both have good bikes, friendly staff, and low rates. The biggest and cheapest (per day) operator is **Take-A-Bike** (Centraal Station/Stationsplein 12, tel 020/624-8391). **Holland Rent A Bike** (Damrak 247, tel 020/622-3207) has higher rates than most but a choice of hundreds of bikes, including children's models, tandems, and mountain bikes (which aren't too common in the city). At **Mac Bike** (Mr. Vis-serplein 2, tel 020/620-0985 and Marnixstraat 220, tel 020/626-6964, www.macbike.nl) you get a basket with a big name on it, but the place also has fast-food service and the option of taking theft insurance, a rare but valu-able benefit. If your rented bike is stolen, it is usually your responsibility. Always use the locks provided, and always ask about the policy on stolen bikes: If insurance isn't available, how much does it cost to replace a bike?

Cycling beyond the city limits... Outside Amsterdam, almost every highway and major country road has a bike lane. The land is as flat as the proverbial pancake, so you can cover a lot of ground, but be aware that frequent, strong head winds can double or triple traveling times. You can either rent a bike in town and cycle out or put your bike on a train (though not during rush hour), or take a train or bus out of Amsterdam and rent a bike where you get off: Bikes are readily available all over Hol-land. A free ferry ride across the IJ River from Centraal Station can put you and your bike on the road to several popular villages, including centuries-old Nieuwendam, exclusive Broek in Waterland, the old fishing ports of Monnickendam and Marken, and the kitschy Volendam and Edam, two tourist-dependent villages that made their names on eels and wax-wrapped cheese, respectively. The ferry crossing to Amsterdam Noord takes under 10 minutes (the *Buikersloterwegveer* operates around the clock from pier 7; the *IJ-Veer*—at pier 8—runs weekdays only and quits just after 6pm), leaving you a short ride to the atmospheric streets of **Nieuwendam**, one of the city's oldest suburbs. From the ferry terminal, head due north on any of the streets paralleling the right, or east, side of the Hollandskanaal until you reach Nieuwendammerdijk, which veers east. South, on your right, is the wooded W. H. Vliegenbos park, the IJ River, and shipyards. On the north side of the road, your left, are scores of narrow streets lined with centuries-old, two-story brick and timbered buildings. You can stop at the Kleine Haven, the small harbor of the village of Nieuwendam, and sit out at a cafe. One-way from Centraal Station to the middle of Nieuwendam, including the ferry, shouldn't take you more than 30 minutes.

To get to the other villages, don't veer east on the Nieuwendammerdijk, but follow the bike lanes along either side of the Hollandskanaal through the Florapark and Volewijkspark. Bike lanes fan out once you reach the picturesque Buikslotermeerdijk and Noord Hollandsch Kanaaldijk, dikes with clearly marked routes to the next closest stops: Broek in Waterland and Monnickendam. **Broek in Waterland** (12 km/7.5 mi from the ferry terminal, also reachable on bus 111) sits at the end of a route that follows canals, overlooks polders, and traverses pasture land. A picture-book village with old wooden houses, many of them white, it's a suburb where A'dam millionaires live, and is known as one of the tidiest—and most conservative—spots on earth. It has a 1628 Protestant church with gorgeous carved pews and painted woodwork; an unbelievably cute central pond (the Havenrak) with a white pagoda gazebo from 1656 (Napoleon was received here by the mayor); and scores of winding lanes with big houses and flower-filled gardens. About 4 miles north, through the same pleasant but never dramatic scenery, is **Monnickendam** (bus 111), a former fishing port on the IJsselmeer noted for its smoked herring and now a favorite on tourist itineraries (the clogs and costumes start to spring up). Among the countless old buildings on winding streets are De Waag, a weigh house similar to the one in Amsterdam's Nieuwemarkt; the hulking, Gothic Grote Sint Nicolaaskerk; the ornate, 18th-century city hall; and the tall Speeltoren, a brick

tower from the 1500s with a tuneful carillon. A few miles
east is **Marken**, once a fishing village on an island, but
since 1957 linked to the mainland by a bridge, and now
totally dependent on tourism. Here is high kitsch: The
traditional Dutch costumes are always in full bloom
(wide, striped dresses and skirts, long dark smocks, and
white caps); clogs are carved to order. The old wooden
houses—matte green with horizontal white stripes—
stand in clumps on pilings because once upon a time, the
tides of the Zuiderzee, closed off in the 1930s, reached
them. **Volendam**, a few miles due north of Monnickendam, was an eel-fishing port but has suffered the same
economic fate as most of the other villages. This is the
quintessence of package-tour Holland, and the place to
see costumes (winged cotton–and–lace caps), clogs, and
wall-to-wall boutiques. Cheesemaking and A'dam com-
muters lend nearby **Edam** (a few miles northeast) a bit of
dignity, though most of the famous, bland curd is made
elsewhere. The Kaasmarkt (cheese market, 10am–noon
on Wed during July and Aug) is purely for tourists—an
exquisitely cheesey theme-park adventure, featuring canal
boats and wagons and men in silly costumes. The town
itself is crammed with picture-postcard Golden Age
houses and the Grote Sint Nicolaaskerk, whose stained
glass is remarkable. The landmark bell tower has a 16th-
century carillon. (See "Tiptoeing through the tulips" and
"The windmills of your mind," below, for other recommended cycling destinations.)

Island hopping... Eastsern Amsterdam is booming: From
the rehab **Pakhuis Amsterdam** warehouse (see Diversions) to the new artifical islands called Java and Borneo,
the city has added thousands of new, wacky buildings to
its repertoire. You pedal from Centraal Station due east
past the new ferry terminal, turn left after Pakhuis, and
cross a wild bridge that looks like a giant grasshopper to
reach Java island. A broad road rings the island, with
views of the IJ river. Finished in late 2001, the buildings
here and on the attiguous Borneo island are a crazy postmodern hodgepodge evoking your kids' Lego creations
and wavy Manhattan Beach houses, with mock Venetian
bridges over tiny canals and grassy inner courtyards. This
is great biking or walking territory: quiet, clean, and fascinating for its unsettling futuristic qualities. The free

ferry *IJ-Veer 35* (see Diversions) links Java island to Central Station's pier 8, with views en route.

Pedaling and paddling on the water... Bike-obsessed Amsterdammers call pedal boats *waterfiets* or *grachtenfiets*, which they have charmingly translated as "canal bikes." Of course they never use them, but who cares? You can pick 'em up and drop 'em off all day, any day at four **Canal Bikes** docks in the city: Rijksmuseum, Leidseplein, Keizersgracht (at Leidsestraat), and the Anne Frank House (tel 020/626-5574 for all locations; rates: Dfl 12.50 per hour per person; deposit required). The only competition in town is **Aan de Wind** (Mauritskade 1, tel 020/692–9124), near the Amstel Inter-Continental Hotel. Their pedalos cost Dfl 30 for two passengers, Dfl 40 for four, per hour, but you've got to bring them back to the same dock. They also rent "lounge boats" for up to 35 passengers (small party boats with bar, heat, toilet); they cost Dfl 225 and up per hour, including a licensed skipper. Motorboats are Dfl 105 per 90 minutes; deposit required. Farther afield, **Duikelaar**, at the western suburban Sloterpark (Noordzijde 41, tel 020/613–8855; deposit and passport required), rents canoes for about half the price, but you're limited to the park's fairly dull waterways. The boat house at the **Amsteldamsebos** south of town (no tel; March–Sept only; rates about Dfl 20 per hour; deposit and ID required) has pedalos and canoes, and the park's Roeibaan rowing lake alone is well over a mile long.

Horsing around... The Amsteldamsebos in Amstelveen is the best place to saddle up for outdoor riding, but you won't find many Western saddles, except on ponies. You can mount there at **Amsterdamse Manege** (Nieuwe Kalfjeslaan 25, tel 020/643-1342; 18 euros per hour; reservations essential; bring your own boots, hat, and crop for dressage), whose stables and indoor riding area are used by the serious horsey set, though kids and beginners are welcome and there are plenty of ponies. Monitors will lead you out into the 2,200-acre wooded park. Closer into town, and housed in a gorgeous 19th-century building, is the **Hollandse Manege** (Vondelstraat 140, tel 020/618-0942; 18 euros; reservations essential), great for a visit even if you don't ride.

The squash and tennis racket... Amsterdam encourages fans of racquet sports to do most of their swinging indoors, but there are a few tennis courts where you can expose your backhand to the elements. Thrifty, unpretentious types wait outside for hours to play on one of the **Vondelpark**'s four free courts. In the suburb of **Buitenvelder**, south, near the Amstelpark, there is a string of indoor and outdoor tennis courts at clubs that stand practically next door to each other. Among them, **Amstelpark Sportcentrum** (Koenenkade 8, tel 020/301–0700; about 20 euros per hour outdoors, 25 euros indoors, racquets free; reservations essential) is Holland's biggest tennis school, with 26 outdoor courts and 16 indoor courts (12 squash courts; tanning and fitness center). A bit farther down the road is **Gold Star Tennis** (Gustav Mahlerlaan 20, tel 020/644-5483; www.goldstar.nl; about 20 euros per hour, racquets 3 euros and up per hour; reservations essential), with 24 outdoor and 12 indoor courts. The hippest thing in high-strung sports these days is whacking a hard, rubber ball around a tiny white court (indoors, of course) at see-and-be-seen **Squash City Body Club** (Ketelmakerstraat 6, tel 020/626-7883; about 30 euros per 45 minutes, racquet rental 3 euros and up; reserve ahead; 14 courts). Of course, squash isn't the only—or perhaps even the main—thing at this hip fitness club in the Western Islands neighborhood. It has a cafe and *gezellig* bar, a sauna, a Turkish bath, a health-food restaurant, and plenty of gorgeous male and female trainers eager to teach you fat-burning step and funk aerobics. Serious, humorless squash fanatics hone their skills next door to Amstelpark Tenniscentrum at **Dicky Squash** (G. Mahlerin 16, tel 020/646-2266; about 12 euros per hour; racquets available; reserve ahead). **Frans Otten Stadion** (Stadionstraat 10, tel 020/662-8767; squash 15 to 18 euros per half-hour slot, tennis about 18 to 20 euros per hour, racquet rental 3 euros and up; reserve ahead), in the distinctly unhip, far-flung southwest of town near the Olympic Stadium, is a place where serious players compete in 20 squash courts and half a dozen indoor tennis courts (plus fitness center).

Jogging and pick-up sports... Basketball isn't big, but try the Vondelpark if you're looking to get in on a pick-up game. **Soccer** (*voetball*, football) is taken very seriously in Amsterdam, and you might be able to pick up a game on the cobbled, exquisitely unforgiving Amstelveld Square on Prinsengracht (just off Reguliersgracht) or in the Vondelpark, Amstelpark, or Amsteldamsebos. The best **jogging** territory is not in the city at all (too many cobbled streets and too much traffic). Again, head out to the Amstelpark and Amsteldamsebos (where you'll find marked hiking paths and fitness circuits). Vondelpark gets too crowded with picnickers, cyclists, and strollers to be ideal for jogging, though if you stick to the (often muddy) perimeter trail you'll be all right. Rollerskaters and 'bladers meet at 8pm at the Café Vertigo in the Vondelpark every Friday night, year-round, and skate in a jolly group around the city. You'd better be good enough to stop at red lights, and avoid speeding bikes and trams!

On ice... As romantic as it may sound, canal skating in Amsterdam has become all but obsolete in the age of global warming; only thrice in the last decade has the ice been thick enough to bring out the crowds. Try pond or rink skating in the parks—**Vondelpark** and **Oosterpark** are favorites—or squares (part of the **Leidseplein** becomes a free rink). Ice skating anywhere in the city is strictly seasonal available from roughly early November through February, depending on temperatures. That includes skating at the recently restored, world-class indoor-outdoor rink in suburban Watergraafsmeer, the **Jaap Eden IJshockeyhal** (Radioweg 64, tel 020/694-9652; 3.50 euros to enter, 4.50 euros to rent skates). You're more likely to be able to skate outdoors farther away from town, where it's colder in winter. Nearby **Broek in Waterland** (bus 111), a picturesque village for millionaires, is a good bet. Wherever you skate outdoors, you had best have skates of your own, since few places rent them.

In the swim... To swim and enjoy Amsterdam School architecture at a single plunge, go to the hip, handsome **Zuiderbad** (Hobbemastraat 26, tel 020/679-2217; about 5 euros admission), a recently renovated indoor pool built just before World War I, with glistening tiles and mosaics, arches, and relief sculptures. Nude swimming is always Sunday afternoons. **Mirandabad** (De Mirandalaan 9, tel 020/546-4444; about 5 euros) is a mock beach resort on the southeast edge of town, with an indoor mock lake complete with sandy beach, wave machine, slides, and in addition, an outdoor Olympic pool (open May 15–Sept 15). On the opposite side of town, at the suburban Sloterpark, **Duikelaar** watersports center (Noordzijde 41, tel 020/613-8855; pools open May–Oct only; about 5 euros to swim) has both indoor and outdoor pools; you can also rent sailboards, canoes, and tiny sailboats for use on the park's waterways. Nearby at the **Sloterparkbad** (Slotermeerlaan 2, tel 020/613-3700; about 5 euros; May–Oct) there's a big outdoor pool with a daunting diving tower, a solarium, and nudist areas.

Tiptoeing through the tulips... How many Netherlanders does it take to screw in the bulbs at the **Nationale Bloemententoonstelling** (Keukenhof Garden; tel 0252/465-555; tickets required)? Several thousand, probably, since there are usually about six million hyacinths, lilies, crocuses, narcissi, and daffodils, 600 kinds of tulips, and myriad other bulb plants blooming from late March to late May at this, the world's biggest bulb garden. The Bloemententoonstelling is seriously spectacular; you won't even notice the other million visitors tiptoeing alongside you through the 70 acres of romantic gardens, with a pond and canals, meandering paths, and a centuries-old hunting lodge that belonged to a Bavarian countess. Regular commuter trains run about every 15 minutes daily until midnight from Centraal Station to Haarlem or Leiden stations; the local bus ride on to Lisse through miles of bulb fields is kaleidoscopic. The 5- to 15-mile ride to Keukenhof is even more spectacular on a bike, which you could bring with you on the train from central Amsterdam. Nothing could be more Dutch than the **Verenigde Bloemenveilingen Aalsmeer** (Aalsmeer Flower Auction; Legmeerdijk 313, tel 0297/392-185; weekdays 6:30–11am; admission required; bus 172 from Centraal Station), where scents of *bloemen* and guilders blend intoxicatingly. Several billion cut flowers and nearly half a billion green plants are auctioned here weekdays year-round, in a vast in- and outdoor sales area practically the size of old Amsterdam. Visitors cannot participate in the auction. The Dutch countdown method is used, whereby a starting price is given and progressively drops as time passes, marked on a huge timer that clicks nervously from one hundred down to one. Hundreds of buyers must guess when colleagues will hit their buzzers. From a viewing platform you see thousands of specimens being shunted around. It's all very exciting; deals are done in seconds, but the spectacle is strictly for early birds since the best bits are over by 9:30am.

The windmills of your mind... Hidden among the smokestacks of heavy industry is the unusual but handsome mock-village of **Zaanse Schans**, 16 kilometers (10 miles) north of Amsterdam (tel 075/616-2221 or 075/635-1747; open daily April–Oct 8:30–6, till 5 Oct–March; admission charged to individual attractions; trains to Koog-Zaandijk, then 10-minute walk across the river). Since about 1950, the Dutch government has been moving old buildings and windmills here from blighted areas around the country to create a habitat that simulates Dutch life of about 200 years ago. A few souls do inhabit the place—after all, someone has to run the souvenir boutiques, restaurants, and workshops. The village draws about 800,000 visitors a year, the big attraction being the working windmills that grind oil seeds, grain for flour, paint pigments, and mustard seeds. From April to October you and the mob can visit the mills and some of the historic buildings. Off-season, the sights close, and you can stroll around alone at no charge and soak up the ghostly atmosphere. Across the Zaan River at the village of Koog an de Zaan is the **Molenmuseum** (Mill Museum), where you can learn how Holland's 9,000 windmills of 150 years ago have been reduced to a mere 900 today. Grist for the mill. A new bonus is the **Zaans Museum,** an ultra-modern cultural-history vessel dedicated to the life and times of the Zaan River region. There are multimedia displays (wonderful 1920s–'30s black-and-white movies about wind, mills, water, and industry), plus a grab bag of tools, objects, paintings, furniture, sleighs, sailboats, and more. Funny to find a fully fledged museum like this on the edge of such a quintessentially Dutch theme park (tel 075/616-8218; open Tue–Sat 10–5; admission charged).

shop

ping

5

As a city with a
long history of
trading, Amster-
dam is loaded
with tempting
wares, at premium
prices, from all

over the world. But as a small burg with a scant tradition in manufacturing or design, it's a bit short on only-in-Amsterdam bargains on world-class merchandise. There are no local crafts industries to speak of, unless you count clog making or ship repair; the best porcelain comes from nearby Delft, or Makkum in Friesland but frankly, you can get the same stuff in American department stores at comparable prices. Much ado is made of mock-antique pewter wares and grandfather clocks, but the less said about these the better (unless you're into high kitsch). The Dutch flower and plant industry is a booming business indeed, but foreign visitors can take home only certain certified bulbs. Nonetheless, there are plenty of creative ways to spend your guilders, especially on imported, used, or antique goods.

What to Buy

Clogs, windmill souvenirs, and tulip bulbs are swell, but you might also consider things like contemporary art—a vibrant activity in this city of young artists (for art gallery listings on the Internet: www.akka.nl). Antiques—maps, prints, objects, books, furniture, genuine old pewter, porcelain, and jewelry—are a major attraction. There are hundreds of reputable dealers, and you're sure to find something worth shipping or carrying home. Diamonds are still a big industry, and prices are competitive, but make sure you take your time to decide on a purchase: Many diamond-cutting houses give you a brisk tour, deposit you in the salesroom, and wait for the pressure to build. Porcelain from the royal factories at Delft and Makkum can be wonderful, but again, most of it is available in America. Sex-toy aficionados will find an embarrassment of riches (but be warned that some pornographic materials, especially films, cannot be imported into the States). Some of the world's best cigars and pipe tobacco are also available—smoke them on the spot or take a box home. Other products primarily or exclusively for immediate consumption include Dutch gin (*genever*) and white wine (yes, it does exist), dozens of varieties of cheeses (Holland is Europe's number-one dairy products exporter), chocolate and pastries, coffee and tea, and hash and grass (in tiny quantities), if you're so inclined (don't even *think* about smuggling dope out of the country).

Target Zones

Go to **Damrak**, **Nieuwendijk**, and **Kalverstraat** in central Amsterdam south of the station for tacky gift stuff and mass-market clothes; nearby Rokin offers upscale fashion, tobacco, and antiques. The antiques dealers' quarter is on and around **Nieuwe Spiegelstraat**, near the Rijksmuseum, with almost 100 stores. Dozens of antiquarian bookshops are between central Spui and the royal palace on **Spuistraat**, **Singel**, and **Nieuwezijds Voorburgwal**.

Dozens of international and Dutch designer boutiques, plus antique and porcelain dealers, are on **P.C. Hooftstraat** ("P.C." to insiders) and adjoining streets near Museumplein in the south. Nearby, **Cornelis Schuytstraat** has been reborn as an upmarket Greenwich Village, with fashion, food, flowers, and collectibles. Small fashion boutiques and one-of-a-kind shops tend to be on side streets (now nicknamed "The Nine Streets") between canals in the **Grachtengordel** neighborhood. The entire **Jordaan** quarter, east of central Amsterdam, is a junk-and-oddity-lover's paradise. The VVV tourist bureau distributes free a detailed city map called "Shopping in Amsterdam"—worth getting for rabid shopaholics.

Outdoor Markets

Amsterdam has as many markets as it does museums, and of the two you can guess which the locals prefer. Markets provide al fresco shopping and free entertainment, and no one seems to mind the permanently lousy weather. The immense, mile-long **Albert Cuypmarkt** south of Singelgracht (Albert Cuypstraat, trams 16, 24, 25; daily 9–5, closed Sun) is the city's biggest outdoor bazaar, happens six days a week, and is a great place to pick up Dutch and exotic food, cheap clothing, and

The spirit of Amsterdam: distiller Cees van Wees

Dynamic giant Cees van Wees stands about 7 feet tall, has a boyish haircut, and looks about 45. He's actually in his mid-60s, and attributes his health, bruising handshake, and booming voice to the regular intake of genever—Dutch gin. Van Wees—and his family—is Amsterdam's only genever, eaux de vie, and liqueur maker, the scion of a spirited dynasty whose distillery, warehouse, and wholesale tasting room have perfumed the Jordaan neighborhood since 1782. He is also reputedly the only distiller in the Netherlands to use only natural, organic, homemade flavors and aromatics. Using old ceramic vats, oak barrels, and alembics, he distills everything from raspberries to apples, cinnamon to chocolate. Unfortunately, unless you're an importer, you can't visit the distillery, but you can sip and buy van Wees's extraordinary wares at the family proeflokaal (tasting house), De Admiraal, which is equipped with comfortable sofas and chairs to help you through the dozens of nectarious beverages on offer (tel 020/625–4334, Herengracht 319; see Dining and Cafes).

ordinary household goods (though you'd be insane to buy and ship them home). Fresh veggies and lots of local color make the Jordaan's **Boerenmarkt**, or farmer's market (Noorderkerkstraat and Westerstraat, trams 3, 10; Sat 9–4, till 3 in winter), a nice place to wander on a lazy Saturday, especially since that's the day when organic-food peddlers take over the **Noordermarkt** (trams 3, 10; Sat 10–4); kids will love the Punch 'n' Judy show (called *Pantijn*), and aging hippies will flip over the whole-grain breads (and the occasional space cake). (On Monday mornings from 7:30 to 1, the Noordermarkt is host to antiques and collectibles—mostly old junk, but great fun to sift through.) Saturday's **Lindengrachtmarkt** (Lindengracht, tram 3 to Nieuwe Willemsstraat; Sat 9–4), a 5-minute walk south of the Noordermarkt, spreads out food, clothes, and sundry other goods. Another general market in the Jordaan, **Westermarkt** (Westerstraat, trams 3, 10; daily 9–5, closed Sun), is open six days a week.

The tourist office and all other guide writers insist that the famous daily flower market, the **Bloemenmarkt** (Singel at Munt Plein/Koningsplein, trams 1, 2, 4, 5, 9, 14, 16, 24, 25; daily 8:30–6, closed Sun), literally floats. In fact, almost all of it occupies a wide sidewalk or spreads across piers—not boats—in the Singel. But afloat or not, the flowers and plants are beautiful, the atmosphere jovial, and the prices ridiculously low on the things you can't take out of the country: cut flowers and live plants (see "Budding prospects," below).

You don't have to be a bibliophile to enjoy the **Boeken-markt**, a book fair where used and antiquarian books, postcards, and prints are sold. There are two locations—near Amsterdam University (Oudemanhuispoort, trams 4, 9, 14, 16, 24, 25; daily 11–4, closed Sun) and at Spui (Fri 10–6) and the **Nieuwemarkt**, a square on the eastern edge of the red-light district (Nieuwemarkt Square, Metro to Nieuwemarkt or all trams and buses to Centraal Station; June–Sept Wed–Sat 9–5). The collectible coins and stamps at the twice-weekly **Postzegelmarkt**, not far from Spui (Nieuwezijds Voorburgwal 280, trams 1, 2, 5 to Spui; Wed, Sat 1–4), draw pimply teenagers, overweight bachelors, and oldsters with grandkids in tow. The **Artmarkt 't Spui** (Spui, trams 1, 2, 5; March–Dec Sun 10–6, www.artplein-spui.nl), a spring-through-fall Sunday market, and its counterpart, **Thorbecke Artmarkt**, near Rembrandtplein (Thorbeckeplein, trams 4, 9, 14; March–Dec Sun 10:30–6), are where local Michelangelos and minor dealers hawk the occasional masterpiece but mostly the kind of paintings that generally look best in motel lobbies.

Finally, there is something disappointingly orderly, clean, and touristy about the daily **Waterloopleinmarkt** flea market (Waterlooplein, trams 9, 14; daily 9–5, closed Sun), a vast affair occupying hundreds of shantytown stands in hideous Waterlooplein, behind city hall. But bargains—on antiquarian books, for example—can be unearthed among the mass-market rubbish and Third-World souvenir elephants, whips, and beads.

Bargain Hunting

Sales, discounts, and wholesale prices to retail customers are an Amsterdam specialty—for locals. A *reclame* is an advertised sale; an *uitverkoop*, *aktie*, or *aanbieding* is a special sale; *alles moet weg* is a clearance sale. Unfortunately, visitors are not encouraged to participate in such savings—in the hope that they will pay full prices—and you'll hardly ever see advertisements in English. Seasonal discounts are largely the same as in America, with significant post-Christmas savings for all. The best sources for bargains are the Waterlooplein and De Looier flea markets and the outdoor markets of the Jordaan or Albert Cuypstraat (see "Outdoor Markets," above), where you can haggle and dicker like the best of them.

Trading with the Natives

The Dutch are canny shoppers, and will phone and shop around to find the best price. They go in for bargaining, but only with other natives and mostly at specific places, like outdoor markets, flea markets, and clearance sales. For visitors unable to wow natives with fluent Dutch, the price on the tag is what you'll pay. Finding flaws in goods and asking for a discount is a favorite trick among locals, but it probably isn't going to work for you. The salesperson will simply set the merchandise aside and return it to the manufacturer or importer (or call a friend and tell them to hurry over and buy it). Most shops displaying the "Duty-Free Shopping" logo will gladly ship your purchases home; others are less willing to do so, but can be coaxed. Waiting your turn in line is essential, especially in crowded food shops, where you'll often have to take a ticket from a dispenser.

Hours of Business

Many shops and businesses are open six days a week, Monday through Saturday (no lunch closing). Galleries, antiques dealers, and one-of-a-kind shops open and shut when they please. Some shops now also open on Sundays, from noon to 6, especially in designated tourist areas around Rembrandtplein, Leidseplein, Damrak and Dam Square, the red-light district, and main shopping streets. Many shops are closed Monday mornings and open late on Thursdays (usually until 9). The rest of the week, hours are usually 9 until 5, or 8.

Sales Tax

A 19-percent VAT, or value-added tax (called BTW in Dutch), is included in prices on consumer goods. Tax-free shopping for tourists is available at participating shops, but the mail-in refund (of 13.5 percent) is only available when you spend 136 euros or more in one day at one shop (see Hotlines or visit info@taxfree.nl or www.easytaxfree.com).

The Lowdown

Budding prospects... Raising its head like a sunflower above the dozen other bloom vendors at the famous floating Bloemenmarkt (see "Outdoor Markets," above) in the Singel is **A.H. Abels en Zoon.** Here the displays are living Dutch miniatures worthy of the Rijksmuseum. You might think that the bulbs you choose are nobody's blooming business, but U.S. and Canadian customs won't let you bring them home if they don't have a "phytosanitary certificate," i.e., a clean bill of health. You can spend a lot of money on bulbs, so make sure the ones you buy are approved for export. You can buy health-certified bulbs at Abels en Zoon, but you'll have to ship them yourself from the post office. Just down the way are **M.M.C. Roozen** and **Aviflora** (on the Internet), equally good and willing to ship your U.S.–approved bulbs (from July–Sept only; the shipping also allows you to dodge the 19 percent VAT). **Laddrak,** less artful, more mass-market (check out the wooden clogs stuffed with tulip bulbs), is well stocked. They also export certified bulbs, which is the main reason to give them your business. Heads with green thumbs can buy marijuana starter kits from Laddrak (and most other flower-market shops); they should produce smokeable plants in 10 days or so. Beware, they're strictly illegal to export. **IVY** on Leidseplein, and **Menno Kroon** on Cornelis Schutstraat, are the city's top florists and the places to go if you're itching for floral art. The bouquets and exotic plants are magnificently baroque, and beautiful people meet here lingering among the orchids. Edible flowers are the house specialty at **Jemi Bloemsierkunst,** a florist/floral art shop in A'dam's oldest house, in the red-light district. Gorgeous—and delicious—bouquets and compositions.

Where you'll be pampered... At **Theresia P.C.** just down the street, you can admire the clothes Beatrix buys (yes, Theresia *does* dress the queen), and perhaps Theresia herself will be the one who escorts you over the polished marble of the ready-to-wear floor and up the spiral staircase to couture heaven. Across and down the street at **Edgar Vos**, matrons, mavens, and 45-ish businesswomen nod their approval as you don the pricey garden-party and socialite attire, while the stylish staff members listen and advise like the psychiatrists they really are. The master himself, **Panc Vergouw**, welcomes you into his tiny couture shop near the Singel canal, and in no time you feel like a minor Grachtengordel socialite yourself, stunned by the magic of sequins and padded black-widow spider outfits suitable for noir society weddings. Across the street at **Dutch Design by Godelief,** Madame Godelief will help you into a white embroidered wedding dress or a tweedy taileur.

Once you've outfitted yourself for serious spending, head to **Kolthoorn Kunst** antiques. You ring the doorbell of a 1662 Golden Bend mansion and are ushered into "the museum where every exhibit can become yours," as the company's slogan runs. The knowledgeable staff manage to make you feel like the owner of the place, and a much greater expert than they, as you gape at the museum-quality Old Dutch furniture, tapestries, and etchings (including several dozen by Rembrandt, for lease). Once you've made your purchase, stride up Rokin to **P.G.C. Hajenius** and celebrate with a cigar in A'dam's "last elegant tobacco shop." As you stand on a thick red carpet under the huge bronze chandelier in the landmark 1915 interior, the genial, portly staff will open a dozen humidors, pouches, and canisters to find you the perfect smoke—possibly the extraordinary house Sumatra cigars, which you can savor in the new backroom cigar-bar and mini tobacco museum. Windmills you may love to hate, but even blowhard cynics can't resist the colorful mobiles at friendly Arianne van der Veen's **Gone With the Wind**, a tiny toy shop that adults and tots will love in equal measure.

SHOPPING | THE LOWDOWN

Everything under one roof... The city's biggest and best-loved department store is **De Bijenkorf** on Dam Square, called the "beehive" by locals. It's a cross between Macy's and Bloomingdale's, with perfume-soaked sales-ladies and a straitlaced, monied feel. Everything under the Dutch sun is there for the taking, if you aren't fazed by steep prices. **Metz & Co.**, an exclusive address at Keizersgracht and Leidsestraat, is worth a visit for the view from the panoramic top-floor cafe. It's a favorite among well-heeled locals in the market for silk scarves, china, art glass, and the like. **Vroom & Dreesmann** is a mass-market outfit on both sides of busy, tacky Kalver-straat that's handy for all the things you forgot to pack (rain gear, notebooks, toothpicks, 220V converters).

Diamonds are a girl's best friend... To believe most guidebooks and promotional brochures, Amsterdam is synonymous with diamonds. Diamond factory tours (see Diversions) are, in fact, among the city's biggest tourist attractions, but several other cities around the globe, including Antwerp, outrank A'dam as diamond-processing centers. No matter. The industry does trace its roots here to the late 1500s, prices are competitive, and there are many long-established, reputable dealers who gladly guarantee in writing the so-called four Cs: carat (weight), cut, color, and clarity. During World War II, when Nazi atrocities wiped out countless other Jewish diamond dynasties, the Van Moppes family escaped to Brazil, returning after the war to reopen what has become prob-ably the biggest operation in town, **Van Moppes Dia-monds**. Their claim to fame is having cut the smallest brilliant in the world, weighing 0.24 milligrams. The **Amsterdam Diamond Center** was created after the war by several big families, including seventh-generation kingpin Paul Asscher, whose family spent eight months cutting the world's biggest diamond—a 3,106-carat rough—into nine gems, including the famed Cullinan I (530 carats) and Cullinan II (317 carats). **Coster Dia-monds** won renown in the 1930s by restyling the 186-carat Koh-i-Noor ("Mountain of Light") into the 108-carat centerpiece of the British royal crown (now in the Tower of London). **Gassan** and **Stoeltie Diamonds** round out the list of the city's top five dealers (there are many others); though smaller, their tours are just as good. Be aware that all the tours end in the salesroom, where you can be made to feel like the least you could do in return is buy a precious stone or two. The Diamond Foundation Amsterdam has a website with info on its many members (www.amsterdam-city-of-diamonds.nl).

Club gear... Clubbing is big in A'dam, and hardcore party fiends outfit themselves at **Clubwear-House**, currently the place for the requisite sequins and feathers and impractical garb needed to stun bouncers into compliance. Buy the latest Dutch, American, British, and German designer duds or used party gear at this Spuistraat boutique, and get party fliers, concert tickets, DJ tapes, and insider's info from the hipsters at the cash register. Similar garments, plus wild hair styling, are on offer at nearby **Housewives on Fire**, a split-level new-and-used clubgear shop and hair salon. After your hair-raising spree, you might even stand a chance of getting into IT or Escape (gee, what a privilege), provided, of course, that your shoes meet the bouncers' standards. When it comes to outrageous footwear—towering clogs, marvelously silly spike heels, FMPs and other un-PC items for the tootsies—try **Antonia by Yvette** or **Shoebaloo**. Further down the club-fashion food chain are **Chill Out,** on the top floor of **De Bijenkorf** department store, and **Velvet Monkees,** at the **Magna Plaza** mall. The best thing about Chill Out isn't the neo-bourgeois, teeny-bopper wear; it's the view. There is no best thing about Velvet Monkeys. For leather, plastic, and S&M club garb, check out **Wasteland,** an aptly named boutique near Spui.

Royal fashions... Yes, everyone knows Amsterdam's worst-kept secret: **Theresia P.C.** dresses Queen Beatrix. Classic but fun, regal but discreet, conservative yet liberal, Theresia's clothes are a miracle of paradox and oxymoron. Even if you can't afford them, go to experience the majesty of her P.C. Hooftstraat premises. Apparently that other P.C. Hooftstraat institution, **Edgar Vos**, has *not* had the privilege of a royal commission. Nonetheless, the reigning lady would doubtless approve of the colorful, classic, richly kitschy creations favored by rich Amsterdam business-women and socialites. The same crowd motors over to **Dutch Design by Godelief** for tweedy taileurs and orientalist evening wear. In a pinch, both the women's and men's floors at **De Bijenkorf**, really the only full-fledged department store in town, would provide the kind of proper, upstanding, practical, yet noble clothes that would suit the royals. The feel is more English than Dutch at **De Jager Country Shop**, but in a sporty moment, Dutch princeling Willem Alexander might find De Jager's stylishly waterproof, laudably masculine clothes suitable for a damp country trot, a canal-boat ride, or a spot of urban cycling. Though there are no women's fashions per se, much of the rain gear and sports clothes, like Barbour rain coats, are unisex. **Metz & Co.**, on the corner of Keizersgracht and Leidsestraat, is the kind of perfumed, exclusive, and specialized department store where monied matrons shop for silk scarves and other accessories with aristocratic flair.

Wacky and one-of-a-kind... You'd think a freewheeling cosmopolis and the gay capital of Europe would be teeming with them, but **De Condomerie** is the city's first and still its lone condoms-only boutique. To prove that there's more to a rubber than meets the eye, this red-light district specialist also sells condom souvenirs, condom T-shirts, edible condoms (try passionfruit), and condom samplers specially designed for anal penetration. Nearby, try the edibles at **Jemi Bloemsierkunst,** a floral art boutique where you munch on tulips and other botanical eye candy. **Trunk Interior Decorators** is an exercise in kitsch, popular with hipsters who've grown allergic to Philippe Starck and his legions of hyper-design Euro imitators. This shop down an alley near Spui is crammed with wacky furnishings and objects, mostly from Morocco and India, including plastic Oriental carpets, suitcases made from recycled tin cans, and mock-silver teapots straight from the souk. For nautical instruments, or anything you ever wanted for your canalboat, try **Andries de Jong b.v.,** the city's most handsome chandler's shop, on Munt Plein near the flower market. The Maritime Museum's gift shop is another great source for ship-related flotsam and jetsam (models, books, posters, accessories; see Diversions for business hours). At the new **Brilmuseum** the spectacles are the spectacle: Every imaginable type of eyeglass frame and lens is on show and for sale at this unusual boutique-museum. No one in town can hold a candle to **Pontifex**, located between the Jordaan and the royal palace, which sells only candles, many handmade right there. The other side of this same

U-shaped shop, **Kramer,** is where a Mr. Kramer runs his celebrated doll hospital, working wonders on ragged Raggedy Anns and beheaded Barbies. **Gone With the Wind** is a wonderland of sculptural mobiles and **Frozen Fountain** showcases plenty of impractical but irresistible *objets* by young Dutch designers.

Bags and beans... The Dutch, among the world's earliest and most active coffee and tea drinkers, continue to import, roast, and consume some of the world's finest aromatic caffeine sources. **Wijs & Zonen** has been at its current location—among the gay bars, smoking coffee shops, and grubby hotels of the red-light district—since 1828, and little of the interior has changed. You can mix and match a dozen kinds of coffee beans, or choose the house blends; tea comes in 24 loose-leaf varieties, as well as in packaged form. **Simon Levelt Koffie & Thee** is almost as old (1839) and just as good. This coffee-roasting and tea shop on the edge of the Jordaan—remodeled in 1999—is still full of old coffee grinders and paraphernalia and offers dozens of fragrant blends. The other equally venerable Simon Levelt shop, facing Centraal Station, is always packed. At age 138 in 2002, the red-light district's **Geels & Co.** is a relative newcomer on the coffee and tea scene, but it's right up there in quality and atmosphere and it has a charming coffee and tea museum on its second floor. Try **Brandmeester's** for a contrast: This sleek, ultra-modern coffee-roasting shop and tasting bar in glitzy Van Baerlestraat, around the corner from P.C. Hooftstraat, has palsy service to counter its hard-edged decor. Its American-style brownies would pass muster stateside.

Fashion forward... Carla V, a custom ladies' leather boutique run by irrepressible Carla Van der Vorst, is one of the big draws at the new Cornelis Schuytstratt shopping area. Choose the color and length of your posh lammycoat, guaranteed "as soft as your own skin." Skinflints should abstain. If silk is what turns you on, **McLennan's** kimonos, ties, scarfs, and accessories are for you, artfully displayed in a chic silk-only boutique between the Jordaan and royal palace. At nearby **Van Ravenstein**, twin Dutch/Belgian designer boutiques, you're likely to bump into media stars, gallerists, and the monied creative crowd of both sexes buying camelhair urban safari suits, vests made from zippers and embroidered evening wear, retro-hip felt or woolen garments, and discreet, darkly hip suits or pantsuits by Dries van Noten et al.

Everything you always wanted to know about sex...
De Condomerie is the first place slavering sex tourists go in the red-light district to gawk at the window displays, much to the irritation of the staff of this exuberant condom boutique. You can pick up more than just flavored rubbers here; there are T-shirts, toys, key rings, and underwear decorated with or incorporating condoms. The red-light district isn't the only—or even the best—place to stock up on goodies made from rubber, leather, and the like. At **Female & Partners**, near the royal palace, you'll find all sorts of women's lingerie and charming sex articles for women who like women, women who like men, and those who like both. If the vibrators make you hesitant to enter this chic shop, you can order your goodies by phone, mail, or over the Internet. Leather is the name of the hardcore game at **Vero-Over**, an extraordinary shop way out by the Western Islands. Expect made-to-order leather couture items (the mind boggles), S&M accessories, pigskin pants, leather undies, plus all the usual off-the-rack leather paraphernalia fresh from the tannery. Closer in but just as outlandish is **Wasteland,** where, when it comes to getting into this boutique's club nights and raves, "the decision of the bitch is final" (their words). Leather, uniforms, plastic, rubber, metal, cross-dress, and fetish-glam. What fun!

For foot fetishists... Finding Dutch-designed shoes is a challenge not always worth the trouble, but **Panara**, a pricey, chic shop on P.C. Hooftstraat, sells seriously attractive, classic, and elegant footwear for well-heeled women, designed by Hans van Paridon but made in Italy. Trendies clatter over to **Antonia by Yvette,** a Grachtengordel boutique for Dutch designer Lola Pagoda's fanciful shoes and clogs. At P.C. Hooftstraat's **Shoebaloo**—make your own fun just repeating the name aloud—the decor may be by celebrated architect/artist/designer Borek Sipek, a Czech who has been in Holland for decades, but the Dutch and European women's footwear itself is surprisingly midmarket conventional.

Home designs... At **Frozen Fountain**, a stylish Grachten-gordel showroom near Nieuwe Spiegelstraat, contemporary Dutch designer furniture and other *objets* by Marcel Wanders—and a dozen other fashioners of the gorgeous-but-impractical—draw the media crowd and beautiful people from surrounding canal houses and converted warehouses. At Peter van Kesteren and Helene van Ruiten's **Galerie Binnen**, another name-dropper's Grachtengordel address, you'll find Italian, Dutch, and international interior and industrial design: furniture, vases, jewelry, and more. Less pricey but still chic are **Koot Light & Design** and **Koot Living**, a series of large shops favored by Jordaan yuppies seeking sleek halogen lamps by Dutch designers Gerard van den Berg or Anette van Edmund, or vaguely art-deco furniture and housewares, including Italian tea kettles and flatware. Koot's chief competition is **Wonen 2000 International Design Centrum,** another set of shops distributed around several multistory buildings on the same busy Jordaan street. This international design shop might be in New York except for the Dutch appliances and garden furniture.

Mosquito nets and hammocks... When the bugs rise from the canals like summer storm clouds, rush over to **Klamboe Unlimited**, Holland's top retail and wholesale supplier of mosquito nets. The plantation-style showroom near the Jordaan and Westerkerk displays a wide variety of round or square nets to cover your bed (and transform it into an exotic love nest), along with several hammocks. **Marañon** is another outfit selling mosquito nets; its hammocks are from the East Indies.

The art scene... Once you've shown at **Galerie Paul Andriesse**, your reputation as an artist is pretty much made. Established avant-garde abstract and figurative artists, international and Dutch, make this Jordaan gallery the Leo Castelli of A'dam. Younger, hungrier talents show at Adriaan ten Have's **Torch** gallery, a prime venue for progressive contemporary art. The occasional international name makes this hip Jordaan gallery *the* place to hobnob with the young, beautiful, and creative. Nearby at **De Praktijk**, Dirk Vermeulen, a dentist until the early 1990s, has converted his practice into a forum for contemporary Dutch artists and is the exclusive (posthumous) agent for the furniture-art of (the recently deceased) monk Dom van der Laan. **Galerie Fons Welters** and **Galerie de Expeditie** are the quintessential Jordaan and Grachtengordel galleries, specializing in functional art and contemporary work by young Dutch and other artists. In a relatively new gallery area on the southern end of Lijnbaansgracht is **Galeriecomplex**, a grouping of six up-and-coming showrooms in adjoining buildings with connecting doors. Each gallery is different in style, taste, and quality, showing trendy Dutch and international contemporary works. Back in the Grachtengordel, **Galerie Binnen**, the world-class interior and industrial design gallery, showcases Dutch and European artists and artisans—its owners, Peter van Kesteren and Helene van Ruiten, are local art-world movers and shakers. A'dam's premier photography foundation, **Huis Marseille,** in the Grachtengordel, shows top international art photographers (see Diversions for more). Note: Most A'dam galleries are on the Internet (www.akka.nl).

Very old things... At Rokin, near Munt Plein, you'll come across two equally grand dealers for serious spenders. One, **Premsela & Hamburger**, is arguably A'dam's most reliable antique silver dealer. Poise and polish are the operative words here, with authentic silver baubles ranging from 19th-century English salt cellars to 18th-century tea strainers and art-deco silverware. Next door, the suave staff at **V. O. F. Mathieu Hart,** discreet antiquarians since 1878, will help you fall in love with rare old prints, lithographs, and 18th-century delftware or grandfather clocks. **Kolthoorn Kunst** is an antiques shop made to look and feel like a museum, and even the Rembrandt etchings are available for lease. Persnickety but knowledgeable, Martin Ex at **Ex Antiquiteiten** specializes in textile artworks (needlepoint) from the 17th through 19th centuries. His tiny Grachtengordel shop is also crammed with priceless furniture and objects. As for the city's premier antiques quarter, there are almost 100 reputable dealers in the Nieuwe Speigelstraat alone—far too many to list. Just stuff your wallet and stride out.

Kid stuff... When the kids clamor for their fair share of conspicuous consumption, head to **Magna Plaza**, a mall housed in the turn-of-the-century former Post & Telephone office facing the royal palace at Dam Square:

upstairs are Bam Bam, one of the city's chicest kiddie-clothes boutiques, and Velvet Monkeys, where the post-pubescent set will go ape for the trendy house duds. **De Looier Kunst & Antiekcentrum**, ostensibly an antiques and art market, is actually a covered flea market in the Jordaan where the kids will flip over the junk, especially the old Barbie dolls, teddy bears, pocket knives, Zippo lighters, and maybe even the Aretha Franklin 45s. There's a Renaissance-fair atmosphere on Saturdays at the organic food market at Noordermarkt in the Jordaan (see "Outdoor Markets," above), where you can get all sorts of healthful treats for the children and entertain them with a lively Dutch version of the Punch 'n' Judy show. **Mechanisch Speelgoed**, an old-fashioned toy shop just down the street from Noorderkerk, again in the Jordaan, is stuffed with wooden toys, traditional games, teddy bears, masks, and costumes. The countless colorful mobiles at **Gone With the Wind** are sure to lift your darling's heart. And should your sprout's favorite doll bust its arm or head in your travels, **Kramer**, a delightfully creepy doll hospital not far from the Jordaan, has a kind surgeon named Mr. Kramer ready to Cabbage-Patch things up.

Incredible edibles... Three of the city's friendliest and best-stocked deli and cheese shops, with all the cheeses, young and old, meats (smoked beef), and specialty foods you'll want for your picnics, are **Ron's** in the Jordaan near Westerkerk, **De Kaaskamer** on Runstraat five minutes from the flower market, and **Loekie**, with two locations, one on Utrechtstraat south of Rembrandtplein, the other on Prinsengracht near Leidestraat. A new, upscale catering and take-out joint with adjoining brasserie, **Van Dam** is *the* place for Dutch-French delicacies at premium prices. Chocoholics will appreciate **J.G. Beune**, an old (1882) and old-fashioned confectionery shop west of Centraal Station. Don't miss the Amsterdammertjes—liquor- or chocolate-filled sweets suggestively modeled on the phallus-shaped no-parking poles that line A'dam's streets. **Holtkamp** is a feast for both palate and eyes: The gorgeous Piet Kramer interior is a 1923 art-deco masterwork; Cees and Petra Holtkamp's chocolates, pastries, and croquettes (there are 12 pastry chefs in the basement) are possibly the best in town. A'dam is famous for its salted licorice—you'll either love or hate it—and **The Natural Health Company** is an excellent source for it. This old shop off Munt Plein has a wide selection of the sticky stuff, an equally wide selection of cheesy delftware, plus a grab-bag of homeopathic cures in case you get indigestion. The brainchild of larger-than-life *genever* and liquor distiller Cees van Wees, De Admiraal (see Dining and Cafes)—a *proeflokaal* (tap house) on Herengracht—is a wonderful place to stock up on A'dam's only locally made gin. Tasty tulips with salmon or strawberries are on offer at **Jemi Bloemsierkunst,** a floral art boutique specializing in edible flowers.

Smokes... Tobacco smoking has been the national pastime since Holland's Golden Age. **P.G.C. Hajenius** is a city landmark on Rokin, a venerable tobacconist whose slogan is "the last of the elegant tobacco shops." Even if you're allergic to smoke and feel like kicking fat cats who puff away on smelly cigars, peek into the lovely 1915 interior: thick red carpet, marble and wood paneling, a huge bronze chandelier hanging from gilt beams. Dozens of wooden cigar boxes, humidors, and canisters of pipe tobacco hold some of the world's best tobaccos, including the celebrated hand-rolled house Sumatra cigars. The back rooms house a cigar-bar, library, and mini cigar museum. **J.N. Andringa Takaben** is the other serious tobacconist in town, and has been purveying top-quality products at Munt Plein since 1902. The interior is simple compared to the competition's, but the handmade cigars and specially selected pipe tobaccos are just as good. If pies are your thing check out **Smokiana,** a pipe museum-shop with tribal, antique, and ultra-modern puffing equipment.

Book nooks... If you've forgotten to pack reading material, don't despair: Most Dutch bookstores carry books in English. The best source, however, is the **American Book Center**, a vast discount operation near Dam, with everything you'd find at home, and at reasonable prices. **Athenaeum Boekhandel**, at central Spui, is both a bookstore and an experience: Some local intellectuals seem to live here, eternally browsing the excellent selection, English-language books, novels, and magazines. **The English Bookshop** is a small, cozy Jordaan shop favored by English expats; the mid- or highbrow novels and literature on its shelves reflect the chatty English owner's taste. The upscale British chain **Waterstone's** has a wide selection from U.K. and U.S. publishers, including literature on Amsterdam and Holland, near Spui. Henk Brinkman, part-owner of atmospheric **Antiquariaat Brinkman**, is the leading light in Amsterdam's antique book trade. One of just a handful of booksellers in the 1950s, Brinkman has seen the trade flourish, turning Amsterdam into a European center for bibliophiles, historians, collectors, and researchers. Today, more than 125 shops specializing in everything from musical scores to medieval medical texts, early cookbooks, 18th-century travel guides, and everything else ever printed anywhere in the world are scattered around the center of town, but concentrated around Spui. Many of these books are in English. A detailed map of antiquarian and secondhand bookshops is on sale all over town, and from the publisher, DE KAN (tel 020/627–5794, Binnenkadijk 237). Check www.nwa.nl for a complete listing of booksellers. **Evenaar**, off Singel, is a travel-only specialist, with a good selection of new and used books in English.

Clogs, china, and kitsch... Dozens of souvenir boutiques around town sell delftware with a small "d" (i.e., junk). At **Galleria d'Arte Rinascimento**, near Westerkerk, you can buy the junk and the real thing, too: Royal Delftware with a capital "D." Both the knockoffs and genuine articles come in sublimely ridiculous shapes: ceramic clogs, Christmas ornaments, contorted vases, and the like. **Gassan,** a diamond-polishing house, has a Royal Delftware painting workshop and boutique. You're just gonna love the high-camp atmosphere at **De Klompenboer**, A'dam's celebrated cloggery, just a few hundred yards south of Nieuwmarkt; live chickens peck at the wood shavings from the *klompen* made by Ye Olde Shoemaker, and a woman in "traditional" costume paints these works of contemporary art before your very eyes. Over at the Bloemenmarkt, **Laddrak** stuffs brightly painted wooden clogs with U.S.-certified tulip bulbs.

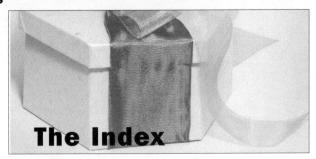

The Index

A.H. Abels en Zoon. Fragrant flower and plant shop in the floating market. Health-certified bulbs, no shipping.... *Tel 020/622–7441, RonAbels@cs.com. Singel 490–494, trams 4, 9, 14, 16, 24, 25 to Munt Plein. Closed Sun.*

(see p. 156)

American Book Center. Multistory discount bookstore.... *Tel 020/625–5537, info@abc.nl or www.abc.nl. Kalverstraat 185, trams 4, 9, 14, 16, 24 to Dam or Spui. Open Mon–Sat 10–8, Thur 10–10, Sun 10–6.* **(see p. 166)**

Amsterdam Diamond Center. Serious gem complex on Dam Square founded by 7th-generation diamond kingpin Paul Asscher.... *Tel 020/624–5787. Rokin 1–5, trams 1, 2, 4, 5, 9, 13, 16, 17, 24, 25 to Dam Square. Open daily 9:45–5:30.* **(see p. 158)**

Andries de Jong b.v. Amsterdam yachtsmen drop anchor at this pricey chandler's shop.... *Tel 020/624–5251, info@andriesdejong.nl or www.andriesdejong.nl. Munt Plein 8, trams 4, 9, 14, 16, 24, 25 to Munt Plein. Closed Sun.*

(see p. 160)

Antiquariaat Brinkman. Leading antique bookstore.... *Tel 020/623–8353, www.nvva.nl/brinkman. Singel 319, trams 1, 2, 5 to Spui. Closed Sun.* **(see p. 167)**

Antonia by Yvette. Grachtengordel boutique for wild or merely hip Dutch shoes and clogs.... *Tel 020/627–2433, www.antoniabyyvette.nl. Gasthuismolensteeg 6, 12 and 16, trams 1, 2, 5, 13, 14, 17 to Paleisstraat or Raadhuisstraat. Open Mon 1–6, Tue–Sat 11–6.* **(see pp. 159, 162)**

Athenaeum Boekhandel. The ultimate A'dam bookstore, at central Spui, with a wide selection of books, novels, and magazines in English.... *Tel 020/622–3933, info@athenaeum.nl or www.athenaeum.nl. Spui 14–16, trams 1, 2, 5 to Spui. Newsstand open daily. Bookstore opens Mon at noon. Closed Sun.* **(see p. 166)**

Aviflora. One of the few flower market shops with U.S.–certified bulbs and Internet ordering.... *Tel 020/622–6592, info@aviflora.nl or www.aviflora.nl. Singel 522, trams 4, 9, 14, 16, 24, 25 to Munt Plein. Closed Sun.* **(see p. 156)**

Brandmeester's. Trendy, updated coffee-roasting shop.... *Tel 020/675–7888. Van Baerlestraat 13, trams 2, 3, 5, 12 to Stedelijk Museum.* **(see p. 161)**

Brilmuseum. Museum-shop for eyeglass aficionados.... *Tel 020/421–2414, www.brilmuseumamsterdam.nl. Gasthuis-molensteeg 7, all trams to Dam square. Closed Sun.*
(see p. 160)

Carla V. Dutch designer Carla van der Vorst's new leather clothing boutique: coats, skirts, bags, and belts. You choose the style and length, Carla dyes the duds whatever color you like.... *Tel 020/672–0404, Cornelis Schuytstraat 45, tram 2 to Cornelis Schuystraat. Tue–Sat 11–5:30.* **(see p. 161)**

Chill Out. See **De Bijenkorf.**

Clubwear-House. Clubwear, DJ tapes, tickets, and club info.... *Tel 020/622–8766, www.clubwearhouse.nl. Spuistraat 242, trams 1, 2, 5 to Spui. Open 11–6, closed Sun–Mon.*
(see p. 159)

Coster Diamonds. One of the biggest, glitziest diamond operations in town.... *Tel 020/305–5555, info@costerdiamonds.com or www.costerdiamonds.com. Paulus Potterstraat 2–6, trams 2, 3, 5, 12 to Museumplein. Open daily 9–5.* **(see p. 158)**

De Bijenkorf/Chill Out. The "beehive," A'dam's biggest and best department store, on Dam Square.... *Tel 020/621–8080. Dam Square 1, trams 1, 2, 4, 5, 9, 13, 16, 17, 24, 25 to Dam Square. Open Thur until 9, Sun noon–6.* **(see pp. 158, 159)**

De Condomerie. The city's first condom boutique.... *Tel 020/ 627–4174, condoms@condomerie.com or www.con*

Singel 348, trams 1, 2, 5, to Spui. Open Mon–Fri 12–6, Sat 11–5. **(see p. 167)**

Ex Antiquiteiten. Tiny Grachtengordel antiques shop selling rare needlepoint art, furniture, and objects.... *Tel 020/625-5180, ex@xs4all.nl. Gasthuismolensteeg 8, trams 1, 2, 5, 13, 14, 17 to Paleisstraat or Raadhuisstraat. Open Thur–Sat 11–6, or by appointment.* **(see p. 164)**

Female & Partners. Chic retail and mail-order boutique for "sex articles for women"—lingerie, dildoes, and other imaginative toys.... *Tel 020/620-9152, www.femaleandpartners.nl. Spuistraat 100, all trams (except 18, 22) to Dam. Open 11–6, Sun–Mon 1–6.* **(see p. 162)**

Frozen Fountain. Dutch designer furniture, neo–Star Trek clothes and *objets* in a trendy showroom near the Nieuwe Spiegelstraat antiques quarter.... *Tel 020/622-9375. Prinsengracht 629, trams 16, 24, 25 to Prinsengracht. Open Mon–Fri 10–5, Sat 12–5. Closed Sun.* **(see pp. 161, 163)**

Galerie Binnen. International interior and industrial design fills this serious Grachtengordel gallery.... *Tel 020/625-9603. Keizersgracht 82, trams 1, 2, 5, 17 to Martelgracht. Open Tue–Sat noon–6 and 1st Sun of month 2–5.* **(see pp. 163, 164)**

Galeriecomplex. Six galleries under the same roof (the Living Room, Lumentravo, Metis NI, Akinci, Van Wijngaarden, Vous etes ici), showing Dutch contemporary works.... *For info call Ron Lang at tel 020/638-9863. Lijnbaansgracht 314–318, trams 6, 7, 10, 16, 24, 25 to Marnixplein. Open Wed–Sat 1–6. Closed Sun except 1st Sun of month.* **(see p. 164)**

Galerie de Expeditie. Grachtengordel contemporary art gallery with up-and-coming talents.... *Tel 020/620-4758, galerie@de-expeditie.com. Leliegracht 47, trams 13, 14, 17 to Westerkerk. Open Tue–Sat 10:30–6.* **(see p. 164)**

Galerie Fons Welters. Hip Jordaan gallery showing functional and avant-garde art and top contemporary work by young artists.... *Tel 020/623-3046. Bloemstraat 140, trams 13, 14, 17 to Lijnsbaangracht/Rozengracht. Open Wed–Sat 1–6, 1st Sun of month 2–5. Closed mid-July–early Sept.* **(see p. 164)**

Galerie Paul Andriesse. Top gallery on the edge of the Jordaan for established avant-garde artists…. *Tel 020/623-6237, andriesse@emonet.nl. Prinsengracht 116, trams 10 to Marnixplein or 13, 14, 17 to Westerkerk. Open Tue–Fri 11–1 and 2–6, Sat 2–6, 1st Sun of month 2–6.* **(see p. 163)**

Galleria d'Arte Rinascimento. Delftware of every conceivable type is sold in this nondescript but well-stocked emporium in the shadow of Westerkerk…. *Tel 020/622-7509. Prinsengracht 170, trams 13, 14, 17 to Westerkerk. Sun 10–5.*
(see p. 167)

Gassan. One of the city's top 5 diamond houses. Good tours; also sells Royal Delftware…. *Tel 020/622-5333. Nieuwe Uilenburgerstraat 173–175, trams 9, 14 to Mr. Visserplein, Metro to Nieuwemarkt. Open daily 9–5.* **(see pp. 158, 167)**

Geels & Co. A coffee-roasting and tea-importing establishment in the red-light district since 1864…. *Tel 020/624-0683. Warmoesstraat 67, trams 4, 9, 16 to Beursplein. Closed Sun.* **(see p. 161)**

Gone With the Wind. Nearly 100 mobiles, plus traditional toys…. *Tel 020/423-0230, info@gonewind-mobiles.com, www.gonewindmobiles.com. Vijzelstraat 22, trams 16, 24, 25 to Herengracht. Closed Mon.* **(see pp. 157, 161, 165)**

Holtkamp. Homemade chocolates, pastries, and croquettes spread out in a gorgeous 1923 art-deco interior…. *Tel 020/624-8757. Vijzelgracht 15, trams 16, 24, 25 to Prinsengracht. Closed Sun.* **(see p. 165)**

Housewives on Fire. Clubwear and hair-styling for serious House fiends…. *Tel 020/622-9818, info@housewiveson fire.a2000.nl or www.xs4all.nl/~housew. Spuistraat 102, trams 1, 2, 5, 13, 17 to Molsteeg. Open daily 10–7, Thur until 9.* **(see pp. 159)**

Huis Marseille. The city's top photo exhibitions, at a nonprofit foundation…. *Tel 020/531-8989, huismarseille@wxs.nl or www.huismarseille.nl. Keizersgracht 401, trams 1, 2, 5, 11 to Keizersgracht. Open Tue–Sun 11–5.* **(see p. 164)**

IVY. Creative, postmodern-baroque florist across from the American Hotel…. *Tel 020/623-6561. Leidseplein 35, trams 1, 2, 5, to Leidseplein. Closed Sun.* **(see p. 156)**

Jemi Bloemsierkunst. Gorgeous bouquets, exotic plants, and the house specialty—edible flowers. In a historic landmark building in the red-light district.... *Tel 020/625-6034, bloemen@jemi.nl. Warmoesstraat 83a, all trams to Centraal Station. Closed Sun.* **(see pp. 157, 160, 166)**

J.G. Beune. Old-fashioned chocolate shop and bakery west of Central Station.... *Tel 020/624-8356. Haarlemmerdijk 156–158, tram 3 to Haarlemmerplein. Closed Sun.* **(see p. 165)**

J.N. Andringa Takaben. A simple shop founded in 1902 on Munt Plein, with excellent handmade cigars and pipe tobacco. Will ship anywhere.... *Tel 020/623-2836. Reguliersbreestraat 2, trams 4, 9, 14, 16, 24, 25 to Munt Plein. Open daily, Sun noon–5.* **(see p. 166)**

Klamboe Unlimited. Top supplier of mosquito nets and other tropi-colonial fare.... *Tel 020/622-9492, info@klamboe-unlimited.com. or www.klambo-unlimited.com. Prinsengracht 232, trams 13, 14, 17 to Westerkerk. Opens Mon at 1. Closed Sun. Oct–Mar weekends only noon–5.* **(see p. 163)**

Kolthoorn Kunst. An antiques showroom in a 17th-century mansion with some of the city's finest Old Dutch furniture, delftware, tapestries, and etchings.... *Tel 020/622-1010, geelvinck@euronet.nl. Herengracht 518, trams 16, 24, 25 to Herengracht. Open by appointment only.* **(see pp. 157, 164)**

Koot Light & Design. 2 hip home-design boutiques west of Dam Square.... *Tel 020/626-4830. Raadhuisstraat 52–54 & 55, trams 13, 14, 17 to Singel. Open Thur until 9. Closed Sun.* **(see p. 163)**

Koot Living. More vaguely art-deco Dutch furnishings.... *Tel 020/625-0770. Rozengracht 10, trams 13, 14, 17 to Westerkerk or Lijnbaansgracht. Open Thur until 9. Closed Sun.* **(see p. 163)**

Laddrak. A Bloemenmarkt florist who will export your health-certified bulbs for you.... *Tel 020/625-4842. Singel 548, trams 4, 9, 14, 16, 24, 25 to Munt Plein. Closed Sun.* **(see pp. 156, 167)**

Loekie. 2 delis stuffed with delicious Dutch cheeses and specialty meats.... *Tel 020/624-3740. Utrechtstraat 57, tram 4 to*

Keizersgracht. Also tel 020/624-4300. Prinsengracht 705, trams 1, 2, 5 to Prinsengracht. Closes Wed at 1, closed Sun. **(see p. 165)**

M.M.C. Roozen. Good source of U.S.–approved bulbs. At flower market.... *Tel 020/625-7176. Singel 496, trams 4, 9, 14, 16, 24, 25 to Munt Plein. Closed Sun.* **(see p. 156)**

Magna Plaza. Upscale 5-level mall in the turn-of-the-century Post & Telephone office building facing the Royal Palace.... *Tel 020/626-9199. Nieuwezijds Voorburgwal 182, all trams (except 18, 22) to Dam. Open daily until 7.*
(see pp. 159, 164)

Marañon. Mosquito nets and hammocks displayed in a colonial atmosphere.... *Tel 020/622-5938, hammocks@mara non.net or www.maranon.net. Singel 488–490, trams 4, 9, 14, 16, 24, 25 to Munt Plein. Open daily 10–5:30, until 6 in summer.* **(see p. 163)**

McLennan's. Pure silk, by the yard or snipped into kimonos, ties, scarves, and other accessories.... *Tel 020/622-7693. Hartenstraat 22, trams 13, 14, 17 to Westerkerk. Opens Mon at 1. Closed Sun.* **(see p. 161)**

Mechanisch Speelgoed. Old-fashioned Jordaan toy store.... *Tel 020/638-1680. Westerstraat 67, trams 3, 10 to Marnix-plein. Closed Sun and Wed.* **(see p. 165)**

Menno Kroon. Hip new floral arts boutique where the beautiful people spend their euros on gorgeous blooms.... *Tel 020/679-1950. Cornelis Schuytstraat 11, tram 2 to Cornelis Schuytstraat. Closed Sun.* **(see p. 156)**

Metz & Co. Exclusive Grachtengordel department store at the junction of Keizersgracht and Leidsestraat. Panoramic cafe on top floor.... *Tel 020/624-8810. Keizersgracht 455, trams 1, 2, 5, to Keizersgracht. Open Thur until 9, Sun 12–5.*
(see pp. 158, 160)

The Natural Health Company. Famous salted licorice, homeo-pathic cures, and tacky souvenirs are stuffed into this atmos-pheric shop facing Munt Plein.... *Tel 020/624-4533. Vijzelstraat 1, trams 4, 9, 14, 16, 24, 25 to Munt Plein. Opens Sun at 1.* **(see p. 165)**

P.G.C. Hajenius. Elegant 1915 tobacco shop, cigar bar, and mini-museum. Will ship anywhere.... *Tel 020/623-7494, www.hajenius.com. Rokin 96, trams 4, 9, 14, 16, 24, 25 to Spui. Open daily, Thur until 9, Sun noon–5.* **(see pp. 157, 166)**

Panara. Elegant yet hip Dutch-designed shoes for women 30 and over.... *Tel 020/622-1908. P.C. Hooftstraat 124, trams 2, 3, 5, 12 to Stedelijk Museum. Opens Mon at 1, open Thur until 9.* **(see p. 162)**

Panc Vergouw. Small couture shop near the Singel canal where businesswomen and socialites order sequined silks or more conservative, tailored woolens and cottons.... *Tel 020/428-0655. Oude Leliestraat 1, trams, 13, 14, 17 to Westerkerk. Opens Mon at 1. Closed Sun.* **(see p. 157)**

Pontifex/Kramer. 2 shops in 1: candles galore at Pontifex; toy repair at Mr. Kramer's creepy doll hospital.... *Tel 020/626-5274. Reestraat 18–20, trams 13, 14, 17 to Westerkerk. Closed Sun.* **(see pp. 160, 161)**

De Praktijk. Jordaan gallery for contemporary Dutch artists; exclusive agents for Dom van der Laan's extraordinary furniture.... *Tel 020/639-1316. Lauriergracht 96, trams 13, 14, 17 to Westerkerk. Wed–Sat and by appointment.* **(see p. 163)**

Premsela & Hamburger. Possibly the city's best source for buying or restoring antique or contemporary silver.... *Tel 020/627-5454, info@premsela.com or www.premsela.com. Rokin 98, trams 4, 9, 14, 16, 24, 25 to Spui. Open Mon–Fri 9:30–5:30, Sun noon–5, or by appointment.* **(see p. 164)**

Ron's. Dutch deli and cheese shop in the Jordaan.... *Tel 020/624-8802. 2e Tuindwarsstraat 3, trams 3, 10 to Marnixplein. Closed Sun.* **(see p. 165)**

Shoebaloo. Chic boutique, selling women's footwear that's not as outrageous as you'd expect from the decor.... *Tel 020/671-2210. P.C. Hooftstraat 80, trams 2, 3, 5, 12 to Stedelijk Museum. Opens Mon at noon, open Thur until 9 and 1st Sun of month.* **(see pp. 159, 162)**

Simon Levelt Koffie & Thee. An 1839 coffee-roasting and tea shop in the shadow of Westerkerk has expanded, with 3 other locations, but the same great coffee.... *Tel 020/624-0823,*

SHOPPING | THE INDEX

www.simonlevelt.nl. Prinsengracht 180, trams 13, 14, 17 to Westerkerk. Closed Sun. **(see p. 161)**

Smokiana. Pipe museum and shop with pipes primitive to postmodern…. *Tel 020/421-1779. Prinsengracht 488, trams 1, 2, 5 to Prinsengracht. Closed Tue and Sun.* **(see p. 166)**

Stoeltie Diamonds. Small, old, reliable diamond dealer near Rembrandtplein…. *Tel 020/623-7601. Wagenstraat 13–17, trams 4, 9, 14 to Rembrandtplein or Muziektheater. Open daily 8:30–5.* **(see p. 158)**

Theresia P.C. Luxurious P.C. boutique, where ready-to-wear (downstairs) ranges from Dfl 800–10,000 for a dress…. *Tel 020/679-6225. P.C. Hooftstraat 55, trams 2, 3, 5, 12 to Stedelijk Museum. Opens Mon at 1. Closed Sun.*
(see pp. 157, 159)

Torch. Progressive contemporary art, theme shows, and the occasional international name give this Jordaan gallery its hipster cachet…. *Tel 020/626–0284. Lauriergracht 94, trams 13, 14, 17 to Westerkerk. Open Thur–Sat 2–6.*
(see p. 163)

Trunk Interior Decorators. This anti-design shop in an alley near Spui has plenty of inexpensive wacky imports…. *Tel 020/638-7095. Rosmarijnsteeg 12, trams 1, 2, 5, to Spui. Tue–Sun 11–6.* **(see p. 160)**

V.O.F. Mathieu Hart. Polished century-old 4th-generation antiques dealer near Spui…. *Tel 020/623-1658, Rokin 122, trams 4, 9, 14, 16, 24, 25 to Spui. Closed Sun.*
(see p. 164)

Van Dam. Franco-Dutch caterer with great takeout at regal rates. Also a hip brasserie…. *Tel 020/670-6570. Cornelis Schuytstraat 8–10, tram 2 to Cornelis Schuytstraat. Open daily.*
(see p. 165)

Van Moppes Diamonds. The biggest diamond operation in town. Draws crowds of tourists…. *Tel 020/676-1242, info@moppesdiamonds.com or www.moppesdiamonds.com. Albert Cuypstraat 2–6, trams 16, 24, 25 to Albert Cuypstraat. Open daily 8:45–5:45.* **(see p. 158)**

Van Ravenstein. Upscale Dutch/Belgian designer boutiques in the Grachtengordel, for women and men; good for handmade sweaters, leather pants, and 2-piece suits.... *Tel 020/639-0067. Runstraat 18–22 and Huidenstraat 27, trams 1, 2, 5, to Spui. Open Mon 1–6, Tue–Fri 11–6, Thur until 9, Sat until 5. Closed Sun.* **(see p. 161)**

Velvet Monkees. See **De Bijenkorf.**

Vero-Over. Off-the-rack and made-to-order leather and rubber couture, mostly for the hardcore S&M crowd.... *Tel 020/625-1989, info@vero-over.com. Oostzaanstraat 60, bus 22 to Oostzaanstraat.. Open Mon–Sat 11–7, until 9 on Thur. Closed Sun.* **(see p. 162)**

Vroom & Dreesmann. Vast, mid- to downmarket department store scattered in several buildings on Kalverstraat.... *Tel 020/622-0171. Kalverstraat 201–221, trams 4, 9, 14, 16, 24, 25 to Dam Square or Spui. Opens Mon at 11, open until 9 on Thur. Closed Sun.* **(see p. 158)**

Wasteland. Kinky latex clubwear, plus all sorts of S & M "toys." Don't bring the kids.... *Tel 061/557-1306. Nieuwezijdsvoorburgwal 332. Open Tue–Sun 1–6, until 9 Thur–Sun, Closed Mon.* **(see pp. 159, 162)**

Waterstone's. British chain bookshop near Spui with a wide variety of English and American books.... *Tel 020/638-3821. Kalverstraat 152, trams 1, 2, 5, to Spui. Opens Mon and Sun at 11, open until 9 Thur.* **(see p. 167)**

Wijs & Zonen. One of Amsterdam's oldest (1828) and best coffee-roasting and tea-importing establishments, stuck in the seedy red-light district.... *Tel 020/624-0436, wijs.zonen@wxs.nl. Warmoesstraat 102, trams 4, 9, 16, 24, 25 to Oude Brugsteeg. Open daily.* **(see p. 161)**

Wonen 2000 International Design Centrum. Dutch and international designer home furnishings distributed around several multistory buildings in the Jordaan.... *Tel 020/521-8710. Rozengracht 202–210 and 215–223, trams 13, 14, 17 to Westerkerk. Opens Mon at 1, open until 9 Thur. Closed Sun.* **(see p. 163)**

nigh

6

tlife

A'dam's reputation
as Europe's sex,
drugs, and rock-
and-roll capital
is as solid as ever.
A steady stream
of European

twentysomethings—particularly British and German—flows into the city solely for the night life. You can drink whenever you want; clubs usually open around 10pm, get lively at midnight, and buzz until 4am Monday to Thursday and Sunday (5am Friday and Saturday). Cover charges are usually a low 4 to 6 euros, with drinks for 1.50 to 4 euros. If you're at least 18, you can buy and consume what you please, where you please. Erotic—i.e., porno—venues are rife. The place is lousy with smoking coffee shops where you can puff dope and hash; most have ear-boggling live or canned music. The gay scene is world-class, with venues that cater to every taste, including hardcore S&M.

Hangouts range from tiny, laid-back cafes and bars to huge, exclusive 100 beats-per-minute discos with *sui generis* dress codes and ferocious bouncers (before leaving, always tip the bouncer 1 to 2 euros if you ever want to get back in). For bureaucratic reasons, some clubs call themselves "societies" and theoretically require you to pay a "membership fee" (2 to 4 euros), nearly always waived at the door. Clubwear boutiques (see Shopping) cater to serious clubbers keen to get into the top venues—IT, Sinners in Heaven, More, the Supperclub, and Escape.

House of ill repute with a great reputation

There's prostitution, and there's prostitution. In A'dam, streetwalkers are illegal (most are desperate young addicts). Bordellos are not. The most celebrated one in town—a decades-old institution—is Yab Yum, owned and managed by affable Théo Heuft and Madame Monique, his Swiss friend. Everyone loves Yab Yum; especially taxi drivers, who get a hefty tip if they deposit you there. The name: a goddess of love heavily featured in the Kama Sutra. The location: a 17th-century mansion on Singel, far from the sleaze of the red-light district (plus a branch in Rotterdam, and one under construction at Schiphol Airport, due to open in 2002). The women: 20 nightly, all Dutch, well-educated, gorgeous, ages 18 to 24 (with one perfectly preserved 45-year-old). Most are reportedly stewardesses, nurses, students, and housewives—all strictly moonlighting. No one is twisting their arms. The clientele: businessmen, jet-setters, and kinky couples into threesomes or orgies.

(continued on p. 181)

Rave parties, organized by professionals and usually held in warehouses or theaters, are no longer the thing unless you're into acid, spasm-inducing noise (i.e. "music"), and pushy creeps in smelly synthetic sweatsuits. Raves and other "events" (such as "fetish fantasy" nights) are announced via leaflets distributed in clubs, bars, and cafes;

the cover charge is usually about 20 euros. Clubs are hipper, and the harder it is to get into them the better they are. Admittance is based on your look, sexual orientation, and the people you hang out with. As elsewhere, clubs and star DJs spring up like proverbial mushrooms; trends in music come and go. What's hip today—a mix of pumping house, grunge, hypnotic techno and progressive trance, drum & bass, 100-bpm club house, rave, speed garage, R & B, soul, jazz-dance—will be passé tomorrow. Most venues listed here have been around awhile and look likely to last in one form or another. Also see the Dining and Cafes chapter for some of the 1,400 or so brown, white, and designer cafes where people of all ages, looks, and sexual orientations spend a great deal of their time day and night.

Smoke Houses

Here's Dutch ambiguity again: Officially, drug menus are illegal, but all smoking coffee shops have them (they are often small, and you must ask specifically to see one). A typical dope menu (when this book went to press) reads as follows:

House of ill repute (continued)

The set up: a musclebound bouncer leads you up the stairs and rings a buzzer. An elegant guy—a banker by day?—shakes your hand, and initiates you into the mysteries. You can change money in the lobby or use a credit card. The decor: quintessential cat house stuff. There are stalagmite chandeliers, nudes, a lounge with a splashing Venus fountain, and a U-shaped bar where the ladies perch on stools. The price: about 70 euros to get in; about 160 to 480 euros for champagne while you chat. Innocent entertainment can stop there. It's about 340 euros per hour per woman should you decide to mount the faux leopard-skin carpet leading to the 11 luxury bedrooms, fitted out like the extravagant whorehouses of Hollywood westerns but with Jacuzzis and beds big enough for, well, use your imagination. Expensive? To paraphrase Sly and the Family Stone: The nicer the nice, the higher the price. (Yab Yum; tel 020/624-9503, www.yabyum.nl. Singel 295; daily 8pm–4am).

per gram cost: "Skunk," 5.70 to 8.40 euros; "Sauraica," 6.40 euros; "Morocco," hash 5.25 to 13 euros; "Afghanistan," hash 3.60 to 10 euros; "India," 10.50 euros. A single joint is about 3.20 euros. Even in smoking coffee shops, though, you are never limited to smoking the dope: You can eat and drink the stuff, too—in space cakes, brownies, or hash tea. So when ordering food or drinks, make sure you're getting what you want. If you don't partake, that's fine, but you might get a free contact high just eating a sandwich (some places serve health food) or drinking fruit juices or soft drinks. The sale and consumption of alcohol in all smoking coffee shops is theoretically forbidden, part of a successful effort by city officials to bring down their numbers.

Sources

The up-to-the-minute entertainment info sources in English are *Day by Day*, the VVV tourism bureau's straitlaced, tri-weekly magazine, *Gay & Night Magazine*, an alternative entertainment monthly written by and for the gay community and *Shark*, a give-away with a twentysomething, outlandish readership. Rave invitations are found in clubs, bars, shops, and cafes, while rave tickets and insider info are available from the city's top clubwear shops, including **Clubwear-House** (tel 020/622–8766; Spuistraat 242, www.clubwearhouse.nl) and **Wasteland** (see Shopping). For one-stop ticketing and information on music, parties, and the club scene, call or visit the **AUB Uitburo** (tel 0900–0191 [40 euro per minute], www.uitlijn.nl; Leidseplein 26; open daily 9–9).

The Lowdown

Kink on stage... If you're dreaming of breaking into the hardcore live Dutch porno scene and would like to leap onstage to display your prowess, **Casa Rosso**, the city's most famous erotic theater, is the place for you. (You'd better be well endowed.) Nearby, operated by the same porno-meisters, is the **Bananenbar**, where the classic Mexican donkey act has been replaced by a piece of artfully wielded fruit. Audience participation is welcome; fruit is distributed free, and the rest I leave to your imagination.

That arty, multi-culti thing... Fun of a less obscene kind is at **Melkweg**, an A'dam institution that started in hippy days and has evolved into an international multi-media cultural center, with everything from a cafe and smoking coffee shop to music and dance spaces.

Dutch drinking songs... Sing-along cafes, where older locals belt beer and *genever* and then break into old Dutch songs, are a dying breed, but a handful still exist, especially in the Jordaan. That's where you'll find both

Cafe Nol, whose red-vinyl stools prop up local rois-terers, and **Cafe Twee Zwaantjes**, with famously tobacco-stained walls, full-throated singers, and live accordion music. In the same vein, though across town in the east, Cafe Ruk & Pluk (see Dining and Cafes) is a neo-brown cafe run by a jovial gay couple, where mixed locals make merry against the Brazilian carnival backdrop, breaking into song when the spirit moves them.

Smoking out... If you'd sooner forget all of Amsterdam's other special attractions, you can enjoy its tolerant approach to soft-drug use by diverting yourself into oblivion at any one of the 250 or so smoking coffee shops found on practically every street (see You Probably Didn't Know). Center-city establishments are almost exclusively frequented by tourists. City officials estimate that 90 percent of these supposedly laid-back, cool places are now owned by international organized crime, a thought to keep in mind as you plonk down your nice, clean euros. **The Bulldog**, a 28-year-old veteran—filled with bleary-eyed tourists oblivious to the deafening music and snarling staff—is the archetype. It has half a dozen locations downtown and in the red-light district. **The Grasshopper** is strictly for curious tourists, because it's bright and clean and has a big terrace overlooking the docks on Damrak. **Paradox** and **Kadinsky** are among the only center-city places with a neighborhood feel. City and police authorities continue to eliminate as many dope-smoking establishments as they can, so these are here-today, possibly gone-tomorrow addresses.

Painting the town pink... Lesbians have few nightclub venues and tend to organize private parties, announced with leaflets. The lesbian community's most celebrated hangout is **Cafe Saarein II**, an old brown cafe in the Jordaan with a pool table, a woman-watching mezzanine, and a bulletin board where lesbian parties are announced. Since 1999 Saarein has also welcomed gay men. Other, less lavender, venues welcome lesbians, too. As of 2000, there's a women-only disco called **You 2**; and some nights are women-only at the **GETTO** (a bar). One Sunday a month at **Melkweg** there's lesbian dancing-clubbing; the party moves to **Vrankrijk,** a wild "squatter's club," every third Sunday of the month (Planet Pussy is the lip-smacking name of these wild theme nights). Since RoXY

NIGHTLIFE | THE LOWDOWN

burned down in 1999, **IT** has taken over as the city's hippest disco, followed by **More;** both are exclusively for gay men on Saturdays and Wednesdays, but mixed the rest of the week. Dress and act like a glamorous lunatic (feathers and sequins are big) and you'll probably get in. **IT** has heart-stopping techno house music, artificial smoke, lightning-storm spotlights, and a grandstand for voyeurs. **More** is less glam, though that's not what the owners think. Reguliersdwarsstraat is currently the hottest gay area in town; **April** bar, **Soho** bar, and **April's Exit** disco are here. They're among the most fashionable venues for beautiful people, gay and lesbian, who begin their night with a drink at the modern-looking bars, then wander down or across the street for DJ dancing and other disco amusements. Nearby at **Havana's**, a gay cafe-club, things get especially hot on Friday and Sunday nights. Hardcore is the specialty at **The Cockring**, in the leather and S&M gay district on Warmoesstraat. There are the usual ear-splitting house music and blinding lights on the vast dance floor, as well as a particularly active back room where tough guys get up to all sorts of tricks. **COC**, just down the street, is tamer, appealing mostly to local guys in their 30s (Saturday nights are women-only).

Dance fever... The post-pubescents who like to wriggle and scream to deafening vintage hard rock or contemporary ear-exploding noise go to **Arena**, a large venue in a former nunnery. Anyone and everyone dances at **Mazzo**, a big disco in the Jordaan with no dress code, where top DJs spin mostly cutting-edge stuff. The cultural center **Melkweg** has popular disco club nights on Thursday, Friday, and Saturday, where a mixed-age crowd dances to funk, jungle music, hip-hop, soul, R&B, and club-house. Sunday nights are Planet Pussy—women only. At nearby **Paradiso**, the DJ theme nights—so-called VIP club nights, like "Drum & Bass," "Big Beat," or "Speedgarage"—can be a big draw, filling the place to capacity. The in crowd, both gay and straight, dances near Rembrandtplein at exclusive venues like **Sinners in Heaven**, **Escape**, and **IT**, famous for its huge dance floor, sound system, and top DJ theme nights. Ditto **More**, a new club in the Jordaan that considers itself the heir to now-defunct Roxy, and on a par with IT and Sinners in Heaven. **The Back Door**, opened in October 2001, has taken over from Soul Kitchen and features funky vocal, house music and catwalk performances. Gay-only dance clubs are **Cockring**, with a big dance floor and blinding lights, and **Soho** or **Exit**, fashionable, upscale discos on Reguliersdwarsstraat, where you can dance or dress up for drag-queen balls. **COC**, a tame gay cafe-club, offers a variety of theme dance and DJ disco nights. Lesbians dance at **You 2,** Amsterdam's sole women-only disco and at Planet Pussy theme nights at **Melkweg** and **Vrankrijk**.

All that jazz... Jazz is big in A'dam, though performance quality isn't consistent. The biggest and unquestionably the best club is **Bimhuis**, in an old shipping warehouse rebuilt entirely in the late 1990s. The atmosphere is like New York's Village Vanguard, with top names and rapt audiences who smoke, grunt, and groove. Tickets are pricey and hard to get; try the VVV and Uitburo. Two less ambitious but good clubs near Leidseplein are almost interchangeable: **Alto Jazz Cafe**—the city's oldest—and **Bourbon Street**. They're smoky, cozy, and crowded with Americans, English expats, and locals 25 and up. As the names suggest, jazz and blues—most of it cool—is the name of the game. Similar, and nearby, the **Bamboo Bar** offers cocktail-lounge jazz and blues plus a grab bag of world music, Brazilian, folk, and country and western. The **Westergasfabriek** is a converted gas plant where trendies groove to jazz and a blend of everything but house; its motto, hanging on the wall: "Jazz is the teacher. Funk is the preacher. And with hip-hop it won't stop." For experimental jazz—more like contemporary atonal chamber music—**De IJsbreker Muziekcentrum** is a vibrant, cutting-edge venue favored by intellectuals and the designer-stubble set. The Engelbewaarder (see Dining and Cafes), a so-called literary brown cafe, is where intellectuals wearing "I'm Cool" badges hang out in a bluish fog and listen to live cool jazz on Sunday afternoons (and some nights). Cristofori, a big piano repair and sales outfit with a fabulous Prinsengracht location, hosts jazz concerts regularly in its fifth floor auditorium. For jazz info call 020/770-0660 or visit www.jazz-in-amsterdam.nl (see Entertainment).

For fabulous, beautiful people... You'll probably make it into **IT** if you spend enough on your clothes—plumes, sequins, foot-high spikes. This huge, nominally gay club/disco is famous for its jet-setting crowd and wild

NIGHTLIFE | THE LOWDOWN

theme nights. Spot the same jet-setters with mega-wardrobes at **Sinners in Heaven**, an outlandish place with mock-medieval decor fit for a torture chamber, and **Escape,** a vast old theater space done over regularly for theme nights. **The Back Door** and **More,** new to the scene, are tamer, with a media-monied and fashion crowd. The owners of More also run the Supperclub, a restaurant-club-cabaret where the gorgeously braindead lie recumbant on sofas while munching to DJ sounds (see Entertainment for details). **Time,** with minimalist, distressed-iron decor and music to match (the gamut of club sounds), attracts a raunchier, tougher crowd. Intellectual and wannabe hipsters go to the **Westergasfabriek,** where everything but house music is on the sound system—funk, jazz, power soul, Latin, hip-hop, R&B, and boom-boom. Designer 25- to 35-year-olds who don't feel like dancing drift into the Cafe Luxemburg on Spui, or the Cafe Wild-schut (see Dining and Cafes for both), where they meld with the worn leather armchairs and sofas, drink, and listen to mellow jazz and 1970s rock tapes.

For youthquakers... Grungy expats, pimply club crawlers, and the smoking-coffee-shop set love **Arena**, an aptly named teenybopper-plus club in an old nunnery, sound-proofed like an asylum, with an atmosphere to match (there's a youth hostel in the building, too). It's great if you like undiscovered DJs who blast out whatever is currently breaking eardrums. The same crew can also be spotted at **The Bulldog**, that celebrated chain of smoking coffee shops, with loud rock and gruff help. Glamorous young-sters dressed elaborately are welcomed at **IT**, a gay club/disco with mixed nights, set in a dark, cavernous hall. House music throbs, and the stunning IT dancers flex on raised platforms at the command of demonic DJs. **Sinners in Heaven** has a medieval-theme interior that junior S&M practitioners will love. Depending on the night, **Escape**, on Rembrandtplein in a vast theater space, can be full of 20- to 30-year-old trendies. Rejects from the top clubs often drift over to **Mazzo**, a big disco with a nondescript interior in the Jordaan; it has no dress code and plays all kinds of music. **Paradiso**, in a deconsecrated church off Leidseplein, is where clubbers go for rock and new-music concerts. Most bands are local or unknown. Paradiso is also popular for warming up before heading out to the discos. **Melkweg** has Friday and Saturday theme house parties.

For baby-boomers and up... It's not as if the bouncers won't let over-30s into IT, Escape, More, The Back Door, or Sinners in Heaven—the top discos—or any of the other 1,001 youth venues in town. But if you prefer to be around a crowd with more mature elements, head for any of the city's 1,400 cafes (see Dining and Cafes). Or try a music club like **Bimhuis**, the city's top jazz venue, and the three smoky, crowded jazz and blues clubs around Leidseplein— **Alto Jazz Cafe**, **Bourbon Street**, and **Bamboo Bar**. West- **ergasfabriek** is fine for the long-in-tooth, provided they're hip. Gray hairs are sometimes spotted at the Engelbe- waarder, a literary cafe with classic cool jazz. **Mazzo** wel- comes anyone—no matter how old or infirm—willing to pay. You're unlikely to see anyone under 30 at **Cafe Twee Zwaantjes** or **Cafe Nol**; ditto their wilder, eastern- Amsterdam counterpart Cafe Ruk & Pluk.

Where to drink hard... Older intellectuals and literary types favor **Grant Cafe De Still**, where owner Henk Eggens pours the world's best whiskies in his tiny bar. Serious drinkers (and American Hotel guests) lounge at the **Nightwatch Bar**, another time warp of a place where the bartender remembers your name and your favorite drink. **Mulligan's** is a typical Irish bar, with live folk music and a friendly crowd that's both straight and gay, old and young.

Erotic play for gays... Scores of gay bars and discos show porno films, and many have the kind of back rooms—also known as dark rooms—that disappeared elsewhere in the AIDS-ravaged '80s. For example, **The Cockring**, an aptly named hardcore club in the leather and S&M district, is renowned for its back room near the upstairs toilets. The biggest, most glamorous gay club/disco, **IT**, also has a back room, reportedly very feral on Saturday nights. **Exit**, the fashionable gay disco on Reguliersdwarsstraat, hosts drag-queen balls and shows gay out films that whip the boys into a frenzy. Lesbians head instead to **You 2**, a women-only disco, or Planet Pussy theme nights (Sundays, once a month each) at **Melkweg** and **Vrankrijk** or Saturday nights at **COC,** a gay cafe- club-disco.

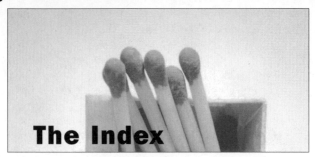

The Index

Alto Jazz Cafe. American and English expats, plus locals, crowd into this smoky, cramped club, the oldest jazz venue in town. Modern and classic tunes are played by the Alto Jazz Ensemble.... *Tel 020/626-3249. Korte Leidsedwars-straat 115, trams 1, 2, 5, 6, 7, 10 to Leidseplein. Open daily until 3–4am.* **(see pp. 185, 187)**

April, Soho, and **April's Exit.** The most famous—and fashion-able—gay bars and discos in town, in the heart of the Reguliersdwarsstraat gay district. Condoms available at all three spots (same owner).... *Tel 020/625-9572 and 625-8788. Reguliersdwarsstraat 36, 37, and 42, trams 1, 2, 5 to Koningsplein. Open daily; bars open until 1–2am, disco until 4–5am.* **(see pp. 184, 185, 187)**

Arena. Huge club on various levels of an old nunnery, where international up-and-comers play very loud crossover rock—or whatever else is breaking—for a decidedly young crowd.... *Tel 020/694-7444. 's Gravesandestraat 51, trams 6, 7, 10 to 's Gravesandestraat. Open Thur–Sun 10pm–3am. Cover charge.* **(see pp. 184, 186)**

The Back Door. Outrageous fashion shows, funky vocal house music, Sunday "tea dance," at this new, hip club disco near Rembrandtplein.... *Tel 020/620-2333, www-backdoor.nl. Amstelstraat 32A, trams 4, 9, 14 to Rembrandtplein. Daily until 4–5am. Cover charge.* **(see pp. 184, 186)**

Bamboo Bar. A mix of jazz, world music, Brazilian, folk, country and western, and blues at this smoky, crowded club.... *Tel 020/624-3993. Lange Leidsedwarsstraat 66, trams 1, 2, 5, 6, 7, 10 to Leidseplein. Open Mon–Sat 10pm–2-3am.* **(see pp. 185, 187)**

Bananenbar. A uniquely appalling place where scantily clad ladies use bananas to surprising effect. Porno emporium crowd; sticky floors.... *Tel 020/627-8945 and 622-4670, www.bananenbar.com. Oude Zijds Achterburgwal 106 and 37, all trams to Centraal Station. Open nightly 8pm–2/3am. Cover charge, but drinks are free.* **(see p. 182)**

Bimhuis. A'dam's prime jazz club for the last 20 years, housed in a landmark building remodeled with a modern bar. American and international big names come here. Free jam sessions several times a week.... *Tel 020/623-1361, www.bimhuis.nl. Oude Schans 73, tram 9, 14 to Mr. Visserplein, Metro to Nieuwemarkt. Tickets usually around Dfl 30.* **(see pp. 185, 187)**

Bourbon Street. More spacious and mainstream than Alto Jazz or Bamboo Bar, this live jazz and blues venue near Leidseplein draws a tame crowd. Minimum age: 23.... *Tel 020/623-3440. Leidsekruisstraat 6, trams 1, 2, 5, 6, 7, 10 to Leidseplein. Open daily until 4–5am.* **(see pp. 185, 187)**

The Bulldog. An institution among smoking coffee shops.... *Tel 020/627-1908. Leidseplein 15, trams 1, 2, 5, 6, 7, 10. Open daily 9–1am.* **(see pp. 183, 186)**

Cafe Nol. There's a U-shaped bar, velvet stools, and lace on the windows at this legendary Jordaan brown cafe. Older crowd, and very, very few tourists. A campy blast from the past.... *Tel 020/624-5380. Westerstraat 109, trams 13, 14, 17 to Westerkerk. Open daily until 2–3am.* **(see pp. 183, 187)**

Cafe Saarein II. Amsterdam's most famous (and notorious) lesbian cafe now welcomes gay men.... *Tel 020/623-4901. Elandsstraat 119, trams 13, 14, 17 to Westerkerk. Open daily 8pm–1am.* **(see p. 183)**

Cafe Twee Zwaantjes. Famous Jordaan sing-along brown cafe, with famously tobacco-stained walls.... *Tel 020/625-2729. Prinsengracht 114, trams 13, 14, 17 to Westerkerk. Open daily until 1am. No cover.* **(see pp. 183, 187)**

Casa Rosso. A bordello-like erotic theater with live sex on stage (audience participation welcome; you'd better be well hung). Brought to you by the same folks who run the Erotic Museum (see Diversions).... *Tel 020/627-8945, www.club casarosso.com. Oudezijds Achterburgwal 106. Open nightly 8pm–2/3am.* **(see p. 182)**

COC. Gay cafe-club and disco in the Jordaan favored by clean-cut locals. No hardcore.... *Tel 020/626-3087. Rozenstraat 14, trams 13, 14, 17 to Westerkerk. Opening hours vary; Saturday nights women only.* **(see pp. 184, 185, 187)**

The Cockring. A hardcore gay club in the center of the leather and S&M district. Condoms available.... *Tel 020/623-9604. Warmoesstraat 96, all trams and buses to Centraal Station. Open daily 11pm–4/5am.* **(see pp. 184, 185, 187)**

De IJsbreker Muziekcentrum. Check out the arty crowd in the cafe if your ears resist departure from the standard 7-tone scale. On the Amstel River south of Singelgracht.... *Tel 020/668-1805. Weesperzijde 23, tram 3 and buses 51, 53, 54 to Wibantstraat.* **(see p. 185)**

Escape. This cavernous club on Rembrandtplein is favored by the hip 20-somethings in silly clothes who flutter like demented butterflies between the other self-consciously cool clubs—Sinners in Heaven, The Back Door, and IT. The decor and sounds change with every party, though the register remains industrial-chic and house. Saturday "Chemistry" theme night is hot. Top DJs. Clubwear and attitude essential.... *Tel 020/622-1111., www.escape.nl and www.chemistry.nl. Rembrandtplein 11, trams 4, 9, 14 to Rembrandtplein. Open Wed–Sun until 4 or 5am.* **(see p. 184, 186)**

GETTO. Popular gay bar-restaurant; Tuesday nights women only.... *Tel 020/421-5151, www.getto.nl. Warmoesstraat 51, all trams to Centraal Station. Open daily 7pm–1am.* **(see p. 183)**

Grant Cafe De Still. A tiny vintage bar in old A'dam. Affable Henk Eggens pours hundreds of the world's oldest and rarest whiskies.... *Tel 020/620-1349. Spuistraat 326, trams 1, 2, 5 to Spui. Open Mon–Sat 4pm–midnight.* **(see p. 187)**

The Grasshopper. Clean, well-lit, and on the cusp of the red-light district, this smoking coffee shop with a regular cafe and steakhouse on the upper floors is a tourist magnet.... *Tel 020/626-1529. Oudebrugsteeg 16, trams 4, 9, 16, 24, 25 to Dam Square, or all trams and buses to Centraal Station. Open Mon–Thur and Sun 10:30–1am, Fri–Sat 8:30–2am.* **(see p. 183)**

Havana's. Gay cafe-club and disco in the Reguliersdwarsstraat gay district, patronized by the same friendly, 20s and 30s crowd as April, Soho, and Exit nearby.... *Tel 020/620-6788. Reguliersdwarsstraat 17–19, trams 1, 2, 5 to Koningsplein. Open daily until 1am, Fri–Sat until 2am.* **(see p. 184)**

IT. Huge gay club-disco with mixed nights Thurs, Fri, and Sun. Sat is strictly gay. There's room for 1,100 hipsters in the black-warehouse interior. Fancy dress required!... *Tel 020/421-6924, www.it.nl. Amstelstraat 24, trams 4, 9, 14 to Rembrandtplein. Open Thur–Sun until 4–5am. Cover charge.* **(see pp. 184, 185, 186, 187)**

Kadinsky. Relaxed, clean smoking coffee shop with neighborhood atmosphere (thick).... *Tel 020/624-7023, www.coffeeshop-amsterdam.com. Rosmarijnsteeg 9, trams 1, 2, 5 to Spui. Open daily 10–1am.* **(see p. 183)**

Mazzo. Unpretentious, large disco club with nondescript interior in the Jordaan. No dress code.... *Tel 020/626-7500. Rozengracht 114, trams 13, 14, 17 to Westerkerk. Open daily until 4–5am. Cover charge.* **(see pp. 184, 186, 187)**

Melkweg. An A'dam institution, this multimedia cultural center near Leidseplein offers a maze of post-industrial-hip spaces in a former dairy (see Entertainment). There's a cafe and smoking coffee shop; a bar and restaurant; an art center; a dance and movement theater; a cinema; and lots of interesting music. There's also a disco club (Thur–Sun 1–5am).... *Tel 020/531-8181. Lijnbaansgracht 234a, trams 1, 2, 5, 6, 7, 10 to Leidseplein. Open daily 3pm–5am. Cover charge plus membership fee.* **(see pp. 182, 183, 184, 185, 186, 187)**

More. When Roxy burned down in 1999 its DJs and clients dispersed and have regrouped, since late 2001, at this glam disco club favored by fashion models, TV dolls and dudes, and other beautiful, self-conscious types. Theme nights Fri and Sat; Wed gay night.... *Tel 06/209-02571. Rozengracht 133, trams 13, 14, 17 to Westerkerk. Daily until 4–5am. Cover charge.* **(see pp. 184, 186)**

Mulligan's. The most appealing of A'dam's half-dozen beery Irish bars, with live folk music, spoon playing, and the like on Fri and Sat. Crowded, noisy, smoky, friendly.... *Tel 020/622-1330, www.mulligans.demon.nl. Amstel 100, trams 4, 9, 14 to Rembrandtplein. Open daily until 1–2am.* **(see p. 187)**

Nightwatch Bar. Classic hardcore drinker's bar, just off the lobby of the American Hotel.... *Tel 020/624-5322. Leidsekade 97, trams 1, 2, 5 to Leidseplein. Open daily until 2–3am.* **(see p. 187)**

Paradiso. A deconsecrated church off Leidseplein—the stairway to heaven for new-music and rock fiends. Occasional theme club nights, with DJs.... *Tel 020/623-7348. Weteringschans 6–8, trams 1, 2, 5, 6, 7, 10 to Leidseplein. Open usually until 3am. Cover charge, plus membership fee of Dfl 4–5.* **(see pp. 184, 186)**

Paradox. A friendly neighborhood smoking coffee shop favored by English expats (see Diversions).... *Tel 020/ 623-5639. 1e Bloemdwarsstraat 2, trams 13, 14, 17 to Westerkerk.* **(see p. 183)**

Sinners in Heaven. Favored by jet-setters, Ajax soccer heroes ,and visiting (and aging) rock stars like Mick Jagger. Top DJs (Gomez, Marnix, Natarcia) and theme nights.... *Tel 020/620-1375, www.sinners.nl. Wagenstraat 3, trams 4, 9, 14 to Rembrandtplein. Open Wed–Sun until 4–5am. Cover charge.* **(see pp. 184, 186)**

Time. Trendy, 20s–30s crowd. Minimalist decor with lots of bashed iron. The usual mix of house music, plus Dutch drum and bass. Strictly no sportswear.... *No telephone. Nieuwe Zijds Voorburgwal 163–165, trams 1, 2, 4 to Paleisstraat or Spui. Open Thur–Sun 11 until 3/5am. Cover charge.* **(see p. 186)**

Vrankrijk. Gay-straight "squatters' club" with "Queer Night" on Mon and "Planet Pussy" lesbian nights every third Sun. Rough 'n' ready scene.... *No telephone. Spuistraat 216,* *trams 1, 2, 4 to Paleisstraat or Spui. Daily 10–4/5 am. Occasional cover charge.* **(see pp. 183, 185, 187)**

Westergasfabriek. Converted industrial site on the western edge of town, now a hip club, bar, and restaurant (there's a barbecue in the middle of the room).... *Tel 020/621-1211 or 597-4458. Westergasfabriek, Haarlemmerweg 6–10, buses 18, 22 to Haarlempoort. Open 11:30–1/2am; lunch served 11:30am–3pm, dinner 6–10:30pm.*
(see pp. 185, 186, 187)

You 2. A'dam's only lesbian disco club.... *Tel 020/421-0900. Amstel 178, trams 4, 9, 14 to Rembrandtplein. Open Thur–Sat 10–4am, Sun 4pm–1am.*
(see pp. 183, 185, 187)

enterta

7

inment

Unless you
speak fluent Dutch
or get your kicks by
sitting through
performances
you can hardly
understand, an

Amsterdam theater is not the best place to spend your entertainment euro (and it doesn't help that the overall quality of the shows and performers is a bit less than world-class). Still, it's remarkable that a city of less than a million boasts some 60 theaters and concert halls. Such stats suggest a culture vulture need never sit at home cursing the language barrier.

The best time of year for the arts in Amsterdam is June, when the innovative Holland Festival (which runs simultaneously in Rotterdam, The Hague, and Utrecht) brings an abundance of international theater (in various languages, including English), dance, opera, and music to the city's stages. The Amsterdam Arts Adventure, running from late May through August, offers music and dance performances aimed primarily at tourists (no theater, no language probs). It, too, occupies a variety of venues. Music is, of course, a good bet year-round since it speaks all languages, but summer is a particularly musical time in the city's ancient but restless churches, whose frequent concerts make regular use of A'dam's 42 historical organs. Movies are a good choice, too, since most are in English; many, in fact, are British- or American-made.

Info Sources and Tickets

Amsterdam keeps no secrets about arts events from the uninitiated: There are posters up all over town all the time, fliers in bars, cafes, and restaurants, and a general sharing of knowledge that you don't necessarily find in other cities. Just walk into a bar, a cafe, or a club and ask whoever's on hand what's going on. Both the city tourist office, known as the **VVV** (tel 0900/400-4040, 9–5 weekdays, 55 euro cents per minute; offices at Stationsplein 10, in front of Centraal Station, 9–5 daily; Leidseplein 1, 9–7 daily; and Stadionplein, 9–5 daily), and the government-sponsored **AUB Uitburo** (tel 0900/0191 or 0201/621-1288, www.uitlijn.nl; Leidseplein 26, daily 9–9) give info by telephone (40 euro cents per minute) or on the spot, and sell tickets to just about everything going on in town (advance telephone/Internet reservations cost 3 euros per ticket; 2 euros at the AUB ticket window).

Getting tickets in A'dam is a straightforward, democratic affair: Either they're available or they're not. Ticket scalping is practically unknown in Amsterdam, so don't count on last-minute purchases on the steps of a concert hall. The best thing to do is to get hold of entertainment listings and make reservations before leaving the United States. You can do this by contacting either the VVV or the Uitburo.

The June **Holland Festival** (tel 020/530-7110) publishes its own free newsletter in Dutch and English. Buy festival tickets through the Uitburo, VVV, National Reservations Center, or at the venues where performances are held. Various season-ticket packages for the festival are sold and should be ordered before mid-April, preferably by mail, through the Uitburo or the NRC.

Three English-language magazines are good sources for entertainment listings: *Day by Day,* a straitlaced, triweekly tourism and entertainment magazine from VVV; *Shark,* a fringe free-sheet; and *Gay & Night Magazine,* written by and for gay hipsters. For movie listings, buy a Dutch daily.

Though Amsterdam is an expensive city, ticket prices are reasonable compared to other European capitals. For example, Holland Festival tickets run about 11.50 to 23 euros per event (or about 9 to 16 euros if you buy a season-ticket package). Movie prices average 7 euros, while rock concerts will set you back anywhere from 5.75 euros for unknowns to 34 to 45 euros for top names. Jazz and classical concerts average about 14 to 23 euros, but can top 60 euros at places like the Concertgebouw. For info on jazz (see Nightlife), call 020/770-0660 or visit www.jazz-in-amsterdam.nl. Opera tickets, at 11.50 to 45 euros, are considerably cheaper than in London or Paris for performances of comparable quality.

The Lowdown

Classical sounds... Classical-music lovers will be in Beethoven's seventh heaven in Amsterdam, where concerts are abundant, relatively cheap, and of world-class quality. Musicians perform all over town—in parks, churches, clubs, concert halls, piano factories—and audiences are enthusiastic and savvy. Contemporary classical is a particular specialty, the Dutch being among Europe's greatest fans of new and challenging musical creations in the classical domain. The excellent **Koninklijk Concertgebouworkest** (Royal Concertgebouw Orchestra), currently under the baton of Riccardo Chailly, plays at the **Concertgebouw**, an 1888 neoclassical hall south of the Singelgracht whose acoustics are so perfect you can hear every atonal instant of the contemporary pieces recently added to the repertoire. Guest performances by the world's best—from the Berlin and Vienna Philharmonic orchestras, to the Borodin Quartet or Frans Bruggen's Orchestra of the 18th Century—make this among Europe's most vibrant concert venues. Chailly's taste for contemporary composers (Nono, Berio) has been a breath of fresh air after the departure of his Brahms-obsessed predecessor, Bernard Haitink, but the ensemble has a vast range, and Bruckner and Mahler remain its fortes. The **Nederlands Philharmonisch Orkest** (Netherlands Philharmonic Orchestra) and its spinoff **Nederlands Kamerorkest** (Netherlands Chamber Orchestra), potentially first-rate ensembles that have been handicapped by administrative struggles and constant shifts from one base to another, finally have a permanent home in **Beurs van Berlage**, Amsterdam's former stock exchange. This Dutch art-nouveau landmark, just a few hundred yards from Centraal Station, was successfully remodeled to improve acoustics. Though used almost exclusively for dance and opera, the **Muziektheater**, the artsy half of Amsterdam's much-loathed 1980s city hall complex, hosts free lunchtime chamber music concerts by the Netherlands Philharmonic, the Netherlands Ballet Orchestra, or the choir of the Netherlands Opera. Bach is the mainstay at **Bachzaal**, part of the New South's Sweelinck Conservatorium, where accomplished students and professionals stage chamber music performances for the public. At **Felix Meritis,** a 200-year-old theater on Keizersgracht, you can listen to a variety of classical and baroque music (and attend musico-cultural seminars and conferences). At **Cristofori,** a vast piano showroom and restoration workshop with a fifth-floor concert hall, you can hear classical and contemporary classical performed by an international mix of top-flight and fledgling musicians.

Music for the masses... Churches are particularly active venues in Amsterdam. The **Waalse Kerk**, a rather unspectacular French Huguenot church in the red-light district, is now a vibrant venue for organ concerts (on a celebrated rococo Christian Muller organ) and baroque music, sometimes performed by top local and international talents. One of the most spectacular organs in town—Casa Rosso customers notwithstanding (see Nightlife)—is at **Nieuwe Kerk**, the 600-year-old Gothic church on Dam Square. Architect Jacob van Campen designed the instrument in the mid-1600s, and it is played regularly by highly regarded resident organist Gustav Leonhardt as well as by visiting performers. The landmark **Westerkerk** has a gorgeous 1686 organ with scenes of David dancing before the Ark painted on its shutters, but its more modest choir organ is usually used for Bach cantatas and other performances. The city's only Golden Age wooden church, **Amstelkerk**, overlooking Reguliersgracht and Prinsengracht canals, hosts chamber music, songs from the Middle Ages, and recitals, while the oldest church in town, **Oude Kerk**, in the middle of the red-light district, is another splendid setting for organ and classical music. Corelli, Bach, Handel, and Purcell are played regularly by local and visiting ensembles at the gorgeous and acoustically stunning 1392 **De Engelse Kerk** (English Reformed Church) in the Begijnhof, where in the summer months free lunchtime concerts are added to the musical calendar. (See Diversions for more about these churches.)

Modern sounds... Wear black, smoke plenty, and don't shave when you visit **De IJsbreker Muziekcentrum**, a distinctly hip venue dedicated to ear-boggling tonal and atonal contemporary work. From post-fusion jazz to concertos for pianoforte and tape to electrified 12-tone Schoenberg, this is strictly 20th-century, angular stuff. Some of it is outstanding, while much is strictly for initiates. But even if you don't pop for tickets (which aren't very expensive), hang out in the cafe or on the terrace overlooking the Amstel River and be entertained by the self-consciously arty regulars. De IJsbreker also coproduces contemporary music concerts at **Artis Planetarium**, in the 19th-century Artis Zoo complex. **Cristofori,** a big piano repair and sales operation, offers contemporary music (and jazz) at its fascinating workshop-concert hall on Prinsengracht. Performers include Wong Wing Tsan, Niek von Dosterum, and Deborah Carter. One of the myriad activities at **Melkweg**—a groundbreaking, 28-year-old multimedia cultural center, theater, club, and art gallery just off Leidseplein (see "On the fringe," below)—is musical performance—everything from world music to indefinable contemporary works by local bands to classic or experimental jazz. **Paradiso**, a deconsecrated church off Leidseplein, keeps you guessing with its eclectic lineup. Part dance club and major rock venue, it also books jazz, occasional classical music performances, and learned music conferences. **Westergasfabriek**, a converted gas plant in a former industrial complex in northwestern Amsterdam, is similarly eclectic, filling its music calendar with experimental jazz, pop, rock, and DJs. The cheapest, airiest concert venue of all is the **Vondelpark**, a lovely 19th-century park where musicians of all kinds—from modern minstrels to execrable bongo players and tone-deaf guitarists—perform daily in summer among the greenery, especially at or around the domed Koepel music stand in the center of the park, about 150 yards from the entrance on Van Eeghenstraat. When big crowds are anticipated for rock stars, teen idols, and so on, the new **ArenA** soccer stadium in the southern suburbs is the top mega-venue.

Kitsch concertos... The fantastically ornate **Tuschinski Theater**, a 1921 art-deco cinema near Rembrandtplein that books mostly mainstream first-run features, spends many of its Saturday mornings mounting tributes to the cinema's glorious past. Typically, a great silent film from the 1920s fills the screen while an organist cranks up the old Wurlitzer to evoke the proper mood. Restored top to bottom in 2001–2, the setting is Saturday-matinee opulence: marble panels, tiled floors, velvet seats, and lots of freshly polished brass and bronze. You can even reserve a special loge and sip champagne. Similar musical fare is served Sunday afternoons in the Jordaan at the Pianola Museum (see Diversions), the coziest museum in town, where player-piano lovers congregate in a front-room brown cafe to listen to any of the 35 old pianolas.

Theater you can understand, sort of... At **Badhuis Theater de Bochel**, a former bathhouse near the Oosterpark, an evening can be exhilarating or baffling when experimental works are performed. A variety of languages are used—sometimes in the same performance—so unless you're polyglot, stick to the visiting American and British companies (though the quality of productions varies widely). Multiethnicity is the byword at the aptly named **Cosmic Theater** smack in the heart of Old Amsterdam, where some of the Third-World companies perform in English. Visiting mainstream and experimental American or British theater troupes—some known, others up and coming—sometimes perform at **Transformatorhuis Toneelgroep Amsterdam**. The setting is industrial-chic: a converted former electrical plant on the western edge of town.

What's opera, doc?... The choice is simple: the **Muziek-theater**, a fascinatingly hideous complex built in 1986 and nicknamed "Stopera" (rhymes with "opera") when activists tried unsuccesfully to stop its construction. Locals may hate the way the venue looks, but the **Netherlands Opera** company, reinvigorated by director Pierre Audi, is winning kudos for everything from Monteverdi to world premieres by unknown Dutch talents. The tickets are unusually cheap, considering the quality. Check *Day by Day* for visiting opera companies performing in a variety of A'dam venues.

Men in tights... The eyesore **Muziektheater** is also the city's top dance venue, home to the **Netherlands National Ballet** and its ballet orchestra and choir. This company is rated among Europe's best and has helped enhance the Muziektheater's status, making an unpopular building a success. Celebrated for performances of works by Balanchine, it also has a strong reputation in contemporary Dutch ballet (especially creations by choreographer Hans van Manen), as well as in classic crowd-pleasers. The top international dance companies perform here, too, and the stage is vast. **Bellevue**, a large theater near Leidseplein with three halls, features dance performances by up-and-coming local companies, with a slant toward minimalist modern works. Amsterdam's municipal theater, the **Stadsschouwburg**, has been opening its Leidseplein stage to cutting-edge Dutch contemporary dance. The setting is stunning: a gorgeous horseshoe-shaped auditorium with gilt colonnades, red velvet, and dozens of chandeliers. Another handsome late-1800s theater, the **Carré Theater**, on the Amstel River just south of the Magere Brug, is primarily for cabaret and musicals (in Dutch), but big-name dance companies (Pina Bausch, for example), and occasional folk-dancing groups make it a viable hall for non–Dutch speakers. Fans of multicultural dance—African, Asian, South American, and combinations thereof—should head for one of two venues. At the **Cosmic Theater**, the "Cosmic Instants" programs—each a collection of 20-minute works by 8 to 10 choreographers—can be fascinating. Similar multiethnic dance and movement can be found at the beautiful **Tropeninstituut** and **Soeterijn**—two halls inside the Tropenmuseum (Tropical Museum) near Oosterpark. Amateurs and accomplished modern dancers perform their sometimes- inspired, sometimes-embarrassing creations at the **Dans Werkplaats Amsterdam** (Amsterdam Dance Workshop), just north of the Vondelpark. More of the same goes on at **Veemtheater**, in a warehouse beyond Westerdok. It's great if you're keen on experimental dance, body movement, and mime theater, but the uninitiated will feel lost. Captivating contemporary dance performances are among the many things going on at **Melkweg**, a pioneering multimedia cultural center (see "On the fringe," below).

On the fringe... By their nature, fringe theater, music, dance, and combinations thereof pose a challenge in any language, so you may enjoy them even more in indecipherable Dutch (actually, some performances are at least partially in English). Twenty-eight years ago, **Melkweg** (its name, which means Milky Way, derives from its location in a former dairy) was the wildest, most cosmic club/theater/art gallery in A'dam. Over the decades it has grown ideologically away from flower power toward a savvy hipness, becoming part of an international network of multimedia cultural centers, and it has spilled into a series of separate spaces—a regular cafe and smoking coffee shop (where hash-laced goodies are sometimes available), a bar and restaurant, an art center, a dance and movement theater, a cinema, a music venue, and a dance club (see Nightlife). The scene is mixed: punks, artists, businesspeople, and the occasional lost socialite. And though it has moved steadily into the mainstream, Melkweg can still shock with lunatic dance, music, and performance art. **OCCII**, which in pre-gentrification days was one of many abandoned buildings near Vondelpark that had been seized by squatters, is now a bar, club, and performance venue where locals bash out electrified sounds and fling themselves into crazy cabaret or stand-up comedy acts. **Badhuis Theater de Bochel**, set in a reconverted bathhouse near Oosterpark, offers wild and wet experimental theater, dance, and music that might leave you feeling wrung out. Out on the western edge of town, the former gas plant **Westergasfabriek** favors experimental theater that's hip but tame. Read *Shark* for the current, ever-changing roster of squats, theaters, and clubs on the fringe.

Life is a gamble... The **Holland Casino**, A'dam's only casino, is a slice of Vegas. Join the bus-tour and provincial-Dutch set for a bit of gaming in smoke-filled rooms over-looking the Singlegracht at Leidseplein.

Life is a cabaret... The **Boom Chicago Theater**, an American improv troupe, landed in Amsterdam about 10 years ago, and contrary to everybody's expectations (and I mean *everybody*), it has not only survived but thrived by making fun of Dutch customs and language, and generally appealing to youngish tourists from America and Britain. They have a permanent venue, the Leidseplein Theater, and even publish their own quarterly, *Boom!*, which they claim is written by "outsider insiders." Hmmm. We've all seen their brand of entertainment before: determinedly wild and wacky guys and gals riffing, rather tamely, off reactions of a mostly embarrassed and bemused audience (do they ever get repeat visitors?). The food (veggie sand-wiches, Mars mousse, Sunday brunch specials) will trans-port you right home. The competition, **Comedy Cafe Amsterdam,** hails and hah-hah-hahs from a modern shopping mall behind the Holland Casino. The stand-up and improv meisters here are American, British, or Dutch. A mixed bag of chuckles, guffaws, and groans, washed down by suds (and, if you're daring, accompanied by deli-cacies such as meat pastries or turkey tournedos swimming in mustard-dill sauce). Altogether different, pricier, and immeasurably more pretentious is **The Supperclub,** a true end-of-the-empire restaurant-club-cabaret where the rich, beautiful and brain-dead stretch out on Roman-style couches in a clinical white interior and spend hours choking down mediocre food while watching videos, fashion shows, and the like to OJ music. A masseuse shows up to help massage down the grub and prepare you to dis-gorge about 60 euros for the "entertainment."

The sporting life... In Amsterdam, **Ajax** is neither a scrubbing powder nor a Trojan war hero: It's the name of the local *voetball* (soccer) club, who thrilled fans in 1995 by winning the European championship. A dominant European force in the early 1970s, the franchise slumped for about a decade before rejoining the game's elite in the late 1980s. Their 1995 title inspired fans to go on a rampage, breaking windows, looting, and attacking bystanders around Leidseplein, behavior that might send any team into a decade-long slump, maybe even intentionally. Indeed, Amsterdammers as a whole are enthusiastic boosters, and tend to go berserk—dancing in the streets, drinking even more than usual, and making lots of noise—whenever their local heroes win. And win they sometimes still do—Ajax is among Europe's most unpredictable teams. The team has settled into its 51,000-seat, high-tech **ArenA** stadium, in the southwest suburbs, and regularly draws capacity-plus crowds. The stadium—now a tourist and soccer fan mecca—is like a mini-city and shopping center. It features about 50 food stands (mostly burgers and pizza), the Soccer World restaurant (there's a giant soccer-ball pattern on the floor, yup, and a bank of TV monitors), a gift and souvenir boutique, and two giant video screens in the mall-like inner halls (so you won't miss a second of the action, even if you are on your way to the can). To pay for your fun, use cash or a credit card to buy an ArenA Card. The Amsterdam **RAI** still exists as a large conference and sporting hall about 2 miles south of central Amsterdam, though the ArenA has largely overshadowed its events.

Amsterdam also boasts professional teams in second-rate knockoffs of a few favorite American pastimes. The Amsterdam **Admirals** challenged for the 1995 championship title in the World League of American Football and have continued to perform admirably since. They bid farewell to the crumbling 1924 Olympic Stadium following their 1996 season (May–June) and have joined Ajax at the new Amsterdam ArenA. Nonetheless, the sport just doesn't seem to be catching on, golly gosh. Likewise, only a few thousand ticket-buyers—mostly American expats and curious young locals—litter the stands any weekend from May to September when Amsterdam's **Pirates,** among the top baseball teams in the Netherlands, take the field at Sportpark Jan van Galen in Bos en Lommer, a western suburb. Amsterdam's basketball team, inexplicably named **Finish Profiles Amsterdam,** or, more commonly, just "Amsterdam," can also boast of being among the best in the Netherlands. You can imagine what the competition's like. Their squad of American and European pros plays Saturday evenings, from September to April, at the Apollohal in the New South neighborhood, south of Vondelpark.

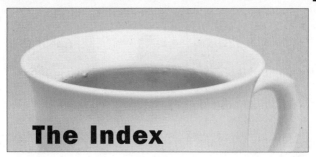

The Index

Admirals. The city's American-football team plays home games Sat, April–June. They now play at the ArenA stadium complex. For info call 020/465-0550. See listing for **ArenA** below. **(see p. 204)**

Ajax. Amsterdam's much-loved soccer team, winners of the 1995 European Cup and fully expected by optimistic locals to win again. They're at ArenA too. See listing for **ArenA** below. **(see pp. 203. 204)**

Amstelkerk. This Golden Age church overlooking Reguliersgracht and Prinsengracht canals hosts classical music, recitals, songs from the Middle Ages, and chamber music…. *Tel 020/ 622-0774. Amstelveld 2, tram 4 to Prinsengracht.* **(see p. 199)**

ArenA. This high-tech stadium with a sliding roof opened in August 1996. Ajax and the Admirals play here. There are also about 7 major rock performances held each year (see Nightlife)…. *Tel 020/311-1333; 020/311-1333 for Ajax Museum. Amsterdam ArenA Zuidoost, Dutch Railways trains to Duivendrecht or Bijlmer, Metro to Strandvliet/ArenA or Bijlmer. Stadium complex open daily from 9–6 (hours vary on soccer or football match days and during rock concert performances).* **(see pp. 200, 204)**

Artis Planetarium. Part of the 19th-century Artis Zoo complex, this handsome, functioning planetarium sometimes hosts interesting, quality concerts, especially contemporary works…. *Tel 020/523-3452. Plantage Kerklaan, trams 7, 9, 14 to Artis Zoo.* **(see p. 199)**

Bachzaal. Part of the Sweelinck Conservatorium, this hall hosts regular chamber-music performances by students and professionals. The quality varies widely. Cheap.... *Tel 020/664–7641. Bachstraat 7, trams 5, 24 to Corellistraat, bus 15 to Handelstraat.* **(see p. 198)**

Badhuis Theater de Bochel. Visiting companies, sometimes American or British, put on a variety of professional and amateur acts at this former bathhouse, but many productions are in Dutch.... *Tel 020/668-5102. Andreas Bonnstraat 28, trams 3, 6, 7, 10 to Weesperplein or Ruyschstraat.* **(see pp. 200, 202)**

Bellevue. There are 3 halls in this theater near Leidseplein, where the dance tends to be minimalist. You need to learn Dutch to appreciate most of its cabaret artists and theater companies.... *Tel 020/530-5301. Leidsekade 90, trams 1, 2, 5, 6, 7, 10 to Leidseplein.* **(see p. 201)**

Beurs van Berlage. The former stock exchange, this Dutch art-nouveau landmark by Hendrick Petrus van Berlage is now a concert venue, the permanent home of the Nederlands Philharmonisch Orkest and its offshoot, the Nederlands Kamerorkest.... *Tel 020/521-7575. Damrak 243, trams 4, 9, 16, 24, 25 to Damrak/Beurs.* **(see p. 198)**

Boom Chicago Theater. This unsinkable American cabaret and improvisational theater company lives by a familiar formula: The audience dines, snacks, and drinks at candlelit tables while the fun-loving troupe plays for laughs in ever-changing yet predictable acts.... *Tel 020/423-0101, office@boom chicago.nl or www.boomchicago.nl. Leidseplein Theater, Leidseplein 12, trams 1, 2, 5, 6, 7, 10 to Leidseplein.*
(see p. 203)

Carré Theater. This 1887 wedding cake of a theater, long used as a circus venue, now hosts ribald Dutch cabaret and Dutch-language versions of British and American musicals. More comprehensible for English-only speakers are the big-name dance performances and the occasional high-spirited folk-dancing group.... *Tel 020/622-5225, www.theatercarre.nl or kassa@theatercarre.nl. Amstel 115–125, trams 6, 7, 10 to Sarphatistraat, Metro to Weesperplein.* **(see p. 201)**

Comedy Cafe Amsterdam. Stand-up and improv routines by an international grab bag of fun-meisters.... *Tel 020/638-*

3971, www.comedycafe.nl. Max Euweplein 43–45, trams 1, 2, 5, 6, 7 to Leidseplein. **(see p. 203)**

Concertgebouw. This acoustically impeccable 1888 venue is the permanent home of the rejuvenated Koninklijk Concert-gebouworkest. Visiting performers include the world's best, and their work ranges as far off the beaten path as obscure saxophone concertos. Monthly schedule in English. Guided tours Sunday mornings at 9:30 (3.50 euros). Reserve ahead.... *Tel 020/671-8345, kassa@concertgebouw.nl or www.concertgebouw.nl. Concertgebouwplein 2–6, trams 2, 3, 5, 12, 16 to Concertgebouwplein.* **(see p. 197)**

Cosmic Theater. Multiethnicity and multiculturalism are the grist for this multimedia mill, which offers avant-garde dance, theater, and combinations of same, mostly in Dutch, occasionally in English.... *Tel 020/622-8858. Nes 75, trams 4, 9, 14, 16, 24, 25 to Spui.* **(see pp. 200, 201)**

Cristofori. Piano repair and sales outfit with a surprising, fifth-floor concert hall (classical, contemporary, and jazz).... *Tel 020/626-8495, salon@cristofori.nl or www.cristofori.nl. Trams 16, 24, 25 to Prinsengracht.* **(see pp. 198, 199)**

Dans Werkplaats Amsterdam. A dance workshop where local performers do their robotic, serpentine, contortionistic thing, while sympathetic aficionados look politely on.... *Tel 020/ 689-1789. Arie Biemondstraat 107b, trams 1, 6, 7, 17 to Jan Pieter Heijestraat.* **(see p. 202)**

De Engelse Kerk (English Reformed Church). This hand-some little 1392 church in the Begijnhof offers up to four classical concerts a week, performed by accomplished Dutch and foreign ensembles. The setting is beautiful and relaxed, the acoustics are good, and the ticket prices rea-sonable.... *Tel 020/624-9665. Begijnhof 48, trams 1, 2, 5 to Spui.* **(see p. 199)**

De IJsbreker Muziekcentrum. Challenging international atonal music is standard fare at this ultra-hip venue on the Amstel River south of the Singelgracht. Check out the arty crowd in the cafe.... *Tel 020/668-1805, post@ysbreker.nl or www.ysbreker.nl. Weesperzijde 23, trams 3, 5, 6, 7, 10 to Ruyschstraat, buses 20, 56 to Wibautstraat.* **(see p. 199)**

Felix Meritis (aka the Shaffy Theater). Classical music, seminars, and conferences have revived the fortunes of this 1780s neoclassical theater long celebrated for its acoustics and unusual architecture.... *Tel 020/626-2321, balie@felix.meritis.nl or www.felix.meritis.nl. Keizersgracht 324, trams 1, 2, 5 to Spui.* **(see p. 198)**

Finish Profiles Amsterdam (aka Amsterdam). The city's basketball club, tops in the Netherlands, plays Sat evenings from Sept to April.... *Tel 020/671-3910. Apollohal, Stadionweg 1–5, tram 24, buses 15, 63 to Sportpark Olympiaplein.* **(see p. 204)**

Holland Casino. Amsterdam's only casino, full of bus-tour groups and provincial Dutch.... *Tel 020/521-1111, www.hollandcasino.nl. Lido complex on Singelgracht at Leidseplein, trams 1, 2, 5, 6, 7, 10 to Leidseplein. Open 1:30pm–3am.* **(see p. 202)**

Koninklijk Concertgebouworkest (Royal Concertgebouw Orchestra). This top-notch orchestra, which excels at Bruckner and Mahler, has recently added contemporary atonal work to its broad repertoire. Find them at the Concertgebouw, the 1888 hall that lends the ensemble its name.... *Tel 020/671-8345, www.concertgebouw.nl. Concertgebouwplein 2–6, trams 3, 12, 16 to Concertgebouwplein.* **(see p. 197)**

Melkweg (Milky Way). A perpetually hip, 30-year-old multimedia cultural center with a smoking coffee shop, a bar and restaurant, an art center, a dance and movement theater, a cinema, a music venue, and a dance club.... *Tel 020/531-8181, www.melkweg.nl. Lijnbaansgracht 234a, trams 1, 2, 5, 6, 7, 10 to Leidseplein.* **(see pp. 199, 202)**

Muziektheater. Multipurpose dance theater and opera house, home to the Netherlands National Ballet and Orchestra and Pierre Audi's highly acclaimed Netherlands Opera company. This is where top international dance and opera companies perform. Each week, for most of the year, it also hosts free lunchtime chamber music concerts (Boekmanzaal, Tue at 12:30, Oct–June).... *Tel 020/625-5455, info@hmth.nl or www.hmth.nl. and www.gastprogrammering.nl. Amstel 3, trams 9, 14 to Muziektheater.* **(see pp. 198, 201)**

Nederlands Kamerorkest (Netherlands Chamber Orchestra). This offshoot of the Nederlands Philharmonisch often attracts top international soloists.... *Tel 020/ 627-1161. Damrak 213, trams 4, 9, 16, 24, 25 to Damrak/Beurs.* **(see p. 198)**

Nederlands Philharmonisch Orkest (Netherlands Philharmonic Orchestra). This reputable ensemble boasts world-class performances now that it's settled permanently at the Beurs van Berlage, Amsterdam's former stock exchange.... *Tel 020/627-1161. Damrak 213, trams 4, 9, 16, 24, 25 to Damrak/Beurs.* **(see p. 198)**

Netherlands National Ballet. This top-flight company, most renowned for its stagings of Balanchine, makes its home at the Muziektheater in the modern city-hall co plex.... *Tel 020/551-8225 info; box office: 020/625-5455, info@het-nationale-ballet.nl or www.het-nationale- ballet.nl. Amstel 3, trams 9, 14 to Muziektheater.* **(see p. 201)**

Netherlands Opera. Everything from old standbys to risky world premieres have won high praise since director Pierre Audi took over this company. The opera performs at the Muziektheater.... *Tel 020/551-8922 info; box office: 020/625-5455. info@nederlandse-opera.nl and www.dno.nl Amstel 3, trams 9, 14 to Muziektheater.* **(see p. 201)**

Nieuwe Kerk (New Church). This 600-year-old Gothic church on Dam Square is now primarily an art and cultural center; its spectacular 17th-century organ is used regularly for concerts by top performers.... *Tel 020/626-8168. Dam Square, trams 1, 2, 4, 5, 9, 13, 14, 16, 17, 24, 25 to Dam Square.* **(see p. 198)**

OCCII. Laid-back fringe venue, once a squat, way out beyond the southeastern edge of Vondelpark. You're likely to see off-the-wall cabaret or stand-up acts by unknowns, and hear unclassifiable music produced by young A'dammers.... *Tel 020/671-7778. Amstelveenseweg 134, trams 2, 6 to Amstelveenseweg at Vondelpark.* **(see p. 202)**

Oude Kerk (Old Church). A 13th- or 14th-century church in the middle of the red-light district, often holds organ and classical music concerts.... *Tel 020/625-8284. Oudekerks-*

ENTERTAINMENT | THE INDEX

plein 23, all trams and buses to Centraal Station.
(see p. 199)

Paradiso. Among the city's top music venues, this deconsecrated old church off Leidseplein has a cafe/club out front and a large performance area in what used to be the nave.... *Tel 020/623-7348. Weteringschans 6–8, trams 1, 2, 5, 6, 7, 10 to Leidseplein.* **(see p. 199)**

Pirates. The city's baseball team plays Sat and Sun from May to Sept at a ball field in the western suburbs.... *Tel 020/616-2151. Sportpark Jan van Galen, Jan van Galenstraat 254, Bos en Lommer, tram 13, buses 19, 43, 45, 48, 193 to Sportpark Jan van Galen. Tickets are about 23 euros.* **(see p. 204)**

RAI. This vast exhibition center in the southern suburbs hosts everything from international boat shows to occasional rock and classical music concerts, though it has been largely eclipsed by the ArenA.... *Tel 020/644-8651. Europaplein 12, tram 4, buses 15, 51, 60, 69, 158, 169 to exhibition center.* **(see p. 204)**

Shaffy Theater. See **Felix Meritis.**

Soeterijn. See **Tropeninstituut.**

Stadsschouwburg (Municipal Theater). Unfortunately, all theater productions are in Dutch at Amsterdam's main theater, but there are frequent contemporary dance performances.... *Tel 020/624-2311. Leidseplein 26, trams 1, 2, 5, 6, 7, 10 to Leidseplein.* **(see p. 201)**

The Supperclub. It started out as a post-provo anarchistic underground club and restaurant and has become an icon of end-of-the-empire A'dam decadence. Roman-style dining sofas, slinky fashion-model "waitresses," post-fusion food on a huge tray, DJ music, fashion shows, dancing, cabaret.... *Tel 020/638-0513, www.supperclub.nl. Jonge Roelensteeg 21, trams 1, 2, 5, 11 to Paleisstraat. Daily 8pm–midnight.* **(see p. 203)**

Transformatorhuis Toneelgroep Amsterdam. This excellent municipal theater company plays in this former electrical plant on the western edge of town. Their performances are in Dutch, but the occasional visiting theater or dance company puts on works intelligible to English-speaking audiences.... *Tel 020/686-9735. Haarlemmerweg 8–10, buses 18, 22 to Haarlempoort.* **(see p. 200)**

Tropeninstituut and **Soeterijn.** These art-deco/art-nouveau halls at the Royal Tropical Institute building (which houses the Tropenmuseum) stage dance, theater, music, and film dedicated to multiethnic, multicultural themes. Very PC.... *Tel 020/568-8711. Mauritskade 63, trams 9, 14 to Tropenmuseum.* **(see p. 201)**

Tuschinski Theater. An opulent 1921 Dutch art-deco cinema—still a first-run theater—where an organ from silent-movie days is used for occasional concerts and to accompany silent films. Totally restored in 2001–2.... *Tel 020/626-2633. Reguliersbreestraat 26, trams 4, 9, 14, 16, 24, 25 to Rembrandtplein or Munt Plein.* **(see p. 200)**

Veemtheater. No language barrier here. This converted warehouse way out beyond Westerdok and the Western Islands now hosts experimental dance, movement, and mime theater. For contemporary dance aficionados.... *Tel 020/626-0112. Van Diemenstraat 410, tram 3 to terminus, bus 35 to Van Diemenstraat.* **(see p. 202)**

Waalse Kerk. This small, simple church set back from a canal in the red-light district is now a vibrant venue for organ concerts (on a celebrated rococo Christian Muller organ) and baroque music, sometimes performed by top names.... *Tel 020/623-2074. Oude Zijds Achterburgwal 157, all trams and buses to Centraal Station.* **(see p. 198)**

Westergasfabriek. In the same former industrial complex as the Transformatorhuis (see above), this converted gas plant on the western edge of town is now a venue for experimental theater, live pop and rock, and DJ theme nights. There's also a hip bar and diner-like restaurant.... *Tel 020/621-1211 or 581-0425. Haarlemmerweg 8–10, buses 18, 22 to Haarlempoort.* **(see pp. 199, 202)**

Westerkerk. Organ music and Bach cantatas are a regular feature at this Golden Age landmark.... *Tel 020/624-7766. Prinsengracht 281, trams 13, 14, 17 to Westerkerk.* **(see p. 199)**

hotlines &
other basics

Airport... **Schiphol** (pronounced skipple) is 15 kilometers (9 miles) from downtown Amsterdam—about 30 minutes by taxi or car, 25 minutes by train, or 12 to 55 minutes by hotel shuttle-bus. It's one of the world's most convenient, efficiently run, and least unpleasant airports, handling more than 20 million passengers a year (only London, Paris, and Frankfurt are busier). It features hotels, a casino, sauna and meditation facilities, shopping, restaurants, and business meeting rooms. Security is state of the art, with iris scanners. For general information tel 0900/724-4746 (10¢ euro per minute); customs tel 020/316-4700; lost luggage tel 020/601-2325; www.schiphol.nl.

Airport transportation to downtown... Trains leave from the airport station to Centraal Station downtown 24 hours a day (every 15 minutes, 5–1am; hourly 1–5am). Tickets cost about $3 one way ($5 round-trip same day). Make sure you board a train to Amsterdam CS (Centraal Station). Note that trains do not originate at Schiphol; there are through trains to and from Rotterdam, Utrecht, and The Hague. Information: **Dutch Railways**, tel 0900–9292 for domestic trains; tel 0900/9296 for international trains. **KLM** runs a hotel **shuttle-bus** (tel 023/515-2652 or 020/405-6565) every 30 minutes from

Schiphol 6:30am–2:30pm, hourly 3–10pm. Buy tickets on board (about $8 one way; about $15 round trip). Hotel stops are: Hilton, Barbizon Centre, Pulitzer, Krasnapolsky, Holiday Inn Crowne Plaza, Amsterdam Renaissance, and Barbizon Palace. You can take the bus even if you're not staying at one of these hotels. It takes only 12 minutes to the Hilton from the airport, but almost an hour to the Barbizon Palace; going the opposite direction, the times are reversed. **Taxis** cost about $25–30 to central Amsterdam (020/653-1000; www.schipholtaxi.nl).

Baby-sitters... Only one organization is approved by Amsterdam's tourist information office (known as the VVV; see "Visitor information," below): **Oppascentrale Kriterion**, also called Onderlinge Studenten Steun (tel 020/624-5848, Valckenierstraat 45). It's been around since the 1950s, and employs male and female students over 18. Reserve by telephone 5:30–7pm daily. Baby-sitters will come to your hotel, but charge a slightly higher fee for the inconvenience. Most four- and five-star hotels will book baby-sitters for you through the concierge's desk.

Banks and exchange offices... Banking hours are usually 9 to 4 weekdays. Most banks have foreign exchange offices. The **GWK** (Grens Wissel Kantoor) exchange offices in Centraal Station and at the main hall of the Schiphol Airport Railway Station are open 24 hours daily. In general, banks and GWK exchanges offer the best rates. Avoid other exchange offices (called Bureau de Change) charging high commissions. The most convenient GWK offices (open daily) are at Damrak 86 (8am–11:45pm), Leidseplein 123 (8am–midnight), and Kalverstraat 150 (8–8). GWK offices also give cash advances on all major credit cards, and they are agents for Western Union (handy for emergency money transfers). GWK also sells telephone cards and *strippenkaart* tickets for city trams, buses, and the Metro. In a pinch, the often-crowded **Dutch Post Bank** at all post offices will exchange foreign currency. **ABN–AMRO** bank has an automatic banknote-exchange machine at Dam Square, corner of Damrak (open 24 hours daily); **Verenigde Spaarbank** (VSB) offers the same service at Singel 548.

Car rentals... Rental cars are listed in the Yellow Pages under "Autoverhuur"; international agencies are at Schiphol Airport. Book from the U.S. for the best rates.

Avis: tel 020/683-6061, Nassaukade 380. **Budget**: tel 020/612-6066 and 0800/0537, Overtoom 121. **Hertz**: tel 020/612-2441 and 0800/235-4378, Overtoom 333. (See "Driving and parking," below.)

Consulates and embassies... All embassies are in The Hague. **United States Embassy**: tel 070/310-9209, Lange Voorhout 102. **Canadian Embassy and Consulate**: tel 070/311-1600, Sophialaan 7. **British Embassy**: tel 070/427-0427, Lange Voorhout 10. **United States Consulate** in Amsterdam: tel 020/575-5309, Museumplein 19. **British Consulate** in Amsterdam: tel 020/676-4343, Koningslaan 44.

Currency... On 1/1/2002, the euro became the official currency all over continental Europe. One euro fluctuates between 88¢ and 96¢ U.S. Do your calculations in US $, then knock off 5–10%. Coins are worth: 1, 2, 3, 5, 10, 20, 50 euro cents and 1 or 2 euros. The paper denominations are: 5, 10, 20, 50, 100, 200, and 500 euros.

Doctors and dentists... Consult the Dutch Yellow Pages under "Tandarts" for dentists (the Yellow Pages Visitors Guide, in English, is in most hotels). The **Dentists Referral Bureau** will refer you 24 hours daily to an approved practitioner (tel 0900/821-2230). Doctors are listed under "Artsen-huisartsen: dokters" in the Dutch Yellow Pages. The **Centrale Doktersdienst** (tel 0900/592-3355) is a 24-hour daily referral service. For medical or dental emergencies call 112, 24 hours daily. (See "Emergencies and police," below.)

Driving and parking... The best advice we can give on driving in Amsterdam is this: Don't drive in Amsterdam. Traffic is horrendous, the normally polite Dutch are demon drivers, and parking is nightmarish. If your car is parked illegally, it will be clamped or towed almost immediately by the dreaded Parkeerbeheer police, and you will need large amounts of cash to get it back (from about $60 to $210; call 020/553-0333 around the clock to recover a towed vehicle). American driver's licenses are valid. Drive on the right-hand side. You can leave your car for 5.70 euros at the "P+R" lot at Amstel Station, south of town, served by taxis and by tram 12 and bus 15 (both run 6am–midnight weekdays, from 6:30 Sat, and from 7:30 Sun). For other "P+R" locations call 020/553-0333. A handful of hotels have garages; some upscale hotels offer a 1- or 3-day tourist parking pass (19.50 euros and 58.50

euros) allowing you to park on the street—if you can find a spot. You can also buy passes from the "parking management office": Bakkerstraat 13 (near Rembrandtplein); Nieuwezijds Kolk (near Kolk garage); Ceintuvrbaan 159 (near Sarphatipark); Kinkerstreet 17 (near Police H.Q.); and Cruquiuskade 25 (on the NW edge of town). A 1-week pass costs 106 euros. Parking meters are now ubiquitous: 2.60 euros per hour (Mon–Sat 9–7), 1.60 euros 7–11pm and Sun noon–11pm. Times and charges can vary in certain zones; check the meter for details. Central city garages' opening hours vary widely, so call ahead: **Europarking BV** (tel 020/623-6694, Marnixstraat 250); **De Bijenkorf** (tel 020/621-8080, Beursplein/Damrak; Mon–Sat 9–midnight); **Parking Plus** (tel 020/626-6141, Centraal Station, enter at 20a Prins Hendrikkade; 24 hours daily); **Kroon & Zn** (tel 020/638–0919, Waterlooplein 1); and **Parking Byzantium** (tel 020/616-6416, Tesselschadestraat 1g; 24 hours daily). Rates are about 2–4 euros per hour.

Electricity... Dutch plugs are the same 220-volt European model used in Italy and France, with two small round poles. Hotels are not equipped for American plugs or appliances that use 110 to 120 volts.

Emergencies and police... For accidents, medical emergencies, burglaries, or fire, call the police, fire department, and ambulance 24 hours daily at **112**. The Amsterdam police central dispatcher is at tel 020/559-9111 (24 hours daily). The main police station is at Elandsgracht 117. Other police stations: Lijnbaansgracht 219; Nieuwezijds Voorburgwal 118; Prinsengracht 1109; Singel 455; Van Leijenberghlaan 15; and Warmoesstraat 44.

Events information... AUB Uitburo (tel 020/621-1288 or 0900/0191 [40 euro cents per minute], www.uitlijn.nl; Leidseplein 26; daily 9–9) is a one-stop entertainment ticketing agency and information office for music, dance, theater, and special events. The VVV (Amsterdam Tourist Office, Stationsplein 10; see "Visitor information," below) has a 55 euro cents-per-minute info line in English (tel 0900/400-4040); find out about everything from concerts and theater programs to bike rentals and baby-sitters.

Festivals and special events...

February: **Carnaval Mokum**, a popular festival, draws big crowds; the 1941 **Dockers' Strike** is commemorated Feb 25.

March: **HISWA te Water** national boat show at RAI convention center fills hotels (mid-month); the **Silent Procession** (Stille Omgang) of about 15,000 people marks the bizarre 1345 "Miracle of Amsterdam" of the fire-resistant Host (closest Sun to March 15).

April: There's a 2-day celebration before and on **Queen's Day** (Koninginnedag), April 30—book your hotel room several months ahead.

April–May: Tulip season.

Late May to end of August: The Amsterdam Arts Adventure features dance and music (see Entertainment for details).

June: **RAI Arts Fair** (KunstRAI) is a major contemporary arts-and-crafts fair (early June); **Canal Run** (Echo Grachtenloop), the closest thing to a marathon, lopes along city canals (routes are 3, 6, and 11 miles; second Sun in June); the month long **Holland Festival** features theater, dance, and concert performances by major artists and companies (also in Rotterdam, The Hague, and Utrecht; see Entertainment for details).

August: **Uitmarkt**, held on the last weekend of the month, ushers in the fall concert/theater/opera season.

September: **Flower Parade** (Bloemencorso) occurs the first week of the month, from Aalsmeer through town to Dam Square (best review spots are Rembrandtplein and Vijzelstraat); on **National Monument Day** (Monumentendag), usually the second Sat of the month, landmark buildings are open to the public; **Jordaan Festival** features arts, crafts, and entertainment (second and third week of the month).

November: **St. Nicholas Parade/Santa Claus** (Sinterklaas), a kiddies' parade, runs from Centraal Station to Dam Square, with Santa Claus and his sidekick Black Peter (Zwarte Pieten), held the second or third week of the month.

Gay and lesbian sources... The **Gay and Lesbian Switchboard** (tel 020/623-6565, www.switchboard.nl or info@switchboard.nl; 10–10 daily) offers English-language info and advice. Tune into **MNS Radio** (106.8 FM, 6–9pm daily) for up-to-the-minute info on gay events and issues. For advice and info from the government-subsidized **COC**, the Dutch Gay and Lesbian Organization, call or visit the local branch at Rozenstraat 14, 626-3087 open Wed–Sat 1–5; English-speaking meetings; cafe). The COC's national branch is at Rozenstraat 8 (tel 020/623-4596, open Mon–Fri 9–4). Call **AIDS Infolijn,** tel 0900/204-2040, for info on AIDS. *Gay News*, a monthly news and listings tabloid, is published in Dutch and English and is sold in bookstores, cafes, and clubs (www.gaynews.nl). *Gay & Night*, a monthly gay events listings guide, is sold in many bookstores, and at clubs and cafes. *Shark*, a twice-monthly give-away, lists clubs, squats, music, film, and gay events.

Holidays... National holidays when businesses shut are: Jan 1 (New Year's Day); Good Friday, Easter, and Easter Monday; April 30 (Queen's Day); Ascension Day (the 40th day after Easter); Pentecost (the seventh Sunday after Easter); May 5 (Liberation Day); Dec 5 (St. Nicholas' Day); and Dec 25 and 26 (Christmas).

Internet... Most hotels, many shops, museums, and galleries, and some restaurants and cafes are on the Internet. There are a dozen Internet cafes or bars in town, most of them seedy (in smoking coffee shops). The exceptions are: In de Waag (tel 020/422-7772; see Dining and Cafes), The Internet Cafe (tel 020/627-1052, www.internetcafe.nl; Martelaarsgracht 11), and Chesterfield Internet Lounge (tel 020/428-0428, www.grandpub.com; Leidesplein 2). There are dozens of blue "Internet Pillars" on sidewalks, usually near telephone booths. They use KPN telephone cards. Surf the Web or receive messages (you cannot send e-mails). Instructions are in English: Insert card, "start" page appears onscreen, surf or go to "e-mail."

Language... Natives speak Dutch, but will not respond if you try to speak to them in Dutch; they speak better English than most Americans and are keen to demonstrate it. They cannot stand hearing their language miscoughed (coughing and spluttering are key to correct pronunciation; just try saying "Fan Ghchoaghch"—Van Gogh). Most Dutch also speak French, German, and more. Warning: If you are a native English speaker do not attempt to speak German in Holland, or pronounce Dutch words as if they were German words. Dutch has a great deal in common with German, but it also resembles English, which the Dutch prefer to speak.

Newspapers... There is no English-language daily in Amsterdam, but the monthly *Day by Day* is widely available. Major British dailies and Sunday papers are sold at many newsstands. Readily available American papers: *USA Today*, *International Herald Tribune,* and *The Wall Street Journal.* The best sources for these publications are: Waterstone's (Kalverstraat 152); American Book Center (Kalverstraat 185); Kiosk (Stationsplein 13, and other locations); Centraal Station newsstands; AKO (Rozengracht 21, and other locations); Athenaeum Nieuwscentruum

(Spui 14); and Bruna (Leidsestraat 89). The main Amsterdam dailies are ***Het Parool*** (center-left afternoon paper); ***NRC Handelsblad*** (centrist, intellectual evening paper); ***De Volkskrant*** (Catholic, left-liberal morning paper); ***De Telegraaf*** (right-wing morning rag).

Opening and closing times... Most shops are open 1–8 Mon; 9–8 Tue, Wed, Fri; 9–9 Thur; and 9–5 Sat. Many businesses and shops are now open Sundays 12–5. Food shops generally open between 8 and 9am and close at 5 or 6pm (3pm Sat). Convenience or late-night shopping remains almost unknown.

Passports and visas... American, Australian, Canadian, New Zealand, and British citizens need only present a valid passport for stays of up to three months. No visas required.

Post office... The main **PTT NL** is at Singel 250 (tel 020/556–3311; Weekdays 9–6, 9–3 Sat). The post office was privatized in 1997. For general information call 0800-0402. Stamps are sold at newsstands and tobacco shops; coin-operated stamp dispensers are attached to some mailboxes. For mail sent outside Amsterdam, use the slot marked "Overige Bestemmingen" (sometimes labeled "Foreign Countries").

Public transportation... There are trams, buses, and a subway system (the Metro/Sneltram), running basically 6am–midnight. Night buses run Mon–Fri 1–5:30am; weekends 1–6:30 (buses 73 to 76 serve central areas). There are no buses from midnight to 1am. The subway, only marginally useful, runs from Centraal Station to eastern and southern suburbs, with center-city stops at Nieuwemarkt, Waterlooplein, and Weesperplein. There are 17 tram lines (streetcars). Trams are the most useful, expedient, and popular form of transit. The Circle Tram (line 20) links many major central-city sights and big hotels. Punch-as-you-go strip tickets, called *strippenkaart*, valid on all types of transit, are sold by drivers or conductors; at the GVB transit authority office in front of the main train station; and at tobacco shops, post offices, and some train station ticket windows. There are also passes for 1 hour, 1 day, multiple days, 1 week, or 1 month, sold at the same places as other tickets. Tram line 5 and Metro cars have automatic ticket dispensers. On board the trams, *strippenkaart*s cost 1.36 euros for 2 strips, 2.04 euros for 3 strips, and 5.45 euros for 8 strips, or 2.73 euros for a 2-hour ticket valid all over town. Buy strip tickets at railway stations or GVB offices and they cost less: 5.67 euros for 15 strips, and 16.68 euros for 45 strips. There are 11 zones in greater Amsterdam. Central-city rides cover 1 zone, requiring 2 strips; 2 zones require 3 strips (always one strip more than the total number of zones). Fold the ticket and time-stamp the strip corresponding to the length of your trip. Once stamped, the ticket is valid for 1 hour for transfers to other trams, buses, and Metro/Sneltram lines. Upon request, drivers or conductors will stamp tickets and tell you when your stop comes up. Drivers cannot sell or stamp tickets on trams with conductors (numbers 4, 6, 7, 9, 10, 13, and 25). For transfers to buses, board in front and show the driver your ticket. Ticket inspectors do spot checks; fines are about $30 plus the ticket price (info tel 0900-9292). Day passes from 1 to 9 days cost from 5 euros to 23.85 euros (see You Probably Didn't Know for more on streetcars; www.ov-info.nl and www.gvb.nl.). A new mini-bus service, De Opstapper, links Centraal Station to the Stopera Opera House, via Prinsengracht.

Radio and TV stations broadcasting in English... Radio stations include Voice of America for Europe, at 99.1 MHz; BBC World Service at 101.3 MHz and 648 kHz on MW; and BBC Radio 4 on 106.6 MHz, 198 kHz AM, and 1500 kHz LW. CNN, BBC 1, and BBC 2 are available in most luxury hotels; some also offer MTV and NBC Superchannel.

Standards of measure... The Netherlands uses the metric system. Clothing size conversions are approximate at best and do not correspond to exact half measures. Clothing sizes: Women's Dutch sizes 36, 38, 40, 42, 44, 46 correspond to U.S. 6/8, 10/11, 12/13, 14/15, 16, 18; women's shoes Dutch sizes 36, 37, 38, 39, 40, 41 equal U.S. 5, 6, 7, 8, 9, 10. Men's shirts Dutch sizes 37, 38, 39, 40, 41, 42, 43, 44, 45 translate to U.S. 14.5, 15, 15.5, 15.5, 16, 16.5, 17, 17.5, 18; men's shoes Dutch are 39, 40, 41, 42, 43, 44, 45, 46, 47 to U.S. sizes 7, 8, 8.5, 9, 10, 11, 11.5, 12, 13.

Taxes and duty free... The murderously high value-added tax (called BTW) of 19 percent is included in the sales price of all consumer goods. Tax-free shopping is possible (though more complicated than you'd think) for non-EU residents (including Americans). You've got to spend 136 euros or more in one day at one participating shop, then take your purchases out of the country within three months. You're actually refunded 13.5–14 percent, less a variable commission fee. Look for the

"Europe Tax-Free Shopping" blue and gray logo (info@taxfree.nl) or the red and blue "Easy Tax Free" logo (www.easytaxfree.com) at participating shops, ask for a Global Refund Cheque when you make your purchases, get a customs officer at Schiphol or Centraal Station to stamp the "cheques" as you leave the country, then rush to the refund office at one of the ABN–AMRO banks in the airport departures halls 1 and 3 or the GWK exchange office at the train station or in Schiphol Plaza Shopping Center. For information: tel 023/524-1909, fax 023/524-6164, info@taxfree.nl.

Taxis and limos... You can hail cabs in Amsterdam, but they are not obliged to stop. Best spots to flag a cab: an artery with a tram line, or central-city streets like Damrak, Rokin, Vijzelstraat, Nieuwezijds Voorburgwal, Raadhuisstraat, and Amstelstraat. Main taxi stands are at Centraal Station, Dam Square, Leidseplein, Spui, Rembrandtplein, Westermarkt, and at the bus station on the corner of Marnixstraat and Kinkerstraat. **Taxi Centrale** (tel 020/677-7777, 24 hours daily) is the central dispatcher for all of these. Radio taxis will pick you up anywhere; the meter runs once you board. Rates are 2.45 euros to start, 1.63 euros per kilometer thereafter; standing time is 28.59 euros per hour. A ride from Centraal Station to a hotel within the Singelgracht costs 8 to 12 euros. Baggage is free. Limousines are listed under "Autoverhuur met chauffeur" in the Yellow Pages. **Devries Business Limousines** (tel 020/669-3889, devries@businesslimo.com and www.businesslimo.com) uses luxury cars and limos. **ETS** (tel 020/659-5333) offers luxury cars and minivans. The **water taxi** rank is in front of Centraal Station; they will pick you up at your hotel or restaurant (Water Taxi Centrale, Stationsplein 8, open 9–1am daily; tel 020/535-6363 or 535-6364, fax 020/535-6369, www.water-taxi.nl or info@water-taxi.nl). Rates for 1–8 passengers: 68.07 euros for the first half hour, 45.38 euros per additional 15 minutes.

Telephones... The Amsterdam area code for calls within the Netherlands is 020; don't dial it inside the city. When calling from abroad, dial 31 (Netherlands), 20 (Amsterdam), then the subscriber's number. Some 0800 or 0900 numbers cost .40–.55 euro cents per minute. Telephone booths are abundant and clearly marked "KPN Telecom/Telefoon." All use telephone or credit cards. KPN Telecom phone cards are sold at post offices and telephone centers, plus GWK exchange offices. Operating instructions are given in English: "Lift handset. Insert card. Dial number." To dial the United States or Canada: 001 + subscriber's 7-digit telephone number. For Country Direct services press "special functions" and follow instructions displayed (the LCD screen allows you to select language and country code and displays the amount of credit on your phone card). To use a credit card, follow the same procedure, but dip your card. Tones, hums, and clicks (all phones are now touch-tone) are similar to those in the United States. **Directory information**: 0900-8008, www.detelefoongids.nl or www.kpn.com; for the yellow pages: www.goudengids.nl; **International info**: 0900-8418; **International collect calls**: 0800-0410. **MCI Worldphone**: 0800/0229-122; **Sprint**: 0800/0229-119; **AT&T**: 0800/0229-111; **Canada Direct**: 0800/0229-116. Mobile phone info: 0800-0106.

Time... Amsterdam's time zone is 6 hours ahead of Eastern Standard Time; 9 ahead of Pacific Time.

Tipping... Don't believe that the Dutch don't appreciate tips. Leave symbolic tips at cafes and bars (loose change, or 1 euro max). Leave about 10 percent at top restaurants (less if the bill is huge). Service is always included in the bill; but as in most European countries, the service charge goes to pay the waiter's miserable salary, so it's good form to leave at least a token tip. Taxi drivers get 1 to 2 euros max. Hotel bell staff: 1 to 3 euros. Bathroom attendants: .25 to .50 euro cents.

Trains... **Centraal Station** (CS) is an unmistakable major landmark on Stationsplein (tel 0900/9292 for info, 6:30am–10pm daily; 030/297-7240 for advance international tickets, daily 9–6, 10–4 Sat, closed Sun). All Continental and UK destinations are served. For international train info: 0900/9296, www.ns.nl.

Travelers with disabilities... Dutch banknotes have braille on the edges to help those with impaired vision, but Amsterdam is a difficult city for the disabled with its uneven pavements, old buildings with narrow stairways, and old buses and trams not equipped with "kneeling" apparatus (some new trams on lines 1, 2, 5, 6, 9, 16, and 24 are being equipped). Metro cars are accessible unless your arms are immobilized. Most curbs are contoured for bikes, which means they're wheelchair-friendly. Museums, concert halls, and public buildings are generally accessible; phone ahead and assistance can be requested almost anywhere. Disabled-friendly hotels are lamentably rare. Best bets are luxury/business establishments. Call the **VVV** (see "Visitor information," below) for hotel addresses; fax your chosen hotel for details. **IHD Schiphol Service** will pick up disabled persons from trains, buses, or taxis and take them to and from their flight (tel 020/316-1417). **Dutch Railways** (NS) distributes a free pamphlet on train travel for the disabled, plus timetables in braille (sold at NS stations, or call 0900/9292 or 030/230-5566); for free escort service at a train station call 24 hours ahead (030/331-253, 8:30am–2pm weekdays).

Visitor information... **VVV** (pronounced fay, fay, fay) is Amsterdam's official tourist office. VVV is what people say and what's on the official literature. No one—not even locals—knows what it stands for. (If you must know, it's Vereniging Voor Vreemdelingen Verkeer.) Its main info number (tel 0900/400-4040, info@amsterdamtourist.nl or www.amsterdamtourist.nl, 9–5 weekdays) at .55 euro cents per minute, often with a long wait, can get ridiculously expensive. Go in person to the VVV offices at: Stationsplein 10 (in front of Centraal Station, 9–5 daily); Leidseplein 1 (9–7 daily); inside Centraal Station, platform 2 (8–8 daily); and farther-flung but uncrowded Stadionplein (9–5 daily). Correspondence: VVV, Box 3901, 1001 AS Amsterdam. The **Netherlands Board of Tourism** (NTB) has offices in the United States at 355 Lexington Ave., 21st floor, New York, NY 10017, tel 212/370-7367, fax 212/370-9507; 225 N. Michigan Ave., Suite 326, Chicago, IL 60601, tel 312/819-0300, fax 312/819-1740; and 9841 Airport Blvd., 10th floor, Los Angeles, CA 90045, tel 310/348-9339, fax 310/348-9344. NBT Canada: 25 Adelaide St. E., Suite 710, Toronto, ON M5C 1Y2, tel 416/363-1577, fax 416/363-1470. The city of Amsterdam now has two websites with cultural/municipal info: www.amsterdam.nl and www.visitamsterdam.nl.

Weather... Amsterdam has an ideal climate—for tulips. Winter is windy, icy, and damp; fall is cold, foggy, and damp; spring is rainy and damp; summer is brief but sticky. Rainy days average 237 per year. February and June are the dry months (17 days of rain on average). Average temperatures (Fahrenheit): Jan: 36, Feb: 36, Mar: 41, Apr: 46, May: 54, June: 59, July: 62, Aug: 62, Sept: 58, Oct: 51, Nov: 44, Dec: 38. Of course, with climate change who can believe in statistics anymore?